MW00787312

A Place in the Sun

A Place in the Sun

Marxism and Fascism in China's Long Revolution

A. James Gregor

A Member of the Perseus Books Group

Copyright © 2000 by Westview Press, A Member of the Perseus Books Group

Published in 2000 in the United States of America by Westview Press, 5500 Central Avenue, Boulder, Colorado 80301-2877, and in the United Kingdom by Westview Press, 12 Hid's Copse Road, Cumnor Hill, Oxford OX2 9JJ

Find us on the World Wide Web at www.westviewpress.com

Library of Congress Cataloging-in-Publication Data
Gregor, A. James (Anthony James), 1929–
    A place in the sun : Marxism and Fascism in China's long revolution / A. James Gregor.
        p.   cm.
    Includes bibliographical references and index.
    ISBN 0-8133-3782-8(hc)
    1. China—Politics and government—20th century.   2. Revolutions—China.
3. Communism—China.   4. Fascism—China.   I. Title: Marxism and Fascism in China's long revolution.   II. Title.

DS775.7.G74   2000
320.951'09'04—dc21   99-089499

The paper used in this publication meets the requirements of the American National Standard for Permanence of Paper for Printed Library Materials Z39.48-1984.

To Maria—For all the years.

Contents

Preface

This work attempts an alternative interpretation of the respective roles played by Marxism and fascism in the complex sequence of events that characterizes the long history of China's revolution. The standard treatment of these subjects involves, at times, loose judgments concerning the "fascist" and "reactionary" character of republican China and the subsequent "Marxist" and "progressive" character of the Maoist regime. At times, such notions, often implicit, provide background for detailed histories. They serve as unacknowledged sorting criteria for the material that enters into historical narrative. The purpose of the present treatment is to review such explicit and implicit judgments—since they do color some China studies.

In general, the discussion that follows remains true to the conviction I have held for most of a lifetime—that there was very little Marxism in the Chinese revolution and that whatever fascism there was, was misunderstood. Time, I think, has demonstrated the merit of those convictions. That so many students of China, for so long, imagined that Marxism had something substantial to do with the long Chinese revolution is the proper object of neither acrimony nor dismay. It could easily have been anticipated. There had been talk of Marxism in China since the turn of the twentieth century, introduced in the waves of European literature that inundated Asia after the incursions of Western imperialism.

Chinese intellectuals did toy with Marxist ideas early in the twentieth century, and after the Bolshevik revolution its themes were common fare in political circles. For a variety of reasons "Marxist theory" became a fad among radical students and university revolutionaries. As a consequence, many imagined it actually had something to do with events.

Whatever the case, very little of classical Marxism could demonstrate any relevance to the critical issues that beset the China of the period. Sun Yat-sen rejected Marxism in its entirety because he saw it as having little of any significance to say about the problems with which the revolution was compelled to contend. At the close of the twentieth century all the evidence indicates that he was right.

Sun Yat-sen probably understood Marxist theory better than any of the founders of the Chinese Communist party—and realized that it could hardly serve any constructive purpose as a guide for China through its long transition to modernity. As though to confirm the correctness of Sun's judgment, the "Marxism" that animated the Chinese Communist party throughout its protracted struggle with the Kuomintang was not a Marxism at all. Mao's "New Democracy" was, in fact, a variant of Sun's program for the development and democratization of China, and it was so recognized by most of Mao's immediate following.

Unhappily, the regime that came to dominate the mainland with Mao's advent had very little to do with the program that the Chinese Communist party advertised for a generation. Abandoning all its solemn commitments to civil and property rights, and the market governance of economic activities, the regime's policies after the seizure of power became an ad hoc patchwork of adaptations of Stalinist tactics and Maoist improvisations that left the people of China helpless in a torrent of events completely beyond their control. The regime's political structures were ramshackle, held together by personal loyalties, illusions, and fears. After all, power was understood to grow out of the barrel of a gun, and the Chinese people constituted a "blank slate" upon which Mao sought to paint the "most beautiful pictures."

Until Mao was swept away by illness and death, "new China" remained perched at the edge of an abyss. For more than a quarter century the leaders of the People's Republic lived in a kind of dream state, in a fog of words that created a universe of illusions in and through which they operated. Only after Mao's death, after the devastation of the "Great Leap Forward"—and the horrors of the "Great Proletarian Cultural Revolution"—did the leadership of the People's Republic publicly acknowledge that Mao, however great a revolutionary, as the ruler of China had made errors so profound that the nation faced catastrophe.

With the passing of Mao, a cohort of "capitalist roaders" arose to transform the bankrupt system he left behind into a form of authoritarian, single-party state capitalism familiar to many developing nations in the twentieth century—and not unfamiliar to the followers of Sun Yat-sen. It will be argued here that with the full emergence of the post-Maoist state, China's "Communism" followed that of the Soviet Union into history. It leaves very little of itself behind. For all the thunder of its coming, Chinese Communism has passed almost silently into oblivion. All of its tattered banners have been folded away—and all the millions who were sacrificed in its name have been buried.

Always more attractive to Western intellectuals at a distance than to any intellectuals at home, Chinese Communism reveals itself to be more shallow than that of the Soviet Union. Those Western academics who counseled us to learn penology, developmental economics, true democracy, education, and the schooling of bureaucrats from Mao's Great Proletarian Cultural Revolution have long since fallen mute. In the empty place where Chinese Communism once stood, an awesome figure is now taking shape. It has yet to be given a name.

A. James Gregor
Berkeley, California

Acknowledgments

Many persons contribute to the making of a book—and many of my students, colleagues, and friends have influenced the making of this one. There are far too many to identify individually, but some have been of particular importance. The field-grade officers of the U.S. Marine Corps with whom I worked as Oppenheimer Professor at the USMC Research Center at Quantico in 1996–1997 impressed on me the potential importance of such a study. I am especially grateful to that entire proud company.

I am indebted to Rear Admiral James B. Linder (Ret.) for his precious insights into that China he knows so well. To Professors John Copper and Jan Prybyla I wish to extend my gratitude for their studies on China. Genevieve Miranda helped with bibliographical material, clerical work, and transcribing notes. Her help was intelligent and her contributions, important.

To my wife, Professor Maria Hsia Chang, I owe thanks for all manner of good things—but most of all for her expertise with the Chinese language materials so essential to the construction of the argument that has become the backbone of this work. Many of the most important references in the exposition below are from her forthcoming works. To the two little boys who resisted knocking almost everything off my desk continuously—and thus allowed me to work—I offer my enduring affection.

Finally, I am grateful to the editors of Westview Press, who thought they found sufficient merit in the work to warrant its publication. To all these people and institutions, I want to extend my sincere gratitude. I hope this work compensates them in some small measure for their kindnesses and their assistance.

A. J. G.

1

On Understanding the
Twentieth Century

The twentieth century was a time of unmitigated horrors. Two world wars and political oppression unknown in the history of humanity, together with the wholesale murder of innocents that accompanied that oppression, seemed to confound the reasoning faculties of some of our most competent thinkers. Right reason seems to have been unable to fathom it all. In the end, many were left with very little confidence that they understood what had in fact transpired.

In looking backward, we recall a time when intellectuals welcomed the Bolshevik revolution as a promise of liberation for the wretched of the earth. It was a time when Beatrice and Sidney Webb could somehow see in the harrowing dictatorship of the Bolsheviks anticipations of a "new democratic civilization"—and in the fabrication of Stalin's elephantine bureaucracy the "withering away" of the state.[1]

Somehow or other, in the confusion of the time, thinkers convinced themselves that the political universe sorted itself into left-wing and right-wing movements and regimes—the first characterized by humanity, democracy, and an abiding concern for the poor, underprivileged, and exploited, the second animated by a pathological commitment to dictatorship, uniforms, violence, and death.[2] It did not seem to matter that the left-wing dictatorships of Josef Stalin and Mao Zedong[3] had murdered millions of "class enemies." Many academics continued to believe in the moral superiority of left-wing regimes and the pathological destructiveness of those on the Right. The pretended differences were offered in the effort to explain what was happening in our time.

For much of the century, the intellectual's world of politics was parsed into evil fascisms as opposed to virtuous antifascisms—a sustained conflict between the purveyors of darkness and the champions of light.[4] Even as the century closed, some academics could still speak of Marxism as a "core project" of the Enlightenment, with fascism its unregenerate opposite.[5]

1

Beneath all of this, there was a persistent suspicion that something was very wrong with the prevailing analyses. Irrespective of the persistence of faith in the Left and Right distinction, there were, by the end of the century, those who argued that the Bolshevik revolution, initially welcomed as the realization of the goals of the Enlightenment, had quickly devolved into a synthesis of "revolutionary radicalism with the most ferocious nationalism" so that by the early 1930s, "the affinity between Soviet ideology and, in general, authoritative fascist types of ideologies was apparent to many."[6] The putative differences between the Fascism of Mussolini[7] and the "Marxism" of Stalin no longer appeared as real as they once did. The distinction between the Left and the Right no longer seemed to provide any serious assistance in coming to understand what caused the twentieth century to develop as it did.[8]

Clearly, theorizing about the twentieth century and the dynamics that governed its fateful evolution had not produced much of persuasive significance. Marxist and fascist regimes shared much in common. However counterintuitive to many academics, Marxist and fascist regimes shared a family resemblance captured in the concept "totalitarianism."[9] As a consequence, it became more and more obvious to more and more academics that much of what had been offered to account for the century's revolutionary history had to be reassessed.

Many academics rejected the notion that the major revolutionary movements and regimes of our time could be distinguished along a continuum from Left to Right. More and more of them conceived the politics of the century in terms of broad "democratic" and "antidemocratic" polities rather than in terms of movements and regimes of the Left and Right. Some began to suggest that a better grasp of left-wing movements and regimes might be obtained through the study of fascist movements and regimes.[10] The comparative study of both would contribute to a deeper comprehension of each.

A similar suggestion has made fitful appearance among Western Sinologists. Distinctions of Left and Right have been employed in almost every contemporary interpretive history of the Chinese revolution. Today the conviction that the ideology of Sun Yat-sen and the Kuomintang was of the Right, whereas that of Mao was of the Left, is no longer as persuasive as it was once thought to be. Considered in that light, the history of China's long revolution takes on an entirely different complexion.

For most of the century, Sinologists regularly divided China's postdynastic history into that of the "reactionary" governance by Sun Yat-sen's Kuomintang nationalists as opposed to the "truly revolutionary" governance of the "Marxists" of Mao Zedong. Because the notion that the "reactionary Right" was devoid of intellectual content had become part of the folk wisdom of political science and history, the ideology of Sun was dismissed without serious reflection.[11] Chinese Communism, on the other hand, as heir to the rich doctrinal traditions of the Left, was the subject of an avalanche of volumes devoted to its explication. Even the diaphanous "thought of Mao Zedong" was treated to sober analysis.[12]

There has never really been a systematic treatment of either Sun or Mao as right- and left-wing revolutionaries—and as a consequence, there was never any general agreement on what was "truly revolutionary" in either. Everyone, on the other hand, seemed certain that Maoism was worlds apart from the ideology of Sun and the regime of Chiang Kai-shek's Kuomintang. As a consequence, we enter the twenty-first century without any clear idea of how to intellectually deal with the China that has emerged after the passing of Mao Zedong and Deng Xiaoping.[13] Sinologists are uncertain how to understand the post-Maoist "socialism with Chinese characteristics" that now occupies the world's attention.

For the one who takes a cue from the most recent studies of Soviet Marxism, as a movement and a regime, and is prepared to entertain the possibility that Marxism and fascism have never been intrinsically opposed revolutionary movements and regimes, the impact on the interpretation of the long Chinese revolution is of major consequence. It is no longer seen as a Manichean struggle between darkness and light, or reaction and revolution. All the major revolutionary forces that shaped contemporary Chinese history are conceived of as sharing some critical properties throughout their common history. The shared properties provide a hitherto unexpected continuity to the entire complex sequence of events that began with the revolution of 1911 and ended with the appearance of Deng's "socialism with Chinese characteristics."

What is missing from our present treatments of China's long revolution is some account that might credibly relate what we know of Sun's nationalist revolution to the revolutionary Marxism of Mao and Deng. That would contribute to our understanding of how the ideologies and the institutionalized features of both bring to mind the ideologies and institutions of Mussolini's Italy and Stalin's Soviet Union.

Some tentative suggestions concerning such an account have been offered in the past.[14] It has been argued that the features of the fascist and Marxist regimes are a function of the demand—made by less-developed nations vegetating on the periphery of the Great Powers—for rapid economic growth and industrialization. A productive and sophisticated economic base was calculated to assure them the resources and power projection capabilities necessary for their survival and prevalence. All of that, in turn, was understood to be a consequence of an abiding sense of inefficacy and humiliation among those in nations that find themselves in unequal contest with those more industrially advanced.

The present effort attempts to relate all this to major cultural, economic, military, and psychological features of twentieth-century life in marginalized countries. Out of a common source, responses emerged that shaped much of the history of our time. Identifying those responses and tracing their effects is the purpose of the present effort.

The Origins of Imperialism

The outward expansion of the industrialized and industrializing powers of northwestern Europe in the nineteenth century is generally spoken of as "imperialism" or "colonialism." In general, the term "imperialism" is taken to mean "the extension of sovereignty or control, whether direct or indirect, political or economic, by one government, nation or society over another."[15]

Although imperialism is not a uniquely European occurrence, no other imperialism in history has exercised such influence over as broad an expanse of territory or over so many human beings. In that sense, the imperialism of northwestern Europe has been unique.

In the case of European imperialism, the most significant phase of European outward expansion began in the eighteenth century. Great Britain and Holland assumed the colonizing role previously played by Spain and Portugal. By the end of the nineteenth century, France, Germany, Belgium, Russia, Japan, and the United States were involved in the process.

By the middle of the nineteenth century, the colonial powers had established claims to about 28 million square miles, or 55 percent, of the earth's surface. By the advent of the First World War, selected Western nations had increased their holdings to more than 43 million square miles, or 84.4 percent, of the globe's entire territory.[16]

France laid claim to 4.25 million square miles, or 37 percent, of the African continent; Great Britain to much of the remainder. Spain seized the Rio de Oro, the "Spanish Sahara," and Portugal laid claim to Angola and Portuguese East Africa. Belgium established its colony in the Congo. In East Asia, Portugal was the pioneer, seizing the island of Macao from China in 1557, and Great Britain and the Netherlands followed.

British colonies in Asia ultimately included India, Ceylon, Burma, Hong Kong, and Malaya. Holland acquired the Dutch East Indies, the islands of Sumatra and Java, the Celebes, Moluccas, Bali, Borneo, and the Timor Archipelago. France colonized Indochina: Cochin-China, Amman, Cambodia, Tonking, and Laos, while the Russians acceded to the control of Sakhalin Island and territories in Northeast Asia. The United States, late to the process, acquired the Philippine Islands as a result of the Spanish–American War of 1898–1899.

Although it seems evident that the Christian imperative to proselytize played an important role throughout the phases of European expansion,[17] it remains reasonably clear that trade and enterprise provided still another motive that drove early European exploration and the search for territory.

With the onset of the industrial revolution and the rise of entrepreneurial capitalism in northwestern Europe, trade and investment loomed ever more emphatically as a force of outward expansion. J. A. Hobson made the case, in 1902,[18] that inequitable income distribution in the industrialized economies produced a lack of effective demand in the domestic market, creating a glut of commodities at one end of the chain of production, and a surfeit of investment capital at the other. The consequence was a frenetic search for both market supplements and opportunities for profitable capital investments wherever they might be found. Industrial capitalism, as an economic force, impelled the Western nations to venture beyond their confines, seeking not only foreign markets for the sale of their excess produce but also virgin territories hospitable to the employment of their excess capital.

All of this was left to the thinkers of the nineteenth and early twentieth centuries to fathom. For those of the first half of the nineteenth century, before the full impact of imperialism had manifested itself, the issue was to attempt to explain the persistence of poverty and oppression in the industrializing nations at a time of extraordinary growth and increasingly liberal thought. For those of the beginning of the twentieth century, on the other hand, questions arose that turned on the reality of "civilized" nations enjoying every competitive advantage vis-à-vis those less-developed—an issue of relative economic and industrial development.

Marxism

Classical Marxism, the Marxism of Karl Marx and Friedrich Engels, was formulated in an effort to explain why the modern world was still host to poverty and oppression at a time when humankind seemed, to all appearances, fully capable of producing unlimited welfare benefits. For Marx and Engels, the world of the mid-1800s had demonstrated a productive capacity that, in principle, could satisfy all material human needs. Industrialization, the substitution of machine power for human muscle, had long since broken through the productivity ceiling that had typified human activity since the establishment of fixed-site agriculture. Organized industrial efforts were capable of more and more amply meeting the needs of humankind. Nonetheless, the modern world suffered poverty and oppression, and Marx and Engels sought to explain the anomaly.

Marx and Engels were Eurocentric in their search for a convincing account. They sought to explain the phenomena of poverty amid potential plenty that they witnessed in the Europe of their time. They attempted to explain the destitution of urban dwellers in London[19] and Paris. They sought to account for the poverty of Western Europeans in economic circumstances that saw the awesome rise of industrial production.

The Communist Manifesto of 1848 was written to illuminate why the workers of Europe were compelled to endure poverty while the economic system to which they gave their labor had demonstrated a capacity to produce an "infinity" of material goods, fully capable of satisfying their every want. Marx and Engels devoted the remainder of their lives to accounting for just that curiosity.

Marx and Engels were committed to the analysis of fully industrialized economic systems. For them, the explanation of poverty amid plenty was a function of acknowledging certain intrinsic features of the industrialized capitalist economic system. Their preoccupation, as a consequence, was with just such systems. They had very little to say about less-developed economic processes on the periphery of the advanced capitalist world of northwestern Europe and North America. For classical Marxism, revolution was a prospect for the advanced industrial nations of Europe and, ultimately, North America. The nations of Asia, Africa, and Latin American did not loom large in their analysis. Such regions languished outside "the flow of history." For Marx and Engels, such areas had no history. They were "asleep" in time.

Whatever Marx and Engels had to say about Asia or Africa, or Latin America, was secondary to their assessment of the revolutionary potential of the developed capitalist nations. The advanced industrial states were the motors of modern history. It was from those states that the liberating revolution would emanate. For Marx and Engels, the revolution that would liberate humankind would be the consequence of the spontaneous mobilization of the industrial proletariat in environments in which they constituted the "vast majority" of the population.

That the majority of the denizens of any given economy would be proletarians—urban dwellers working for wages—meant that revolution would manifest itself in the main capitalist countries of northwestern Europe and North America. Since those countries shared a common system of production, they would all experience proletarian revolution at essentially the same time.[20] In the circumstances they anticipated, the proletariat would be the heirs of the vast productive system produced by the "bourgeoisie." There would no longer be poverty amid plenty.

Revolution, for the founders of classical Marxism, was a product of the fact that, in the industrialized nations, the prevailing "relations of production" had begun to act as a "fetter" on the growing "productive forces." In the industrialized economies, as long as the "means of production" remained in private hands, the distribution of product (as a consequence of the established "relations of production") proceeded only if inventory could be cleared at a profit. Profit provided capital for continued investment—and the realization of profit required a continuous growth of effective demand. Marx argued, however, that at some stage in the growth of the "bourgeois mode of production," industry, because of the very nature of commodity production for sale, would suffer a persistent underconsumptionism. The result would be a secular downward pressure on the overall rate of profit.[21]

If capitalist enterprise could not generate profit in the course of its activities, it was destined to fail. As the system-wide rate of profit fell to zero, industrial capitalism must necessarily succumb. At that point, the industrial proletariat, fully cognizant of what was required to sustain and foster industrial enterprise, must accede to revolutionary control. The entire industrial system of capitalism would pass into the hands of the proletariat, who would then engage industry in the service of production for use rather than profit.

The final crisis of capitalist production would come when the entire system could no longer generate profit and would fail not only to expand production but to sustain itself. That would follow full industrial maturation in market circumstances in which effective demand had been maximally reduced. The revolution that would follow would see the rise of the proletariat to power.

With the advent of proletarian rule, the market would be abolished and production would be governed by "an overall plan," itself fashioned by the working class. The working class, educated and trained in the industrial system that preceded it, would arrange itself in voluntary associations that would administer the new system. Planning and administration would proceed through universal suffrage, together with recourse to referenda and recall, in order to preclude even the hint of elite dominance.

Postrevolutionary society required a mature economy as well as a mature proletariat. Democratically governed by the proletariat, the overall plan would supply the wherewithal for the liberated society. Given the logic of the analysis, the site for the proletarian revolution could only be in the advanced industrial economies.

Marx and Engels imagined themselves as having resolved the anomaly of growing poverty in the midst of increasing wealth. They imagined themselves having supplied a political solution as well. They saw the process of intensive and extensive industrial development as creating a class of liberators, those industrial workers who suffer most acutely under the system.

When the system closed down as a consequence of the declining rate of profit, the proletariat would assume the ownership and governance of the productive processes—eliminating class and ownership distinctions, and producing the equality amid abundance that was the historic promise of the capitalist mode of production.

Karl Marx had answered, to his own satisfaction, the most important social questions his time had posed. His answers define for us what it means to be "left-wing." The leftism of tradition is characterized by the liberation of society's oppressed and impoverished. It opposes elitism and privilege. It seeks harmony and the unity of all in universal tranquility. If there was to be violence in revolutionizing society, it would be relatively mild and brief in duration.

Traditional leftism anticipated the eventual disappearance of industrial capitalism, the political state, police forces, and the standing military. Traditional leftists anticipated a revolution that would see the abolition of classes, the liberation of individuals, and the end of the oppression of man by man. According to Marx's utopian vision, all the advanced industrial nations, "at essentially one and the same time," would transcend capitalism and begin the socialist epoch of individual freedom, universal peace, and collective abundance.

Classical Marxism and the Peripheral, Less-Developed Regions

Neither Marx nor Engels had anything particularly profound to say about the less-developed regions that languished on the edges of the world's industrial systems. Neither made little more than general allusion to some of the peripheral economies in eastern and southern Europe and North Africa. Neither said anything of any real substance about Africa, and surprisingly little about Asia in general. Everything Marx and Engels said about China is contained in one small volume, a miniscule part of the Marx-Engels corpus.[22] The political, social, and economic systems of the peripheral regions were only of tangential interest to the founders of Marxism.

Marx and Engels were convinced that the very dynamics of modern capitalism would drive capitalism outside the confines of northwestern Europe. For the first Marxists, the underconsumptionist biases of expanding industrial economies would drive capitalists into the less-developed world in the search for market supplements and investment opportunities. Surplus inventory and surplus capital would accumulate in maturing European economies. The necessary consequence would be the marketing of goods and the investment of capital in parts of the world that still were lodged in the anachronisms of agricultural and extractive economies. The bourgeoisie was compelled, by the very character of industrial capitalism, to remake the world in its own image.

For Marx and Engels, industrial capitalism would expand to absorb the entire globe in its enterprise. Long before the world would be industrialized, the capitalist system would have succumbed to that inevitable decline in the rate of overall profit. The proletariat would have succeeded to power and, once ensconced, would assume tutelary control over the uplift of less-developed nations.

For the founders of classical Marxism, the expansion of the advanced industrial systems pursued an irrepressible logic. The "modern mode of production" was destined to invest the entire globe—until it had recreated the world "in its own image." In the process of that recreation, "many small national flowers" were to be "crushed." Modern industry requires all the economies of scale. Engels was painfully candid.

When the "energetic Yankees" expanded into the southwestern areas of the North American continent, annexing territories that had, hitherto, been Mexican, Engels could only applaud what he took to be an expansion that served the "interests of civilization," wresting land from "lazy Mexicans who did not know what to do with it." The Americans would "concentrate a heavy population and an extensive trade on the most suitable part of the Pacific Coast, . . . build great cities, . . . [and open] steamship lines. . . . Because of this the 'independence' of a few Spanish Californians and Texans may be injured, but what do they count compared to such world historic events?" All of this was simply the "influence of the more highly developed nation on the undeveloped one."

For Engels, all of that was simply part of the process of historical development. The more highly developed industrial nations would bind "tiny, crippled, powerless little nations together in a great Empire, and thereby [enable] them to take part in an historical development which, if left to themselves, would [remain] entirely foreign to them! To be sure such a thing is not carried through without forcibly crushing many a delicate little national flower. But without force and without an iron ruthlessness nothing is accomplished in history."[23]

For the first Marxists, when peoples of "two completely different levels of civilization" came into contact, the more developed had the historic right to dominion. It was not a question of "abstract" rights, Engels argued, but of "the level of social development of the individual peoples."[24]

What was eminently clear was the conviction that the expansion of the industrial system of production was the consequence of the correlative expansion of the imperialist powers.[25] The advanced industrial nations would bring industrialization in their train. Less-developed nations would suffer in the process, but that was the nature of progress in a cursed and unredeemed creation.[26]

Marx acknowledged that the methods employed by the British in India and China were reprehensible, but they were, in his judgment, inevitable. They responded to the "logic of history." They opened India and China to the "annihilation of old Asiatic society, and the laying of the material foundation of Western society in Asia"—all of which furthered the purposes of the worldwide proletarian revolution.[27] For Marx, the incursions of the British in Asia served as "the unconscious tool of history in bringing about . . . revolution."[28]

The process in China was more complicated for Marx. China was a vast nation, and direct colonization would have taxed the resources of the Western industrialized powers. But that in no way diminished the consequences of Western incursions on the Chinese mainland of Asia. The industrial mode of production would insinuate itself between and among all the features of a somnolent agrarian Asia.

Equally clear was Marx's judgment that the immediate consequence of contacts between the industrialized West and an industrially retrograde China was cultural and military conflict. Those conflicts would be painful and bloody, and out of them would emerge a Chinese "bourgeois" revolution, comparable to the bourgeois revolution in France in 1789. In terms of Marx's analysis, the economic and industrial development of China was a "bourgeois task" to be undertaken in Asia by the bourgeoisie, just as the same task was undertaken by the bourgeoisie in Western Europe.

In the interim, the proletariat of Europe and North America would mature to their liberating tasks. Consequent to revolution in the advanced industrial economies, the European and North American revolutionary proletariat would then extend tutelary control to the industrially less developed "primitive" communities on the margins of mature capitalism and uplift them to full participation in "civilization."[29]

The "civilizing" process anticipated by the first Marxists followed the inevitable logic of history and terminated in the universal liberation of all mankind from the burdens of class domination, national distinctions, and the exploitation of man by man. The industrialized powers would bring economic growth and industrial expansion to the peripheral nations in a process that would culminate in universal human harmony. Actually, history had more to say than either Marx or Engels envisioned in the last half of the nineteenth century. Industrialization and imperialism were to script an entirely different scenario.

Imperialism in the Twentieth Century

For all their densely written volumes, Marx and Engels succeeded in forecasting very little of the reality that imperialism would generate in the twentieth century. That is somewhat surprising, since there is much they should have known and more they might have guessed.

At about the same time that Marx and Engels were writing the *Communist Manifesto*, Friedrich List, an author known to Marx, was finishing his *National System of Political Economy*. For List, the problems of the mid-nineteenth century had very little to do with proletarian revolutions, and more to do with the struggles of less-developed economies to survive and prosper in an environment dominated by more industrially advanced systems.

Marx dismissed List's analysis as irrelevant in a world soon to be liberated by the spontaneous revolution of the working class.[30] For Marx, the very talk of nations serving as vehicles of industrial development was wrongheaded. He understood industrial development as an inevitable process in which industries swallowed up nations, the larger absorbing the smaller until the time when nations simply ceased to exist. The task was not to develop nations but to anticipate a postindustrial society freed from national identities, poverty, and class distinctions.

For List, the issue was none of that. Rather, it turned on how a politically organized but industrially retrograde community of human beings could attain the industrial maturity and economic sophistication that was the necessary condition for material wellbeing, culture, justice, and self-defense capabilities in the modern world. List argued that the advanced industrialized nations possessed power projection potential that intimidated those less advanced. The industrialized nations controlled the financial and trade institutions essential to success in the international markets. For those nations without power, and capital poor, the prevailing international environment offered scant chance of competitive success. Less-developed countries faced the prospect of perpetual "underdevelopment" and inextricable subordination to more industrially advanced nations.[31]

For the purposes of the present account, more than the prospect of simple economic subordination to other nations, the cultural and political impact of that subordination has ignited a reactive and developmental nationalist response among economically retrograde nations that has fueled revolution and international violence over the last century. To identify that revolution and the violence that attended it as explicitly left- or right-wing has become increasingly difficult.

The developmental strategy first recommended by Friedrich List over a century and a half ago has appeared and reappeared in the revolutionary literature of the twentieth century. In economically retrograde Italy, at the turn of the century, Alfredo Rocco, who was to serve as a major ideologue of Italian Fascism, recommended the same strategy for precisely the reasons advanced by List.

Rocco argued that if the "little Italy" of his time, newly reunited a scant few decades before, ever expected to occupy a place as a major European power, it would have to undertake a massive program of rapid economic growth and industrial development.[32] Other nationalists almost immediately took up the litany. Giovanni Papini and Giuseppe Prezzolini called upon Italians to recognize that the demands of the twentieth century necessitated a fulsome commitment to rapid industrialization and economic expansion.[33]

These enjoinments were animated by a deep and abiding sense of frustration and humiliation. That the Italy that had hosted the Rome of the caesars and the universal Roman Church should languish disdained and reviled on the margins of Europe was unacceptable for an articulate minority of intellectuals who collected around themselves an increasing number of business, commercial, and working-class elements. It was clear that many in Italy were not prepared to wait until the "natural" process of industrialization through economic colonization provided the nation the wherewithal for self-defense and survival in a world of exacerbated competition. Many Italians were not prepared to suffer collective inferiority until such time as the advanced industrial powers were ready to extend to them some semblance of equality. They sought timely justice for the oppressed and the exploited.

On the other side of the world, China's first modern revolutionaries had collected themselves around a program of change calculated to make their nation strong and capable of resisting the impostures of the industrially advanced nations of the West. By the first decade of the twentieth century, the first Chinese revolutionaries sought to mobilize all available elements in order to usher the nation through the stages of late economic and industrial development in the search for equity and justice.[34] By that time, China had suffered her "half century of humiliation." The Middle Kingdom had been reduced to a pawn in an international game of supererogation, advantage, and exploitation played by the industrialized powers.

What Marx and Engels had failed to understand, and what List understood perfectly well, was that the variable rates of growth and development that distinguished the advanced and the retrograde national economies were not simple statistical variances. The less developed nations suffered degrees of national humiliation that sparked a totally unanticipated response. A sense of inefficacy, inferiority, and status deflation drove nationals of the less-industrialized nations to revolutionary desperation. A flurry of fierce nationalisms filled the time between the middle of the nineteenth and the end of the twentieth century. Millions were left dead in their train. Marx and Engels had misunderstood some of the more critical consequences of the entire process of differential economic growth and industrialization. The process did not foster the growth of international harmony and economic union. It was not the harbinger of a world without nations. It did not prefigure a world in which workingmen had no fatherland. It was the leavening of a world composed of reactive nationalisms, multiclass revolutions, ideocratic systems, irredentisms, and the search, by each nation, for a place in the sun.

Marxism, Fascism, and Revolution in the Twentieth Century

These were the circumstances out of which Leninism and Fascism were to emerge. The First World War provided the massive dislocations that fueled revolution throughout Europe.

Lenin's Bolsheviks came to power animated by a vision of Marxism that anticipated a worldwide proletarian upheaval that would culminate in a universal, egalitarian utopia. The seizure of power in Russia was to be preliminary to the international communist revolution.

Only with the failure of revolution in the advanced industrial nations did Lenin retreat to the alternative that saw the internationalist Bolsheviks attempting to create a *national* industrial economy out of the agrarianism that largely characterized Russia at the beginning of the twentieth century. Lenin's New Economic Policy followed, in which limited forms of private property were introduced together with the selective restoration of some form of commodity markets. There was an increasing appeal to the "Soviet Fatherland" in the effort to engage the commitment of the nation's "working classes."

As early as 1918, Lenin had characterized the Bolshevik revolution as a "Russian revolt against foreign imperialism."[35] He spoke without embarrassment of "Russian independence and freedom" in a struggle against those nations better armed because more industrially developed.

With the advent of Josef Stalin, the entire program of classical Marxism was more fully transformed into a variant of *national socialism*, in which the citizens of the Soviet Union were called upon to sacrifice for the revolution, contributing the tribute of their labor and commitment to the rapid economic growth and industrial development of the national community. By 1928, the invocation of national sentiment against an international and imperialist enemy, the enjoinments to sacrifice and labor for the nation, and the insistence upon loyalty to a hegemonic and elitist revolutionary leadership were properties already made manifest in the Fascist revolution on the Italian peninsula.

Whatever "internationalism" there was in the ideology of Stalin's Communist International was made to work for the Soviet Union. The price to be paid by those foreign "proletarian" parties attracted to the Comintern was complete and supine subordination to the leadership in

Moscow. The "world's workers" were called upon "to protect the proletariat's motherland."[36] Thus, all mixed together with the call to worldwide proletarian revolution were the unmistakable elements of reactive nationalism combined with a clarion call to rapid, national economic, and specifically industrial development.[37] Whatever else Stalinism was, it was an ideology that satisfied some of the major sentiments of reactive and redemptive nationalism.[38] The "Red patriotism" that became the common currency of the Soviet Union had found expression in the invocation to Russia's greatness, the fulfillment of its messianic destiny.[39]

In the course of this "creative development" of Marxism, proletarian internationalism was to be "reconciled" with Russian nationalism.[40] The Bolshevik revolution was committed to the restoration of the independence and integrity of "Mother Russia" in its long conflict with the advanced industrial powers of the West.

In retrospect, the frenzied nationalism, the etatization of the developing economy, the unmitigated resistance to the pretenses of the West, the "vanguard" role of the elitist revolutionary party, and the imposition of a special form of "democratic centralizing" dictatorship under the "charismatic" leadership of Stalin as *Vozhd*—all signaled the advent of one form of modern mass-mobilizing, reactive nationalist, developmental political system with which the twentieth century has become all too familiar. Stalin's version was a confused variant of the form that had already fully manifested itself on the Italian peninsula.

On that peninsula, the most "subversive" of the revolutionary Marxists had already made the transition from Marx's projected universal proletarian revolution to revolutions of "proletarian nations" against the imperialism of the established "plutocracies." Before the advent of the Great War of 1914–1918, Italy's revolutionary syndicalists argued that a working-class "socialist" revolution on the peninsula was impossible.[41] Italy was an industrially backward nation with a exiguous and politically retrograde proletariat,[42] not unlike czarist Russia at the time of the Bolshevik revolution. As a consequence, many Italian Marxists argued that there could be no "international socialism" in Italy, nor could there be any real expectation that a working-class revolution in the advanced industrial nations would solve Italy's specific and intrinsic disabilities.

By the end of the First World War, the most radical syndicalists in Italy had opted for a form of reactive developmental nationalism that saw in the sentiment of nationality the cement that would infrangibly unite an entire population in pursuit of national integrity and international equity. For Italy's most exacerbated socialists, Benito Mussolini among them, international proletarian revolution was a theoretical construct having very little to do with prevailing realities.[43]

What was real for the socialist heretics in Italy was the disparity between nations that were industrially advanced and those that were less advanced. The "plutocracies" of the world, the "early developers," had arrogated to themselves three quarters of the earth's surface and as much of its resources as they chose.[44] "Proletarian nations" found themselves not only denied resources and living space but threatened by the military power of the more advanced nations. Moreover, they suffered further disadvantage in having their economic growth and development obstructed by the conditions of international trade and capital transfers established, to their own purpose, by the "plutocracies." International socialism, if it were to exist, would have to be the consequence of resolving the problems that arose out of the existence of poor nations struggling in an environment shaped by the interests of the rich. Only upon the resolution of such inequities could there be talk of an international "socialization" in which all would enjoy civil and political rights.[45]

The immediate issue faced by economically backward communities was bridging the distance between economic and industrial underdevelopment and that level of quantitative and qualitative abundance that typified the "plutocracies." It was national economic *productivity* that was to be at the center of the revolution—a productivity that would ensure the material foundation for *national redemption* and *national grandeur*.[46]

By 1925, Fascism, born of nationalism and Marxist revolutionary syndicalism, had fabricated its ideology. It was nationalist, developmental, and etatist. Inspired by the vision of a "Third Rome" that would restore Italy to the grandeur of the caesars and the church universal, Italians were called to sacrifice and commitment in the service of a mission under the leadership of the "charismatic" Duce.

In Asia, half a world away, at almost the same time, Sun Yat-sen was reorganizing his revolutionary party to better discharge what he understood to be its political, social, and economic responsibilities. Having squandered its impetus after the success of the antidynastic revolution of 1911, Sun's Kuomintang had been unable to assure China's integrity or defend the nation against the imperialists of the West.

In 1919, Sun had already outlined an intricate program for the industrial development of China, and in 1924 he delivered the basic outlines of an ideology of national redemption that saw China not only the equal of every other nation but as the bearer of a salvific world civilization.[47] In that same year, with the assistance of Soviet advisers, Sun reorganized the Kuomintang into a mass-mobilizing party.

Sun's ideology occupies a curious place in the history of twentieth-century political thought. Clearly a determined anti-Marxist, Sun was convinced that whatever Lenin had wrought in czarist Russia had very little to do with classical Marxism.[48]

Sun anticipated, rather, that the revolutions of the twentieth century would share features with his own. They would commence as reactive nationalisms, seeking to restore the lost grandeur of nations that had delivered millennial civilizations to humankind. They would seek to economically and politically develop nations that had allowed themselves to be overwhelmed by the imperialism of those communities that had industrialized first.

For Sun, classical Marxism with its emiserated proletariat living at or below subsistence, and an industrial capitalism no longer capable of sustaining itself, was little more than a failed diagnosis of the century's problems. The search for a resolution of China's humiliation through an international proletarian revolution, as a consequence, was, for Sun, little more than a utopian fancy.

Sun saw revolution in the twentieth century as a search for national palingenesis, the rebirth and redemption of nations in an environment of bitter international struggle between imperialist and industrially retrograde communities. Sun anticipated that revolutions, in our time, would be nationalist, etatist, and developmental—led by an elite, unitary party. For China, that party was the Kuomintang and its "charismatic" leader was Sun Yat-sen as *Tsungli*.

Sun anticipated an authoritarian period of indeterminate length that would first see the military reunification of China and a subsequent interim of political tutelage under the unitary party. At some stage, constitutional government, remarkably like that of the United States, would be introduced, to be called a "Chinese neo-democracy."

For Sun, all this involved a developmental regime, typified by qualified private property rights, market guidance, and major state intervention in the process. As it was understood, it would constitute a modified capitalism—a form of market-governed, developmental national socialism[49]—calculated to accelerate industrialization. A strong state, armed with a modern military, would assure China its rightful place in the modern world.[50]

Revolution in Our Time

In retrospect, at the close of the twentieth century, it seems reasonably clear what revolution has meant in our time. We can be equally sure about what it has not meant. It has precious little to do, for example, with the classical Marxism of Karl Marx and Friedrich Engels. By the end of the 1920s, it was evident, to anyone who would see, that "socialism" or "communism" had taken on features that would forever distinguish it from the Marxism of the Second International.

That few actually attempted to understand the nature of Soviet socialism was, in part, the consequence of the canonical left-wing interpretation of "fascism" as a "right-wing" bourgeois product designed to defend capitalism in its final crisis—and Stalinism as a "left-wing" antifascism dedicated to the empowerment of "workers."[51] In fact, the academic community in the West had settled on a left-, and right-wing, dichotomy to typologize revolution. Rarely was the Soviet Union seen for what it was.[52] Over the years intellectuals like Sidney Webb, John Reed, Romain Rolland, Lion Feuchtwanger, Howard Fast, and Upton Sinclair chose to characterize Stalin's Soviet Union as a "workers' state" with clearly "democratic" goals. The Soviet Union was in the "Enlightenment tradition," the culmination of left-wing aspirations.

In fact, by the late 1920s and early 1930s, "socialist" or "communist" revolutions had resolved themselves into one or another form of reactive nationalism, pledged to the uplift and renewal of an economically less-developed community. To accomplish its purposes, "left-wing" revolution took on the institutional form of unitary party rule under charismatic leadership. The inculcation of an ethic of sacrifice, obedience, and duty became common to all such revolutions, however academics chose to identify them.

The fact of the matter is that "leftism" is entirely irrelevant to the revolutions of the twentieth century. Under the pressure of reality, Leninists transformed themselves into Stalinists—just as national syndicalists, Italian Marxists, transformed themselves into Fascists. In turn, the antidynastic revolutionaries of China transformed themselves into a singular kind of Chinese socialism. No one in the nineteenth century could have envisioned such developments. Certainly the first Marxists foresaw none of it.

Classical Marxists foresaw none of it largely because they had no clear conception of what nationalism might be or how it could influence events. They foresaw none of it because of their fundamentally economistic and deterministic interpretation of the world and the behavior of people in it. In the twentieth century, Mussolini, Stalin, Sun, and Mao Zedong understood history to be shaped by human will and human determination—and they understood that will and that determination to be a function of real or fancied foreign oppression and the collective humiliation that attends it. Reactive nationalism was to be at the critical center of the entire process.

In that context, the notion of imperialism occupies center stage. Industrialization, which essentially began in the United Kingdom in the eighteenth century, created a dynamic that saw the first industrialized nations extending their reach over the furthest portions of the globe. With the extension of their military, political, economic, and cultural influence, the reaction of less-developed nations became critical to our century.

When Dino Grandi, who was to become one of the principal ideologues of Fascism, predicted that the twentieth century would be tormented by a "class war" between poor and rich nations, he could not know how accurate his forecast was to prove.[53]

The millions who have perished in the "class war" between nations in our time testify to the intensity of the reaction of less-developed nations to the afflictions, and attendant humiliations, that follow in the train of economic backwardness. Our century is marred by the unnatural deaths of millions of innocents caught up in the tragedy of the contest between "proletarian" and "imperialist" nations.

Until the end of the century, few academics seemed to fully understand what was transpiring. They saw Marxism-Leninism opposed to fascism as the key to interpret contemporary revolution—with each pursuing radically different purpose. It was an interpretative strategy that has proved to be of little cognitive consequence. Rather, the twentieth century has been host to revolutions that have been neither of the Left nor the Right. It has witnessed a series of "anti-imperialist" revolutions that, over time, gradually approximated each other—to distinguish themselves not necessarily from each other but from the class of market-governed, industrialized democracies.

A class of revolutionary movements and regimes emerged in the twentieth century, all of which share a marked family resemblance. Throughout much of the century the resemblances were either neglected or explained away. In fact, the resemblances were defining attributes that identified those movements and those regimes as members of a family, genus, or class: reactive developmental nationalism, of which the Bolshevik, Fascist, or Maoist revolutions were species or subspecies.

That was obscured by the protracted insistence upon the "right-wing" and "left-wing" distinction. In retrospect, it is possible to trace the confusion produced by that putative distinction. There are few places in which that pretended distinction generated more confusion than in revolutionary China.

What follows is a selective account of the revolutionary processes that developed on the mainland of China in terms of "Marxism" and "fascism," as understood by those directly involved in the conflict. The account is not a history as such. It is an effort to trace the impact of the attempts by the protagonists, and those who would understand them, to employ the contested concepts "Marxism" and "fascism" to some cognitive purpose in taking the measure of China's long revolution.

Notes

1. Sidney and Beatrice Webb, *Soviet Communism: A New Civilization?* 2 vols. (London: Longmans, Green, 1935).

2. See Roger Griffin, *The Nature of Fascism* (New York: Routledge, 1993), pp. xi, 183, 229.

3. The transliteration of Chinese into English will follow the pinyin system (hence Mao Zedong), except for names or words that have become familiar as transliterations from the Wade-Giles system (e.g., Sun Yat-sen and Chiang Kai-shek).

4. See the discussion in François Furet, *The Passing of an Illusion: The Idea of Communism in the Twentieth Century* (Chicago: University of Chicago Press, 1999), chaps. 6–7.

5. See Mark Neocleous, *Fascism* (Minneapolis: University of Minnesota Press, 1997).

6. Dmitry Shlapentokh, "Bolshevism, Nationalism, and Statism: Soviet Ideology in Formation," in *The Bolsheviks in Russian Society*, ed. Vladimir N. Brovkin (New Haven: Yale University Press, 1995), pp. 276–277, 294.

7. As a generic concept, "fascism" refers to the indeterminate collection of movements and regimes that satisfy a criterial list of identifying properties. The term "Fascism" refers to the movement and regime founded by Benito Mussolini. Throughout the discussion below, Mussolini's Fascism is treated as the paradigmatic instance of generic fascism. Adolf Hitler's National Socialism is a variant of generic fascism but displayed features (a fundamentally *racist* rather than a *nationalist* political disposition) that made it idiosyncratic and poorly suited to comparative analysis. Marxist-Leninist revolutions, which displayed almost the entire syndrome of fascist traits, chose *class* rather than *nation* as the primary human association and therefore cannot serve as paradigmatic. See the discussion in George Mosse, *The Fascist Revolution: Toward a General Theory of Fascism* (New York: Howard Fertig, 1999), pp. xiv, xvi, 31, 35–36, 40; and A. James Gregor, *Contemporary Radical Ideologies: Totalitarian Thought in the Twentieth Century* (New York: Random House, 1968), chaps. 3–4, 5.

8. By the end of the century, many notable intellectuals called attention to substantial affinities between Marxist-Leninist systems and fascism. Paul Johnson, Richard Pipes, and Renzo De Felice all identified fascism as a "Marxist heresy." Paul Johnson, *Modern Times: The World from the Twenties to the Nineties*, rev. ed. (New York: Harper Perennial, 1991), p. 102; Richard Pipes, *Russia Under the Bolshevik Regime* (New York: Vintage, 1995), p. 253; Renzo De Felice, "Il fascismo," *Nuova storia contemporanea* 1 (November-December 1997): 26.

9. See A. James Gregor, "'Totalitarianism' Revisited," in *Totalitarianism Reconsidered*, ed. Ernest A. Menze (London: Kennikat, 1981), pp. 130–145.

10. See the discussion in Pipes, *Russia*, chap. 5; and A. James Gregor, *The Faces of Janus: Marxism and Fascism in the Twentieth Century* (New Haven: Yale University Press, 2000).

11. See the discussion in A. James Gregor, *Ideology and Development: Sun Yat-sen and the Economic History of Taiwan* (Berkeley: Center for Chinese Studies, 1981), chap. 1.

12. There were some studied academic exegeses of Mao's thought; see, for example, Frederic Wakeman Jr., *History and Will: Philosophical Perspectives of Mao Tse-tung's Thought* (Berkeley: University of California Press, 1973). See the more con-

temporary discussion of that same subject in Maria Hsia Chang, *The Labors of Sisyphus: The Economic Development of Communist China* (New Brunswick, N.J.: Transaction, 1998), chap. 2.

13. In this context, see the interesting work by Thomas A. Marks, *Counterrevolution in China: Wang Sheng and the Kuomintang* (London: Frank Cass, 1998); and Wei Wou, *KMT-CCP Paradox: Guiding a Market Economy in China* (Indianapolis: University of Indianapolis Press, 1993).

14. See, for example, A. James Gregor, *The Fascist Persuasion in Radical Politics* (Princeton: Princeton University Press, 1974); and Gregor, *Italian Fascism and Developmental Dictatorship* (Princeton: Princeton University Press, 1979).

15. George H. Nadel and Perry Curtis, introduction to *Imperialism and Colonialism* (New York: Macmillan, 1964), p. 1.

16. See Grover Clark, *The Balance Sheets of Imperialism: Facts and Figures on Colonies* (New York: Columbia University, 1936), p. 5.

17. See V. G. Kiernan, *The Lords of Human Kind: Black Man, Yellow Man and White Man in an Age of Empire* (Boston: Little, Brown, 1969), pp. 9, 23.

18. J. A. Hobson, *Imperialism: A Study* (Ann Arbor: University of Michigan Press, 1965).

19. See Friedrich Engels, *The Conditions of the Working Class in England in 1844* (London: George Allen & Unwin, 1950).

20. See the more ample discussion in A. James Gregor, *A Survey of Marxism: Problems in Philosophy and the Theory of History* (New York: Random House, 1965), pp. 158–169, 175–185.

21. Marx entertained a much more complicated notion of why the profit rates of industrial capitalism must necessarily decline. Underconsumptionism was only one of the surface features of the central "contradiction" of modern capitalism. For the purposes of the present discussion, underconsumptionism is sufficient to outline the circumstances on which proletarian revolution was predicated. See Gregor, *Fascist Persuasion*, chaps. 2–3.

22. Dona Torr, ed., *Marx on China, 1853–1860* (London: Lawrence & Wishart, 1968).

23. See Friedrich Engels, "Democratic Panslavism," in *The Russian Menace to Europe*, ed. P. W. Blackstock and B. F. Hoselitz (Glencoe: Free Press, 1952), pp. 71–76.

24. See Engels, "Po und Rhein," in *Werke* (Berlin: Dietz, 1961–1968), 13:267; cf. Engels, "Hungary and Panslavism" and "Democratic Panslavism" in *Russian Menace*.

25. In the more than forty years of their analysis, Marx and Engels complicated their account by alluding to "progressive revolutions" in less-developed countries. What is perfectly clear is that revolution in Poland or Ireland was anticipated not because it was intrinsically "progressive" but because Polish unrest would weaken Russian reaction, which would contribute, directly and/or indirectly, to proletarian revolution in the advanced industrial countries. Irish revolution would directly weaken reactionary capitalist rule in Great Britain. The essential argument remained the same throughout their analysis. The support of Marx and Engels "for the right to self-determination in the Irish and Polish cases . . . can be . . . explained in terms of the rigid evolutionary model, epiphenomenal

economism and the eurocentric approach which permeated their interpretations of the processes of social change." Ephraim Nimni, *Marxism and Nationalism: Theoretical Origins of a Political Crisis* (London: Pluto, 1991), p. 25. See the discussion in Horace B. Davis, *Nationalism and Socialism* (New York: Monthly Review Press, 1967), chap. 1.

26. For one of the better discussions of this process of "colonization" or "imperialism," see the introduction to *Karl Marx on Colonialism and Modernization*, by Shlomo Avineri (Garden City, N.Y.: Doubleday, 1968), pp. 1–28.

27. Karl Marx, "The Future Results of British Rule in India," in ibid., p. 125.

28. Marx, "British Rule in India," pp. 88–89.

29. For a more extensive discussion, see Gregor, *Fascist Persuasion*, chap. 4.

30. See the discussion in Roman Szporluk, *Communism and Nationalism: Karl Marx versus Friedrich List* (New York: Oxford, 1988).

31. "Under the existing conditions of the world, the result of general free trade would not be a universal republic, but, on the contrary, a universal subjection of the less advanced nations to the supremacy of the predominant manufacturing, commercial and naval power, is a conclusion for which the reasons are very strong and, according to our views, irrefragable." Friedrich List, *The National System of Political Economy* (New York: Longmans, Green, 1916), p. 103; see pp. 145–146 and J. Shield Nicholson's introductory essay in ibid., pp. xiii–xxvii.

32. Alfredo Rocco, "Economia liberale, economia socialista ed economia nazionale," in *Scritti e discorsi politici*, vol. 1 (Milan: Giuffre, 1938), sec. l.

33. See Giovanni Papini and Giuseppe Prezzolini, *Vecchio e nuovo nazionalismo* (1914; Rome: Volpe, 1967).

34. See Mary Backus Rankin, *Early Chinese Revolutionaries: Radical Intellectuals in Shanghai and Chekiang, 1902–1911* (Cambridge: Harvard University Press, 1971).

35. See Mikhail Agursky, *The Third Rome: National Bolshevism in the USSR* (Boulder: Westview, 1987), p. 204.

36. See the decision of the Second Congress of the Communist Party of China, 1922, in Warren Kuo, *Analytic History of the Chinese Communist Party* (Taipei: Institute of International Relations, 1968), 1:106.

37. See the discussion in Pipes, *Russia*, chaps. 4–5.

38. See the discussion in Agursky, *Third Rome*, pp. 203–213.

39. See ibid., p. 211.

40. Since the Bolshevik revolution, Marxist-Leninists have sought to discretely distinguish "nationalism" from "patriotism," considering the one "bourgeois" and the other "revolutionary." The actual basis for the distinction lay in the fact that both Bolshevik and Chinese Communist revolutions had captured nations with substantial minorities. The nationalism of ethnic minorities threatened to fragment such compound "Marxist" nations. Patriotism, on the other hand, identified as *loyalty to the political regime*, could serve as a stabilizing influence. Although trafficking on essentially the same sentiment of in-group identification and out-group diffidence, the sentiment could be employed in defense of the Marxist-Leninist state. For all that, it is generally recognized that the distinction between "nationalism" and "patriotism," in the case of Marxist-Leninist regimes, is largely contrived and artificial. (See the comments in Pipes, *Russia*, pp. 135 136, 471–472.) The present treatment of "nationalism" in post-Soviet Russia and post-

Maoist China more generally corresponds to what is called "nationalism" in the West. In the discussion of contemporary China, the term "nationalism" will be used interchangeably with "patriotism" to identify the nation-sustaining and enhancing sentiments that have arisen among the people of contemporary Communist China. As Walter Laqueur has simply stated, "Chinese Communism . . . was a predominantly nationalist movement" (see *The Dream That Failed: Reflections on the Soviet Union* [New York: Oxford University Press, 1994], p. 108). It is now commonly recognized that Mao entertained a "sense of nationalism" that was traditional (see the comments by Frank Dikoetter, *The Discourse of Race in Modern China* [Stanford: Stanford University Press, 1992], p. 192). The term "nationalism" is regularly employed by scholars in describing the national politics of the People's Republic of China (see Maria Hsia Chang and Xiaoyu Chen, "The Nationalist Ideology of the Chinese Military," *Journal of Strategic Studies* 21, no. 1 [1998]: 44–64). When specialists do tender qualifications, they are of the following sort: "Anyone who has heard Chinese talk of their patriotism knows that . . . it comprises an admixture of political nationalism, ethnic Han identity, and a culturalist pride" (Jonathan Unger, introduction to *Chinese Nationalism*, ed. Jonathan Unger [Armonk, N.Y.: M. E. Sharpe, 1996], p. xiii). That kind of admixture is typical of almost all ethnic nationalisms and characteristic of Fascist nationalism.

41. See the more ample discussion in Gregor, *Italian Fascism*, chaps. 1–3, 9.

42. See the insightful discussion by one of Italy's most radical syndicalists immediately before his death in the First World War. Filippo Corridoni, *Sindacalismo e repubblica* (1915; reprint, Milan: SAREP, 1945).

43. For a more detailed discussion, see A. James Gregor, *Phoenix: Fascism in the Twentieth Century* (New Brunswick, N.J.: Transaction, 1999), chaps. 2–4.

44. Raw materials remained a constant issue with Fascist authors. See, for example, Vito Beltrani, *Il problema delle materie prime* (Rome: Tupini, 1940).

45. Throughout his life, Mussolini spoke of the "socialization" of the world as a result of resolving the disparities among nations. In his final "testament," Mussolini spoke of the provision of all the civil and political rights that characterize modern democracies in that socialized world. See Benito Mussolini, *Testamento politico di Mussolini* (Rome: Tosi, 1948), particularly pp. 35–36.

46. See the more ample discussion in A. James Gregor, *Young Mussolini and the Intellectual Origins of Fascism* (Berkeley: University of California Press, 1979), chaps. 9–10.

47. Sun Yat-sen, *The International Development of China* (1922; reprint, Taipei: China Cultural Service, 1953). Sun's *Sanmin zhuyi* (The Three Principles of the People) is available in an English edition that is faithful to the original as *The Triple Demism of Sun Yat-sen* (1931; reprint, New York: AMS, 1974). Reprint of the Wuchang edition of 1931.

48. See the first lecture of the third part of Sun's *Triple Demism*, pp. 403–444. See also Sun's comments on Lenin's "revisions" of the internationalism of Karl Marx, making Leninism a variant of the Three Principles of the People. Sun Yat-sen, "Statement on the Formation of National Government," in *Fundamentals of National Reconstruction* (Taipei: China Cultural Service, 1953), pp. 162–163.

49. Sun, *International Development of China*, p. 208.

50. See the discussion in A. James Gregor, *Marxism, China and Development: Reflections on Theory and Reality* (New Brunswick, N.J.: Transaction, 1995), chaps. 7–8.

51. See the comments of Pipes, *Russia,* pp. 241–245.

52. See the account in Christopher Lasch, *The American Liberals and the Russian Revolution* (New York: Oxford University, 1962).

53. "Modern wars, the wars of tomorrow, will inevitably be between poor nations and rich nations, between those nations that labor and produce, and those nations already in possession of capital and wealth. Those wars will have an eminently revolutionary character. They will be wars between those who can do more and those who have more. They will constitute class war between nations." Dino Grandi, *Giovani* (Bologna: Zanichelli, 1941), p. 39.

2

Marxist Theory and Fascism in Republican China

In the years between the two world wars, the century endured a series of revolutions. Not one of them was the revolution anticipated by Karl Marx and Friedrich Engels. Not one of them was a "proletarian revolution" in an advanced industrial environment. Almost all took place in peripheral economies, in which to speak of monopoly capitalism in a society hosting a proletarian majority made no sense whatever. Where revolution took place in an advanced industrial environment—in Weimar Germany—it took on a shape and substance totally unanticipated by Marxists of whatever persuasion.

In the avalanche of events, Marxists of whatever sort sought desperately to understand what was happening. In their attempts, they employed theoretical notions fashioned more than half a century before. It was during those years that Fascism arose in the largely agrarian economy of Italy, National Socialism acceded to power in Germany, and, in Asia, the Kuomintang (KMT)[1] undertook to unify China and develop it economically.

While the KMT attempted to discharge what it conceived to be its obligations, the newly formed Chinese Communist Party (CCP) promoted "proletarian" revolution. Innocent of Marxist sophistication, the CCP enlisted in the Communist International (Comintern) organized by the leaders of Bolshevik Russia almost immediately after the October revolution.

Unlettered in Marxist theory, the founders of the CCP turned to Bolshevik theoreticians to instruct them in the making of revolution in a noncapitalist and nonindustrial environment. Convinced that the Bolsheviks must be profoundly well-informed concerning Marxist theory because they had made a successful revolution in czarist Russia, the first Chinese Communists surrendered their intellectual and tactical independence to the Soviet leaders of the Comintern.

The decision, at best, was unfortunate. The Bolshevik theoreticians were caught up in an intellectual inheritance that originated over half a hundred years before, in the European home of monopoly capitalism. The Marxists of revolutionary Russia attempted to understand what was transpiring by appealing to theoretical formulations calculated to answer questions that had been considered important by Karl Marx and Friedrich Engels in the mid-nineteenth century, half a world away. The extent to which Marxist intellectuals achieved some measure of comprehension in the enormously complex environment of their time has been the subject of an entire library of books, and remains a matter of unresolved dispute.

Rather than attempt a review of all the literature devoted to these issues, an effort will be made here to achieve some appreciation of how Marxists themselves attempted to understand and vindicate the changing "eastern" policies of their leaders in Moscow, when it was not at all evident that those leaders understood what was happening in the Russia they had captured—much less in East Asia, about which they knew so little.

Marxists, in general, have persisted in the notion that the lucubrations of Karl Marx and Friedrich Engels were keys to understanding the modern world. As a consequence, Marxists were convinced that they had answers for every economic, social, and/or political question that might arise in our time.

In that context there will be *selective* scrutiny of the Marxist use of a number of contested concepts: "Marxism," "Marxism-Leninism," "class," "nationalism," and "fascism"—as those concepts were applied to the complex sequence of events that unfolded in China between the two world wars. What emerges will be a more penetrating understanding of both Marxist methodology and the concepts that are under scrutiny. At the same time, it is not inconceivable that some novel insights into China's long revolution might be forthcoming.

Revolutionary China and V. I. Lenin's Comintern

In 1928, Leon Trotsky insisted that developments in China might well be of decisive importance for the anticipated "proletarian world revolution."[2] At about that time, Karl Wittfogel, then an orthodox Marxist, was preparing an account of the revolutionary significance of the thought of Sun Yat-sen, founder of the KMT and the most readily recognized leader of the 1911 uprising that brought an end to dynastic rule in China.[3]

The years between 1922 and 1928 were critical to the Oriental policy of the Comintern. They were the years in which the Executive Committee of the Comintern (ECCI) first attempted to formulate and then implement a coherent and consistent Marxist policy for a China caught up in the throes of revolution. They were the years of the "first united front"—engineered by the ECCI—between the KMT and the CCP. They were also the years that saw the catastrophic close of what the Chinese Communists later called the "first phase" of the communist revolution.[4]

During the lifetime of Karl Marx and Friedrich Engels, two "Internationals" had given expression to Marxist views on world revolution. Lenin's International, the Comintern, was the third. Founded in 1919, years after the death of both Marx and Engels, the Comintern, as an institution, was predicated on the conviction that Bolshevik Russia would perish without the direct support of the Western European proletariat, and the collateral support of massive "national bourgeois" insurgencies in the economically backward East.[5] In 1920, the Second Congress of the Comintern, under the direction of Lenin, put together an appropriate rationale intended to support just such a policy for the economically less developed regions of the East.

With Lenin's death in 1924, Josef Stalin and his immediate entourage assumed responsibility for the formulation of an effective Oriental policy. By that time, the outlines of a Marxist-Leninist conception of "revolution in the East" had been cobbled together.

In substantial part, the Oriental policy of the Comintern was based on the judgment that industrial capitalism had entered a "new phase" since the death of Engels in 1896. That new phase was identified as "imperialism"—the "highest stage of capitalism"—and it presumably created circumstances that transformed the revolutionary expectations and the corresponding revolutionary strategies of those Marxists now identified as "Leninists."

For Marxist-Leninists, the circumstances surrounding "proletarian" revolution in the twentieth century had been profoundly altered. As early as 1900, Lenin maintained that the productive capacity of industrial capitalism had already exceeded the absorptive capacity of its domestic markets and the system had exhausted its internal investment opportunities. Just as Marx had predicted half a century before, industrial capitalism had finally entered into its "general crisis." In its struggle to survive, capitalism was being driven into those regions of the globe "in which industry is weakly developed . . . and which [could] serve as a market for manufactured goods and a source of high profits."[6]

None of this was particularly novel. Marx had suggested as much in 1848. What was different was the emphasis given to the influence of peripheral, less-developed economies on the industrially advanced systems at the European center. International capitalism was understood to have become increasingly dependent upon the relatively primitive economies on its periphery, while, at the same time, its efforts to extract profits created a repository of hostility among the millions upon millions of toiling persons living there. What Marxists like to call the "parallelogram of forces" had changed.

Revolution in the era of imperialism was no longer conceived as spontaneous response on the part of the "vast majority" of a working population in mature industrial environments. Where Marx and Engels had anticipated that periodic crises or the final decline in the overall rate of profit would drive proletarians to overthrow their oppressive domestic system,[7] the Marxists of the twentieth century understood social revolution to be a complex product of proletarian resistance in the advanced industrial economies and uprisings in the economically retrograde communities outside the immediate confines of the world capitalist system.

By 1916, Lenin was prepared to argue that even though industrial capitalism had exhausted its growth potential, it had not succumbed—as Marx had predicted—to a final, fatal stagnation because it had succeeded in extracting "superprofits" from the less-developed economies on its periphery.[8] Not only had the profits from market supplements and the investment outlets in the less-developed economies succeeded in extending the life of industrial capitalism, the profits collected "outside" the system provided the wherewithal to bribe the venal leaders of the working class in the capitalist "center." The "revolutionary proletariat" of the West was being misled by suborned leaders.[9] Only if the integrity of the proletarian revolutionary movement were restored could socialism succeed.

For Leninists, the revolutionary emphasis had shifted from the advanced industrial countries to their dependencies. Leninists were to argue that, given the changed circumstances, the "proletarian revolution" could hardly be expected to be the consequence of the "spontaneous" uprising of the "vast majority" of the population in capital-saturated environments. If socialism was to triumph, there was to be nothing spontaneous about revolution. World revolution was to be the consequence of the calculated intervention into events by a self-selected cohort of professional revolutionaries organized as a "vanguard party." A professional "vanguard," equipped with "the one true social science," would provide principled revolutionary leadership to the misguided "toiling masses" in the industrial center as well as in the marginally developed periphery.[10] They would offset the countervailing influence of the paid lackies of capitalism as well as lead the peasantry of noncapitalist economies.

"The social revolution," Lenin argued in 1916, "can come only in the form of an epoch in which are combined civil war by the proletariat against the bourgeoisie in the advanced countries and a whole series of democratic and revolutionary movements, including the national liberation movement, in the undeveloped, backward and oppressed nations."[11] In the advanced economies, the vanguard party would lead the urban proletariat. In the "backward nations," the vanguard party of the proletariat would make common cause with "bourgeois democratic" and "bourgeois national liberation" movements, in the anti-imperialist service of "world proletarian revolution."

Not only did these notions provide a rationale for Bolshevik foreign policy after the October revolution, but the policies recommended would help to insulate revolutionary Russia from the predations of imperialism and prepare the ground for the "saving revolution." If imperialism could be distracted by proletarian unrest at home and undermined by "bourgeois" nationalism on its periphery, it was reasonable to expect that pressure on the still fragile Bolshevik Russia would diminish.

Successful revolutions on the periphery of world capitalism would separate imperialism from its external support system—and industrial capitalism would once again find itself facing an "inevitable" and irreversible decline in its rate of profit. In the course of that systemic decline, the proletariat of the West once more would be driven to assume their revolutionary "historical responsibilities." Much of the substance of this "creative" and "dialectical" development of classical Marxism came from a book entitled *Imperialism*, written at the turn of the century by an English social reformer, J. A. Hobson. His work, a critique of British imperial policy, exercised its influence on the thought of a number of Marxist theoreticians—Lenin not the least among them.[12]

Hobson argued that the "great financial houses" acted as "the governor of the imperial engine, directing the energy and determining its work." It was "finance" that "manipulated" the energies of nameless masses, soldiers, and politicians.[13] The Leninist conviction that "finance capitalism" was the éminence grise behind reaction and counterrevolution everywhere in the world received much of its impetus from the work of Hobson.

The notion that "finance capitalism" acted as the executive agency for all of capitalism,[14] taken together with the conviction that "imperialism" constituted the final, desperate stand of history's last oppressors, shaped the policy orientation of revolutionary Marxism-Leninism throughout the first half of the twentieth century. Much of the Comintern's behavior is explicable in terms of just such a set of beliefs.

As has been argued, the founders of Marxism had anticipated proletarian revolution in the most industrially advanced economies, where the productive base of a distributive socialism already existed and where urban workers, long enured to factory production, were prepared to assume the material responsibilities of rule. Marxist-Leninists, on the other hand, argued that nationalist uprisings on the periphery of the more advanced economies would be a necessary preamble to world revolution. World revolution would commence at the "weakest links" along the chain of world imperialism. Ruptures in the chain would precipitate the humane and liberating revolution in the advanced industrial nations anticipated by the founders of Marxism.

Thus, in 1917, Lenin acknowledged that the revolution in czarist Russia could only be a "prologue to the world socialist revolution."[15] There was not the least doubt that the economic base of imperial Russia was inadequate to support socialism. The Bolsheviks had undertaken a revolution in Russia in order to deal a blow to international imperialism. It was a political act at one of the weaker links of the chain of international oppression. Such revolutions would fatally weaken industrial capitalism in the economically advanced West. In the pursuit of socialist revolution, Bolsheviks were to recommend "bourgeois nationalist" uprisings all along the perimeter of the industrial core of imperialism.

According to these conjectures, in order to fully succeed, socialism required a series of uprisings throughout the colonialized and semicolonialized regions of the globe. That would neutralize the "resource and reserve base" of international capitalism.[16] Only that would ensure the decisive "proletarian" victory in the industrialized West.

This was the theoretical context in which the Comintern's assessment of China was to be understood. By the time of the Second Congress of the Comintern, conducted during July-August 1920, the first intimations of the policy toward the East had crystallized.

Those who formulated the "Oriental policy" of the Comintern recommended that material and moral support be supplied to the revolutionary nationalist forces of Sun Yat-sen's Kuomintang. China was understood to be one of the more important links in world imperialism—and the Kuomintang was perceived as the only real agent of revolution in China.

The theoreticians of the Comintern argued that precapitalist China had already begun the "bourgeois" revolution that would bring it into the twentieth century. True to some of the basic notions of classical Marxism, it was argued that before China could set itself socialist goals, it would have to resolve those political, social, and economic problems that history has shown can only be solved by the emerging bourgeoisie.

China had embarked on a "bourgeois nationalist revolution" whose responsibility it was to overthrow and supplant the "feudal" economic and political arrangements that had prevailed on the mainland for thousands of years. The bourgeoisie was "destined"[17] to ultimately create the economic foundations for an inevitable socialism.

To accomplish all that for China, and to strike a blow against imperialism, the Comintern urged a policy on the newly organized Chinese Communist Party that would necessarily involve "temporary agreements" with the "national bourgeoisie." In the judgment of the ECCI, the bourgeoisie would lead a "national revolution" committed to national economic development and provide revolutionary resistance to the impostures of imperialism.

Having committed themselves to such a general strategy, upon the insistence of the Third International, Communist party members in China were expected to seek out, foster, and sustain collaboration with "bourgeois national" undertakings as long as any "temporary arrangements" entered into did not "obstruct the revolutionary organization of the workers and peasants" in a "genuine struggle against imperialism."[18] For the theoreticians of the Comintern, the bourgeois national revolution in China, as would be the case everywhere else, would be the necessary first phase in the ultimate "proletarian world revolution."

That understood, Marxist-Leninists in China would employ the opportunities offered by temporary collaboration with the "bourgeoisie" to "facilitate the proletariat's role of hegemon in the Chinese bourgeois-democratic revolution, and to hasten the moment of transition to the proletarian revolution."[19] The anticipated relationship with the "bourgeoisie" would clearly involve considerable subterfuge, political cunning, and sometimes deception.

The "temporary agreements" anticipated by the Comintern in China were those with the Kuomintang, the Nationalist party of Sun Yat-sen. The ideology sustaining the "bourgeois" movement for national liberation would be the essentially anti-Marxist "Three Principles of the People" (*Sanmin zhuyi*), left as an intellectual legacy to the Kuomintang by Sun.

Because the projected relationship involved potential conflict, much of the Oriental policy of the Comintern was composed of directives attempting to govern the inevitable tensions inherent in the "temporary agreements" between the Chinese Communist party and Sun Yat-sen's Nationalists. In an attempt to effectively supervise the proposed relationship, the Comintern sent its representatives to China.

It was in its tortured association with the Kuomintang, and in its intervention in events on the mainland of China, that the Comintern revealed a great deal not only about its methods but about the conceptual materials it employed in the formulation and vindication of policy. Over the course of time, as will be indicated, some of the major theoreticians and principal spokesmen of the Comintern invoked "fascism" as a conceptual tool in the effort to explain events in China and justify their "Oriental policy." How this was expected to make any sense to an objective audience can only be appreciated by reviewing something of the assessments about China and its leaders offered by Marxists during the preceding half century.

The Theoretical Background

In the middle of the nineteenth century, Karl Marx and Friedrich Engels had argued that the industrial bourgeoisie of the West, with their cheap commodities and rapid means of communication, would "batter down all Chinese walls" and would compel "all nations . . . to introduce what it calls civilization into their midst, i.e., to become bourgeois themselves."[20] A decade later, in 1858, both Marx and Engels identified the "particular task of bourgeois society" to be "the establishment of the world market" and "of production based upon [that] market."[21]

In those circumstances, Marx and those who followed him fully expected the expansion of the "bourgeois mode of production" to overwhelm China. The European bourgeoisie, through aggressive trade policies and a penetrative flow of investment capital, would awaken an economically backward China that had long "vegetated in the teeth of time."

Once awakened, an economically developing China would predictably resist the incursions of foreign cultural, political, and economic influences. It would be the native bourgeoisie of retrograde China—the small traders, the founders of factories, the importers of foreign commodities, and the intellectuals who collected around them—who would provide the leavening of resistance to the "foreign devils." Marx and Engels clearly expected anti-imperialism in economically backward China to be "bourgeois" and nationalist in essence.[22]

China's bourgeois resistance was expected to be nationalist in inspiration and antiforeign in expression. Marx acknowledged the intensity of the antiforeign violence that would accompany the mounting nationalism in China. The dislocations that would necessarily accompany the protracted process of irregular warfare and anti-Western revolution on the Chinese mainland could only negatively impact the trade and investment arrangements that had already been forged between the capitalist West and the emerging East. That critical contraction of the export markets and investment outlets would seriously impair the survival capacity of the Western industrial system, increasingly incapable of profitably clearing its inventories.[23] Given such a set of beliefs, Marx was prepared to accept the proposition that the "national bourgeoisie" of industrially less developed regions peripheral to the capitalist "metropole" could significantly contribute to the ultimate victory of the revolutionary proletariat in the advanced capitalist states. The Comintern would accept the essence of that account with special emphasis, as has already been indicated, on the singular role to be played by "bourgeois national liberation" movements in the era of imperialism.

Years before the outbreak of the First World War, Lenin had offered his first opinions concerning revolution in China. In 1900, he spoke of the

Chinese suffering the "oppression of capital" and harboring a revolutionary hatred of "European capitalists,"[24] apparently anticipating an "anti-imperialist bourgeois national revolution."

A dozen years later, armed with these conceptions, Lenin tendered his first judgments with respect to the revolutionary who had emerged as the leader of China's antidynastic revolution. In 1912, Lenin spoke of Sun Yat-sen as an "enlightened spokesman of militant and victorious Chinese democracy." For Lenin, Sun, as leader of the Chinese revolution, was the advocate of a "truly great ideology of a truly great people . . . fighting the age-long oppressors of China." For Lenin, Sun was a "revolutionary democrat, endowed with the nobility and heroism of a class that is rising, not declining, a class that does not dread the future, but believes in it and fights for it selflessly."[25] In Lenin's judgment, Sun's ideology, the Three Principles of the People, was "truly great" and inspired a "truly great" people to a nationalist revolution that would critically wound international imperialism—the implacable enemy of the proletariat.

At the same time, it was equally clear to Lenin that Sun Yat-sen was the spokesman for a "reactionary economic theory" that predicated the development of China on an intensive and comprehensive capitalist program of agrarian and industrial growth and technological sophistication. Not only an advocate of class collaboration in the pursuit of development, Sun was prepared to seek capital investments and foreign loans from "imperialists." Lenin was convinced that only as an emerging China generated its own proletariat would the "petty bourgeois utopias and reactionary views of Sun Yat-sen" be stripped away to reveal the truly revolutionary implications of the Chinese revolution.[26]

By 1925, both Lenin and Sun Yat-sen were dead. Lenin had died on January 21, 1924, and Sun, after a life devoted to revolutionary activity, followed him in death on March 12, 1925. Like Lenin, Sun left his heirs a complex ideological legacy—as well as domestic and international political, social, and economic problems of harrowing magnitude. Not the least of the problems left to their respective followers was the issue of how both communist and nationalist revolutionary movements were to deal with each other in an increasingly complex and threatening world environment.[27]

For Marxists, of whatever persuasion, it was evident that revolutionaries in less-developed economic environments, given the absence of proletarians, could only be "bourgeois." Both Marx and Lenin had recognized as much. Revolutionaries in colonial or "semicolonial" economic circumstances, given their origins, their social base, and their ideological purposes, would be unqualifiedly bourgeois. At the same time, the "bourgeois nationalists" in the economically less developed nations—by the very disturbances they create and the concessions they extract from their oppressors—would deny "world imperialism . . . its 'most reliable' rear and 'inexhaustible' reserve." Without that, "the definite triumph of socialism" would be "unthinkable."[28]

As a consequence of all these notions, Marxists have always hosted a deep ambivalence about nationalist revolutionaries that emerge in primitive economic environments. Although Lenin insisted that the thought of Sun Yat-sen gave expression to a "truly great ideology,"[29] that ideology was inescapably "petty bourgeois" and "reactionary."[30] In the years that followed the founding of the Third International and the formulation of a "revolutionary Marxist-Leninist Oriental policy," that intrinsic ambivalence was to generate fateful difficulties for the representatives of the Comintern, the leaders of the Chinese Communist party, and those responsible for the governance of Nationalist China.[31]

J. V. Stalin and the
Comintern's Oriental Policy

Stalin's Comintern had every pragmatic, foreign policy, and theoretical reason to continue to advocate collaboration between the newly formed Chinese Communist party and the Chinese Nationalists. By 1923, Chen Duxiu, one of the founders of the Chinese Communist party, having accepted in principle the leadership of the Third International, had been compelled to accept the Comintern thesis that China was undergoing a "bourgeois nationalist revolution" and that the Kuomintang was its natural leader.[32]

The initial response on the part of the leadership of the new Chinese Communist party was resistance. "Proletarians" were understood to have no business in a "bourgeois" movement. In reply, the representative of the Comintern, Henricus Maring (Sneevliet), insisted that collaboration between the Chinese Communists and the Kuomintang need not cause difficulty because the Kuomintang was not actually a "bourgeois" party. It was, in fact, an "alliance of all classes," a "united front" to which the "party of the proletariat" could accommodate itself without trepidation.[33]

Pressed for specificity, Maring proceeded to argue that the Kuomintang could best be characterized as a party of "four classes": the intelligentsia, the liberal democratic bourgeoisie, the petty bourgeoisie, and the workers.[34] United against imperialism, the "four-class bloc" of a revolutionary China would participate in the anti-imperialist international of workers.

For anyone with any theoretical sophistication, it was immediately evident that the "intelligentsia" could hardly constitute an independent "class"—but then, neither could the "liberal bourgeoisie" or the "petty bourgeoisie." Whatever the case, the theoreticians of the Comintern finally settled on what they considered a more suitable formulation of the thesis. In the Comintern literature of the time, the most consistent characterization of the "united front" appeared as a claim that it was composed of the "national bourgeoisie, the urban petty bourgeoisie, the peasantry and the proletariat."[35]

However strange the thesis—given the class orientation of Marxism—it was one that represented the official theoretical judgment of the executive committee of the Comintern. Throughout most of the period of the first united front between the CCP and the KMT, and as late as 1927, the ECCI continued to argue that the Kuomintang government was not "bourgeois." It was a "four class bloc government."[36]

Leon Trotsky consistently opposed every such formulation. However much the constituent members of the "bloc" might change, the fact remained that according to Marxist theory there could only be *two* classes: the revolutionary proletariat and the reactionary bourgeoisie. Whatever subsets there might be—"petty bourgeoisie," the "liberal democratic bourgeoisie," the "peasantry," or the "intelligentsia"—they were all unmistakably and irredeemably "bourgeois." A Kuomintang government could not be composed of "four classes." It could only be composed of two classes, with one class, the bourgeoisie, divided into ill-defined and sometimes mercurial subsets.

If Marxists had difficulty with the analysis of the bourgeoisie as a class, no less could be said about their cavalier conceptual treatment of the "proletariat." That "proletariat" was the designation of a homogeneous economic class was clearly a presupposition even less convincing than the notion that the "bourgeoisie" could be parsed into discrete subgroups, each possessed of a peculiar class or subclass consciousness.

The workers of China, during the years between the First and Second World Wars, made up a numerically small, heterogeneous, geographically dispersed, and stratified collection of young and old, skilled and unskilled members, some recent inmigrants from the rural areas and others long-time urban dwellers. Some were members of secret societies while others were members of one or another political association. Some were religious in the Western sense of the term while others were not. Some were members of intact family groups while others were unattached. Some lived in collective housing and others did not. Many of the workers were traditionalists while others had caught the fever of modernization. Some of the workers were of local origin while others came from distant parts of the republic. In many areas, women and girls made up about half the workforce of small factories and collective enterprises, with attitudes that distinguished them from their male counterparts.[37]

It would be hard to imagine that such an aggregate could be possessed of a common consciousness, whether that consciousness be conceived "proletarian" or "anti-imperialist." To suggest that any party, "prole-tariat" or "bourgeois," simply represented the "interests" of such a col-lection would betray a harrowing innocence of the complexities involved in giving any group interest political expression.

In fact, many Marxists admitted that classes, however they were un-derstood, often behaved in ways that belied their putative "class inter-ests." Thus, it was argued that classes could be influenced by their "im-mediate sectional interests" in such measure that it would "blind them to the much greater benefits that might accrue to their class from the victory of the revolution." In many cases, the "world proletarian revolution" that was supposed to resolve all their ultimate interests was only "remotely associated" with immediate concerns. Often the consciousness of entire classes and subclasses was simply "clouded and confused."[38]

There were some classes, like the peasantry, critical to the "proletarian revolution" in China, whose "proprietor psychology" was antithetical to socialism. Lenin had counseled Marxists to be "distrustful" of them; they were to be led by a "vanguard" that appreciated their ultimate "true" in-terests.[39]

Given these methodological complexities, much of the theorizing of the representatives of the Comintern was unfortunate at best. At its worst, it brought ruin on the Chinese Communist party in the late 1920s and death to many thousands of its members.[40]

The argument made by the Marxist-Leninist opposition, and non-Marxists alike, was that the Comintern, for reasons difficult to fathom,[41] had compelled the Chinese Communist party to participate as a junior member in a bourgeois party, animated by bourgeois interests and guided by a bourgeois ideology.[42] Behind that objection was the clear in-timation that the leaders of the Communist International had a very un-certain grasp of "class analysis." The criticism has every appearance of being justified.

Whenever any responsible member of the Comintern attempted to ex-plain some sequence of events, a stereotypic "class analysis" was almost immediately forthcoming. Without any reliable statistics or documentary evidence whatever, representatives of the Comintern would invariably identify some class interest or other behind the most complex and in-scrutable behaviors. Thus, when G. N. Voitinsky, one of the Comintern's China specialists, was called on to explain some behavior of the "right wing" of the Kuomintang, he identified it without hesitation as the con-sequence of the influence of "merchant capitalists" attempting to protect themselves against the "industrial capitalists" in the North.[43] The most complex political behaviors were imagined to be susceptible to that kind of explanatory simplism.

Thus, for the representatives of the Comintern, some particular piece of behavior on the part of Chiang Kai-shek was explained as a consequence of "the bourgeoisie's" attempt to assure their "hegemony" in the "class struggle" taking place in China in the mid-1920s. The omnibus "bourgeoisie" worked "through Chiang Kai-shek,"[44] as though Chiang were the compliant instrument of their bidding.

These kinds of interpretations were commonplace in the deliberations of the theoreticians of the Comintern. Thus, in 1926, the Sixth Plenum of the Executive Committee of the Comintern invited Hu Han-min, one of the late Sun Yat-sen's most trusted compatriots and a leader of the Kuomintang, to Moscow. He was presented to the membership of the Comintern as a revolutionary "representative of the peasantry of China."[45] Needless to say, to this day it remains a mystery why Hu was identified with the Chinese peasantry by the analysts of the Comintern.

This quaint identification of individuals with entire classes or fragments of classes was typical of the analyses made available to the members of the Comintern by its leadership. The explanation of the behavior of individuals or groups of individuals as a function of their supposed class membership was more common still. Thus Mikhail Borodin, one of the Comintern's most important agents, explained the Kuomintang's indisposition to confiscate private property by pointing out its "mixed class composition."[46]

Marxists were simply not prepared to grant that the leadership of the Kuomintang, true to the convictions of Sun Yat-sen, might refuse to consider the confiscation of private property because they were convinced that any such policy would impair the effectiveness of the party's plans for the rapid economic growth and industrial development of China. Together with his insistence on class collaboration in the effort to industrialize China, Sun had made the existence of private property, and its protection in law, central to his program for economic expansion as early as the first decade of the twentieth century. For Marxists, class collaboration and the protection of private property could not be the consequence of the Kuomintang obeying the ideological injunctions of its founder; it could only be the Kuomintang's submissive response to specific class demands of the bourgeoisie.

Most curious of all, of course, irrespective of whatever "class analysis" informed Marxist-Leninist policies, there was Stalin's judgment that in China a preoccupation with class interests was really of little practical importance. As late as April 1927, when the Comintern's united front policy was disintegrating into tragedy, Stalin could still insist that the respective interests of classes involved in the Chinese revolution were of relatively minor consequence because "a powerful national factor" had drawn all "revolutionary forces of the country together into one camp." In his judgment, it was the nationalist "struggle against imperialism" that was the "*predominating* factor . . . determining the character of the relations between the revolutionary forces of China within the Kuomintang."[47]

Stalin had decided that it was the "international class war" —the colonial or semicolonial nations against the "imperialist" powers—that determined the political behaviors of all participants in the Chinese revolution. Class divisions within the "oppressed nations" were matters of relatively little interpretive significance. The critical enemy of less-developed nations was "world imperialism," and the animating revolutionary sentiment was nationalism. Recognition of those realities defined the political options available to revolutionary forces. All "revolutionaries" in economically primitive environments would commit themselves to the international "class struggle" against the "imperialist" oppressor. As a consequence, in the "oppressed nations" the Comintern could advocate the construction of a multiclass "single national revolutionary front" to confront the imperialist enemy. In China, that united front was marshaled under the nationalist leadership of the Kuomintang.[48]

Stalin tendered those judgments in April 1927, immediately before the collapse of the Comintern's policy in China. Between April and May of that year, seeking to unify all of China under their rule, the victorious Nationalists entered Shanghai. On May 5, the Kuomintang Central Standing Committee mandated a purge of all Communists from the party and imposed a reign of terror on all their real or fancied allies. Communists were deemed anti-Nationalists committed to a foreign power.

By August 1927, Chiang Kai-shek had put down the resistance of his opponents in Wuhan. By the end of the year, Nationalist China severed diplomatic relations with the Soviet Union.[49] The Oriental policies of the Stalinist Comintern had shown themselves to be singularly incompetent.

Stalin had entirely misunderstood nationalism. Nationalism was predicated on commitment to one's own nation. Subordination to the directives of a foreign, essentially international organization could only be considered a treasonous betrayal.

Failing to understand that, the Comintern had led the Communists of China into a tragedy of cataclysmic proportions. Stalin had gambled that his policies in China would result in the victory of the "national bourgeoisie" and a setback for "imperialism"—all to the benefit of the Soviet Union. The readiness of China's national bourgeoisie to engage "imperialism" would make the Kuomintang an "objective ally" of the international proletarian revolution. Nationalist China would constitute a buffer for the Soviet Union in the East, and the Kuomintang would be the Soviet Union's ally against the advanced industrial powers of the West.

By mid-1927, it was evident to almost everyone but Stalin that his gamble in China had been a monumental failure.[50] The opponents of Stalin's policies recognized them to have been an unmitigated catastrophe.

Marxists have always maintained that the special virtue of their belief system was its "scientific" character. "Scientific socialism" dealt with the "science of society," with its "laws of development." The special "strength of Marxism" lay "in its ability to foretell" events and predict outcomes.[51]

In their policies in the East, the theoreticians of the Comintern displayed none of the presumed strengths of their "dialectical methods." They had been wrong in China in almost every way possible. The theoreticians of the Comintern had failed to understand the character and the nature of the events that made up much of the history of China between 1920 and the first incursions of the Japanese into Chinese territory in September 1931.

In the years that were to follow, Marxists of all sorts attempted to vindicate the eastern policies of the Third International. There was a bold effort to reinterpret events. The responsibility for failure was showered on the leadership of the Chinese Communist party itself, as though they had somehow failed to understand the theoretical brilliance of the "eastern specialists" of the Comintern. By the middle of 1927, the theoreticians of the Comintern had discovered that the Kuomintang, long identified as "anti-imperialist," had succumbed to imperialist blandishments and was no longer a "party of a *bloc* of oppressed classes." Chiang Kai-shek had "made a deal" with the imperialists.[52] The Comintern had resolved its ambivalence. Chiang Kai-shek, who had tirelessly "waged a war against imperialism" with a party composed of "workers and peasants" in the service of the "international proletarian revolution,"[53] had become an "open agent of imperialism"[54] and a "potential Mussolini."[55]

M. N. Roy, Sun Yat-sen, and
Fascism in Republican China

After the dimensions of the debacle in China had become evident, the theoreticians of the Comintern undertook a reformulation of theory. By the end of the 1920s, the defeated Chinese Communist party had separated itself from the Kuomintang, and it was to pursue a course taking it into the rural reaches of agrarian China. It was to enter into fretful unity with KMT once again to resist the Japanese invasion after 1937, to ultimately engage the followers of Sun Yat-sen and Chiang Kai-shek in civil war immediately after the Second World War. In 1949, Mao Zedong, successful in his military campaign against the KMT, emerged as leader of the newly proclaimed People's Republic of China.

For our purposes, the Marxist attempt to understand the catastrophe that befell the first effort at a Chinese Communist party and Kuomintang "united front" in China is of particular interest. Some of the major protagonists of the Comintern's failed policy offered a reassessment that reveals a great deal not only about what Marxism was expected to accomplish in less-developed economic environments but what the Marxist interpretation of fascism was all about. In fact, it was M. N. Roy, a representative of the Comintern, dispatched to China at the time of critical developments in 1927, who has provided one of the most suggestive and controversial accounts.[56]

Roy was a major figure during the early years of the Comintern. A young Indian Marxist, he debated Lenin on the nature of revolution along the boundaries of world capitalism. He was charged with the responsibility of providing official counsel to the leaders of the Chinese Communist party during the final phase of the direct involvement of the Comintern in the Chinese revolution. As a consequence, Roy was caught up in the recriminations that followed the failure of Comintern policy.[57] As early as 1930, he wrote his first account of the sequence of events that ended in the virtual destruction of the Chinese Communist party. In 1946, almost twenty years after the events in question, Roy provided a revised English-language account of the failure of Comintern policy in China.[58] In that retrospective, Roy revealed that Marxists should have known from their first contacts with Sun Yat-sen's Kuomintang that they were dealing not with "petty bourgeois" and "anti-imperialist" elements but with anti-Marxist and nationalist "counterrevolutionaries."

Having met Sun Yat-sen as early as 1916, Roy claimed to have recognized that Sun, having been raised in Hawaii under the influence of American capitalism, was forever "on the point of becoming an admirer of foreign imperialism." In fact, Roy continued, Sun imagined that retrograde China might be economically developed with "the aid of its worst enemy. . . . The country was to be economically developed with the aid of foreign capital."[59]

According to his account, Roy had immediately recognized that Sun was a spokesman for "petty bourgeois political radicalism." That disability apparently led him to imagine that a "gigantic plan" for the economic and industrial development of China might be "carried out not only by foreign capital, but under the supervision of foreign experts." Sun was prepared to embark on the nationalist and statist development of China by collaborating with "international finance." Not only was such a policy anti-Marxist and "reactionary," Roy insisted, it cast before it the "ominous shadow of fascism." In fact, the economic system anticipated by Sun "was evidently an anticipation of the totalitarian economy of the fascist state."[60]

In retrospect, all of this was transparent to Roy. Somehow or other, the theoreticians of the Comintern had failed to notice what Roy had apparently divined as early as 1916. Sun Yat-sen, having mobilized the petty bourgeoisie behind a program of national development, was a tool of international finance and a servant of imperialism. No one seemed to have recognized all that prior to the late 1920s. Only years later did the truth become apparent to Marxists. "Scientific socialism" had failed to anticipate events.

Only after Mao Zedong acceded to power on the mainland of China did Chen Boda, one of the major theoreticians in the entourage of the "Great Helmsman," acknowledge that fascism had been a major problem in the course of the Chinese revolution.[61] Sun Yat-sen's Kuomintang ultimately and inevitably came to represent "the big bourgeoisie, and counted on the support of foreign imperialism" in order to defeat the Chinese "proletarian revolution."[62]

By the 1940s, the Chinese Communists had learned from the experience of 1927 and had recognized that the Kuomintang was, and had always been, "fascist."[63] As early as 1943, Chen Boda identified the book *China's Destiny*, published that year by Chiang Kai-shek, as "advocating fascism" for China.[64] In that same year, Mao Zedong identified the government of Chiang Kai-shek as a "fascist dictatorship."[65] Somehow or other, what had been obvious to Roy for decades had escaped the theoreticians of the Comintern throughout the years between 1920 and 1927 and only became clear to the Maoist leadership of the Communist party in the early 1940s.

All of this suggested that, for Marxist practitioners, a great deal of confusion surrounded the nature of revolution in the industrially less developed peripheral economies. It also revealed something about the Marxist-Leninist employments of the term "fascist" in any given circumstance.

Although the "standard version" of the Marxist interpretation of fascism had been common property since the first years of the 1930s, the theoreticians of the Comintern had introduced a number of significant qualifiers. According to the standard version, "fascism" was understood to be a quintessential "bourgeois" and nationalist phenomenon, meaning that, in principle, it opposed itself to the "international proletarian revolution." But the leaders of the Soviet Union were prepared to allow that "bourgeois national" revolutions could count as "progressive" if those revolutions served the defense needs of "the Socialist Motherland." There were some nationalist movements that apparently fell within the pale of Marxist-Leninist orthodoxy.

More than that, although Marxist theoreticians, in general, argued that only "proletarian" revolutionary movements could count as "revolutionary," Stalin had insisted that in retrograde economic circumstances, nationalism might serve to mobilize "all classes" around anti-imperialism. However much Leninists might decry the multiclass character of Italian

Fascism, they were prepared to recognize the legitimacy of such class in-
clusiveness in some ill-defined circumstances. Thus, the simple fact that
a revolutionary movement abjured "class struggle" in the pursuit of a
unified front against imperialism did not automatically make it "counterrevolutionary."

Finally, although Marxist-Leninists recognized the social base of fascism to be "petty bourgeois," they acknowledged a similar socioeconomic
base for the bourgeois nationalist movements of the less-developed nations on the periphery of international capitalism. That did not necessarily disqualify such movements as either progressive or revolutionary.
Bourgeois national revolutions in countries like postdynastic China were
considered part of the worldwide revolutionary tide.

Marxist-Leninists somehow "knew" that fascism served the class interests of the "big bourgeoisie"—the agrarian capitalists and large-scale
industrial entrepreneurs—whereas bourgeois national revolutions on the
periphery of industrial capitalism did not. Ultimately, in some uncertain
sense, fascism was dominated by national or international "finance capital" but the bourgeois nationalists in other less-developed nations were
not.

These were some of the confusions that attended any effort to distinguish "fascism" from "progressive" bourgeois nationalist movements on
the margins of world capitalism. In retrospect, the fact that the unfortunate leaders of Chinese Communism failed to identify Sun Yat-sen or the
Kuomintang as fascist before the catastrophe that overwhelmed their
movement is perfectly understandable. The fact is that Stalin himself did
not make the connection until after disaster struck.

Years later, some of the foremost intellectuals of Chinese Communism
divined that one of Stalin's "great theoretical contributions to the Chinese revolution" was his belated discovery—after 1927—that the Kuomintang and its leader were "fascist."[66] Like Roy, Stalin discovered only in
retrospect that the Kuomintang had really always been fascist. The
Kuomintang, characterized by the Comintern until 1927 as a revolutionary party of workers and peasants committed to the revolutionary struggle against imperialism, was exposed after 1927 as having always been
fascist. Only after the abject defeat of his policies in China did Stalin discover the true political character of both the Kuomintang and Chiang
Kai-shek.

Although he gave no evidence of it before the catastrophe that devastated the Chinese Communist party and decimated its membership in
1927, it seems evident that Roy believed that he could have done better
than Stalin in anticipating the political behavior of the Kuomintang and
its leaders. Roy seems to have had the unremarkable faculty of retroac-
tively "deducing" truths from Marxist premises. Thus, years after the

events in question, he informed his audience that he had always known that Sun Yat-sen was a "protofascist" and that the Kuomintang, unable to "liberate itself from [Sun's] reactionary principles," would simply commit itself to "petty bourgeois radical nationalism" and surrender to the influence of the "big merchants, industrialists and bankers"—all of whom, in turn, were to fall under the fateful influence of Wall Street.[67]

Possessed of the "scientific sociology" of Marxism, Roy had apparently foreseen all of that. He had seen the "ominous shadow of fascism" in the political principles of Sun Yat-sen even before there was a fascism.[68] Roy had apparently known that every principle to which Sun Yat-sen had committed himself was "reactionary." He knew that because he was in possession of a scientific sorting device. He could unfailingly tell what was reactionary by employing a simple test: A doctrine is revolutionary "when it leads to an agreement with Marx. Otherwise, it is reactionary."[69]

Should that test fail, Roy informed his audience, one could measure a political ideology against the verdict of history. If an ideology attempted to resist "the verdict of death pronounced [on capitalism] by history," that ideology is clearly reactionary.[70] By both tests, Sun Yat-sun's ideological principles were unavailingly bourgeois and unrelievedly reactionary. That Sun's plans for China's future would allow "international finance . . . absolute control" over its industry and trade clearly suggested that Sun was the tool of "finance capital."[71]

Sun's readiness to "compromise" with agrarian capitalists and industrialists, his rejection of the "class struggle," and his "demogogic nationalism" all signaled to Roy the advent of a Chinese fascism.[72] Sun's ideology, the Three Principles of the People, had implied as much.

This matter had apparently escaped the attention of all the theoreticians of the Comintern and the Communist intellectuals of the Chinese Communist party. As late as 1927, Georgi Zinoviev could still report that the ideology of Sun Yat-sen was a form of Chinese nationalist populism that had a "progressive and democratic essence."[73] On 1 May 1927, Wang Ching-wei of the "Left" Kuomintang and Chen Duxiu issued a "joint statement" affirming that "the Chinese Communist Party is fully aware of the fact that the Kuomintang with its Three Principles of the People is doubtless what the Chinese revolution needs."[74] Seemingly, neither the Comintern nor the Chinese Communist party recognized fascism when it was in their midst.

To make matters worse, in July 1926, Chen Duxiu, leader of the Chinese Communist party, still referred to Chiang Kai-shek as a "pillar of the Chinese national revolution."[75] Chen apparently failed to recognize fascism as an ideology, as a party, or in the behaviors of a political leader.

In effect, there was more confusion than science in the Marxist assessment of the role and historic significance of fascism, Sun Yat-sen, his ideology, Chiang Kai-shek, and the Kuomintang. Stalin had counseled the members of the Comintern that a "bourgeois nationalism," multiclass in membership, that opposed itself to the industrialized "imperialist" powers was an "ally of the proletarian revolution." Stalin's characterization was all but indistinguishable from Fascism's characterization of itself. Mussolini had opposed "proletarian revolution" in Italy for the same reasons Stalin opposed it in the China of the 1920s. By the 1930s, Moscow had settled on a hopelessly incompetent definition of generic fascism[76] that obscured its affinities with what was transpiring in China. Between the 1930s and the 1940s, the judgments of Communist theoreticians in Moscow and among the leadership of the Chinese Communist party remained confused.

In all of this, a curious fact merits reflection. Although the Communist party of Mao Zedong regularly identified the Kuomintang of Chiang Kai-shek as fascist after the early 1940s,[77] Mao continued to support Sun Yat-sen and the ideology he had formulated until the middle of the decade.[78] Whatever fascism there was to be found in the Kuomintang, it apparently was not to be attributed to Sun as founder of the party.

By the mid-1940s, it was seemingly evident to the leadership of the Chinese Communist party that Chiang Kai-shek was the "representative" of the "big landlords, and the big bankers" as well as the "tool" of international imperialism—and, by implication, the creature of "finance capitalism."[79] Chiang was a fascist, but Sun apparently had not been.

The "science" of Marxism has thus left the interwar political history of China in considerable confusion. It seems clear that all the "orthodox" Marxist-Leninists of the Comintern and the Chinese Communist party, between the early 1920s until the end of the Second World War, remained unsure of the analysis appropriate to the major events we have here considered. The concern turns on the Marxist employment, years later, of the concept "fascism" in order to understand what had transpired between 1920 and 1927. Their invocation of the concept has left us with two subsets of problems, each of which can best be considered separately. The first deals with the "fascism" of Sun Yat-sen and the "fascism" of his ideology. The second deals with the "fascism" of Chiang Kai-shek and the "fascism" of his Kuomintang. It is to those problems that we can profitably turn our attention.

Notes

1. The Wade-Giles transliteration of Chinese terms will be used throughout for Nationalist Chinese names (e.g., Chiang Kai-shek) because they are most familiar to English-language readers in that form. The pinyin system will otherwise be used.

2. See Leon Trotsky, "Summary and Perspectives of the Chinese Revolution," in *The Third International After Lenin* (New York: Pioneer, 1937), pp. 167–230.

3. K. A. Wittfogel, *Sun Yat Sen: Aufzeichnungen eines chinesischen Revolutionaraers* (Berlin: Agis, n.d.).

4. See the discussion in Mao Zedong, "The Situation and Our Policy After the Victory in the War of Resistance Against Japan," in *Selected Works* (Beijing: Foreign Languages, 1967), 4:11–26.

5. "The breaking up of the colonial empire, together with the proletarian revolution in the home country, will overthrow the capitalist system." *Theses and Statutes of the III Communist International Adopted by the II Congress, July 17th–August 7th 1920* (Moscow: Communist International, 1920), p. 71. See the discussion in Trotsky, "The Program of the International Revolution or a Program of Socialism in One Country?" in *Third International*, pp. 12f.

6. V. I. Lenin, "The War in China," in *Collected Works* (Moscow: Foreign Languages, 1960), 4:373.

7. See the account of revolution suggested in Marx's *Communist Manifesto*. A reasonably detailed account can be found in A. James Gregor, *The Fascist Persuasion in Radical Politics* (Princeton: Princeton University Press, 1974), chap. 4; and Gregor, *A Survey of Marxism: Problems in Philosophy and the Theory of History* (New York: Random House, 1968), chap. 5.

8. V. I. Lenin, *Imperialism: The Highest Stage of Capitalism* (New York: International, 1939).

9. See the more ample discussion in Gregor, *Survey of Marxism*, chap. 6.

10. Lenin's notions about imperialism and the "vanguard party" are found in *What Is to Be Done?* and *Imperialism: The Highest Stage of Capitalism*. For a convenient review of how Lenin's notions entered into the deliberations of the newly formed Chinese Communist Party in the early 1920s, see Lee Feigon, *Chen Duxiu: Founder of the Chinese Communist Party* (Princeton: Princeton University Press, 1983), pp. 176–178.

11. V. I. Lenin, "A Caricature of Marxism and Imperialist Economism," in *Collected Works*, 23:60.

12. See the discussion in Philip Siegelman, introduction to *Imperialism*, by J. A. Hobson (Ann Arbor: University of Michigan Press, 1967), pp. v–xvi. Lenin's disagreements with Hobson turned on the analysis of underconsumption in capitalist environments. Lenin understood Hobson's notion of underconsumption to be a product of a conviction that underconsumption could be remedied through higher wages, thereby making Hobson a "reformist." Lenin insisted that the profit rate of capitalist enterprise was destined to decline because of the "intrinsic contradiction" of industrial capitalism—which derives profit exclusively from the "surplus labor," or workers being increasingly replaced by fixed, not "living," capital.

13. Ibid., p. 59.

14. Lenin, "Caricature of Marxism," p. 47.

15. Lenin, "Farewell Letter to the Swiss Workers," in *Collected Works*, 23:371.

16. See the discussion in Franz Borkenau, *World Communism: A History of the Communist International* (Ann Arbor: University of Michigan Press, 1962), pp. 285–287.

17. The theoreticians of the Comintern regularly spoke of the "historical roles" of various classes. Each class was "destined" to discharge its role. See, for exam-

ple, M. N. Roy, *Revolution and Counter-Revolution in China* (Calcutta: Renaissance, 1946), pp. 294–296.

18. As cited, Trotsky, *Third International*, pp. 167f.

19. J. V. Stalin, "The Revolution in China and the Tasks of the Comintern," in *Works* (Moscow: Foreign Languages, 1954), 9:314–315.

20. Karl Marx and Friedrich Engels, *The Communist Manifesto* (London: Penguin, 1967), p. 84.

21. As cited, Dona Torr, introduction to *Marx on China: 1853–1860* (London: Lawrence & Wishart, 1968), p. xvi.

22. Marx was fully convinced of the "bourgeois" character of the Chinese Republic. It would inscribe on its portals the revolutionary cry of the French bourgeoisie during its own revolution: "Liberty, Equality, and Fraternity." Marx, "Neue Rheinische Revue" [31 January 1850], in *Karl Marx on Colonialism and Modernization*, ed. Shlomo Avineri (New York: Doubleday, 1968), pp. 44f.

23. See the discussion in Marx, "Revolution in China and Europe," and "Persia–China," in *Marx on China*, pp. 1–10, 48–51.

24. Lenin, "The War in China," in *Collected Works*, 4:373, 377.

25. Lenin, "Democracy and Narodism in China," in *Collected Works*, 18:163–165.

26. Ibid., pp. 166–167, 169.

27. See Hu Sheng, ed., *The 1911 Revolution—A Retrospective After 70 years* (Beijing: New World, 1983); and [Compilation Group for the History of Modern China Series] *The Revolution of 1911* (Beijing: Foreign Languages, 1976).

28. Stalin, "Don't Forget the East," in *Works*, 4:175.

29. See the discussion in Shlomo Avineri, *Karl Marx*, pp. 1–28.

30. See the relevant comments made in 1928 by Karl Wittfogel, representing the thought of the Marxist-Leninists of the period, in *Sun Yat Sen: Aufzeichnungen eines chinesischen Revolutionaers* (Vienna: Agis Verlag, 1928), pp. 42, 48f., 65–67, 112–126, 140.

31. See the detailed discussion in Kuo Heng-yu, *Die Komintern und die Chinesische Revolution: Die Einheitsfront zwischen der KP Chinas und der Kuomintang, 1924–1927* (Paderborn: Schoeningh, 1979); Jane Degras, *The Communist International, 1919–1943: Documents Selected and Edited by Jane Degras* 3 vols. (London: Oxford University, 1956–1965); Xenia J. Eudin and Robert C. North, *Soviet Russia in the East, 1920–1927: A Documentary Survey* (Stanford: Stanford University Press, 1957). The Chinese Nationalist account is detailed and instructive; see Warren Kuo, *Analytic History of the Chinese Communist Party* (Taipei: Institute of International Relations, 1968), particularly book 1. For a Marxist-Leninist account of all these issues, see A. M. Grigoriev, "The Comintern and the Revolutionary Movement in China in the Late 1920s and the Early 1930s"; and A. B. Reznikov, "The Comintern's Oriental Policy," in *The Comintern and the East*, ed. R. A. Ulyanovsky (Moscow: Progress, 1978), pp. 25–106, 410–451.

32. Kuo, *Analytic History*, 1:34, 59f., 90–92; see "The First Program of the Communist Party of China 1921," in ibid., p. 45.

33. Chen Duxiu, "A Letter to All Comrades of the Party," *Chinese Studies in History*, Spring 1970, p. 226.

34. Dov Bing, "Sneevliet and the Early Years of the Chinese Communist Party," *China Quarterly* 48 (October-December 1971): 67–97.

35. See V. I. Glunin, "Comintern Policy for China (1921–1927)," in Ulyanovsky, *Comintern*, p. 271.

36. See Trotsky's commentary in "First Speech on the Chinese Question," in *Problems of the Chinese Revolution*, trans. Max Shachtman (New York: Paragon Book Reprint, 1966), pp. 86f.

37. See the fragmentary and anecdotal evidence in Shih Kuo-heng, *China Enters the Machine Age* (Cambridge: Harvard University Press, 1944).

38. See the discussion in Roy, *Revolution and Counter-Revolution*, pp. 290, 449, 451f.

39. See the insightful discussion in Trotsky, "Summary and Perspectives," pp. 215–223.

40. See the discussion in Dietrich Geyer, "Kommunistische Internationale," in *Sowjetsystem und demokratische Gesellschaft: Eine vergleichende Enzyklopaedie* (Freiburg: Herder, 1969), 3:771–791; Branko Lazitch and Milorad M. Drachkovitch, *Lenin and the Comintern*, vols. 1–2 (Stanford: Hoover Institution, 1972); and Harold R. Isaacs, *The Tragedy of the Chinese Revolution*, 2d rev. ed. (Stanford: Stanford University Press, 1961), particularly chaps. 15–18.

41. Although Trotsky made very clear his conviction that Stalin persisted in his "China policy" in an "opportunistic" effort to insulate the Soviet Union from "imperialist" threats. Disturbances in China would purchase some "little profit" in security for the Soviet Union. See Trotsky, *Problems of the Chinese Revolution*, pp. 229f.

42. See the discussion by non-Soviet Marxists in Franz Borkenau, *World Communism. A History of the Communist International* (Ann Arbor: University of Michigan Press, 1961); Arthur Rosenberg, *Geschichte des Bolschewismus* (Frankfurt a.m.: Europaeische Verlagsanstalt, 1966); and Julius Braunthal, *Geschichte der Internationale* (Berlin: Dietz, 1963).

43. See G. N. Voitinsky, "Der Angriff des Imperialismus auf China," *Imprekorr*, 9 September 1924, p. 1523.

44. N. Nassonov, N. Fokine, and A. Albrecht, "The Letter from Shanghai, 17 March 1927," in Trotsky, *Problems of the Chinese Revolution*, p. 403.

45. Isaacs, *Tragedy of the Chinese Revolution*, p. 86.

46. Louis Fischer, *The Soviets in World Affairs* (New York: 1930), 2:647.

47. J. V. Stalin, "Letter to Chugunov," in *Works*, 9:206.

48. "Resolution on the Chinese Question" by the Comintern Press Correspondence, as cited in Isaacs, *Tragedy of the Chinese Revolution*, p. 87.

49. See Chiang Kai-shek, *Soviet Russia in China* (Taipei: China Publishing, 1969), chap. 1.

50. See the discussion in Isaacs, *Tragedy of the Chinese Revolution*, chap. 12.

51. Trotsky, *Third International*, p. 198.

52. See Stalin, "Talk with the Students of the Sun Yat-sen University" and "Questions of the Chinese Revolution," in *Works*, 9:229, 246.

53. See the discussion in Trotsky, *Third International*, pp. 172–173; and *Problems of the Chinese Revolution*, p. 47.

54. See the discussion in Trotsky, *Problems of the Chinese Revolution*, pp. 45, 57.

55. See Stalin's comments, "Talk with Students," p. 263.

56. A reasonably detailed account of Roy as a Marxist revolutionary is available in O. V. Martyshin, "Some Problems of the Strategy and Tactics of the Indian National Liberation and Communist Movement," in *Comintern*, pp. 173–234.

57. See M. N. Roy, *Memoirs* (New Delhi: Allied, 1964).

58. See the account in Roy, introduction to *Revolution and Counter-Revolution*, pp. 1–11.

59. Ibid., pp. 253, 265.

60. Ibid., pp. 267, 269, 279, 283, 309.

61. Chen Boda, *Stalin and the Chinese Revolution* (Beijing: Foreign Languages, 1953), p. 7.

62. Roy, *Revolution and Counter-Revolution*, p. 389.

63. See "Appendix: Resolution on Certain Questions in the History of Our Party," in Mao, *Selected Works*, 3:210; and "On Chiang Kai-shek's Speech on the Double Tenth Festival," in ibid., p. 230.

64. Chen Boda's review of *China's Destiny* is available in English only in a mimeographed form. Copies are available in major China study centers. The copy used here is available at the Center for Chinese Studies, University of California, Berkeley. See pp. 1, 12, 21, 23.

65. Mao, "A Comment on the Sessions of the Kuomintang Central Executive Committee and the People's Political Council," in *Selected Works*, 3:138, 144f.

66. "Since 1927, a series of events have occurred in China. Chiang Kai-shek became the Mussolini of China." Chen Boda, *Stalin and the Chinese Revolution*, pp. 3, 9.

67. Roy, *Revolution and Counter-Revolution*, pp. 459–460, 500, 525, 603.

68. Ibid., p. 283.

69. Ibid., p. 290.

70. Ibid., p. 282.

71. Ibid., p. 269.

72. Ibid., p. 253.

73. Georgi Zinoviev, "Theses on the Chinese Revolution," in Trotsky, *Problems of the Chinese Revolution*, pp. 331–332.

74. "The Joint Statement of Wang Ching-wei and Chen Tu-hsiu" [1 May 1927], in ibid., p. 307.

75. Chen Duxiu, "CCP's Proposal on Current Situation, Adopted by the Enlarged Session of the Central Executive Committee, CCP, 12 July 1926," cited in Kuo, *Analytic History*, 1:231.

76. See the discussion in A. James Gregor, *The Faces of Janus: Marxism and Fascism in the Twentieth Century* (New Haven: Yale University Press, 2000), chaps. 2–4.

77. Mao, "A Comment on the Sessions of the Kuomintang Central Executive Committee and the People's Political Council"; "On Coalition Government"; "Chiang Kai-shek Is Provoking Civil War"; and "Greet the New High Tide of the Chinese Revolution," in *Selected Works*, 3:138, 144f., 230, 270f., 276; 4:27, 120.

78. Mao, "Current Problems of Tactics in the Anti-Japanese United Front"; "On New Democracy"; "A Comment on the Sessions of the Kuomintang Central Executive Committee and the People's Political Council"; "On Coalition Govern-

ment"; and "On a Statement by Chiang Kai-shek's Spokesman," in *Selected Works*, 2:343, 353, 360ff., 367; 3:127, 147, 280f., 284; 4:42.

79. Mao, "On New Democracy,"; "The Situation After the Repulse of the Second Anti-Communist Onslaught"; "Conclusions on the Repulse of the Second Anti-Communist Onslaught"; "On Coalition Government"; and "The Situation and Our Policy After the Victory in the War of Resistance Against Japan," in *Selected Works*, 2:349, 376, 423, 460, 464; 3:270ff.; 4:11.

3

Fascism and Sun Yat-sen

The inability of Marxist theory to understand what was transpiring in postdynastic China is testimony of its general failure. Not only was Marxist theory incapable of understanding the political dynamics of China after the revolution of 1911, but it gave every evidence of having misunderstood the doctrines of Sun Yat-sen and the Kuomintang. In retrospect, it is clear that Marxist intellectuals failed to understand not only China's antidynastic revolution but also revolutionary reactive nationalism.

M. N. Roy's conviction that Sun Yat-sen's Three Principles of the People "foreshadowed fascism" was not initially shared by many Marxist-Leninists. There is very little to suggest that any of the important Soviet advisers or Comintern representatives to Nationalist China—dispatched between 1923 and 1927—entertained any notion of the implicit "fascism" of the thought of Sun Yat-sen.[1]

For the Marxists charged with the responsibility of guiding the Chinese revolution, Sun Yat-sen, his ideology, and the movement he founded and led were all "petty bourgeois"—as though such a characterization provided serious insights. For Marxists, all ideologies and all movements other than Marxism were petty bourgeois.

That recognition is a matter of some significance for our purposes. The fact that at least one Marxist imagined Sun Yat-sen's ideology to be not only "petty bourgeois" but fascistic as well reflects on the pretense that Marxism—as a theory—is capable of making meaningful typological and classificatory distinctions. Such distinctions are the basic preliminaries in theory generation. If the Marxists of the Third International imagined themselves equipped with the insights necessary to identify "reactionary" nationalism in general or fascism in particular whenever they made their appearance, events in China during the interwar years clearly provided a test case.

Mikhail Markovich Borodin, who served as the Comintern's principal representative to Sun Yat-sen during the most critical years of the Soviet

Union's collaboration with the Kuomintang, never once suggested any misgivings about Sun's revolutionary ideology.[2] However "petty bourgeois" Sun's ideology might have been, Borodin apparently never saw either fascism or reaction in it. For their part, the Chinese Communists similarly failed to find fascism or reaction in the ideology of Sun throughout the 1920s.[3] After the collapse of the first united front in the late 1920s, some of the leaders of the Chinese Communist party found something like fascism in the Kuomintang. But by that time, "fascism" seems to have meant simply anti-Communist and counterrevolutionary to most Marxists. Other than Roy, no Marxists seemed to trace fascism back to the thought of Sun Yat-sen.

For the intellectuals of Communist China, Sun Yat-sen was a "patriot" and a "bourgeois" democrat. Even in the post-Maoist literature of Communist China, he is nowhere identified as a "reactionary," a "fascist," or a "protofascist."[4] Sun advocated the "capitalist development" of China and in doing so appealed to "Western models" as a guide to the transformation of postdynastic China. But in all of that, for almost all Marxists, he remained simply a "bourgeois nationalist" and nothing more. In the millions of words written about the Chinese revolution, few Marxists of whatever persuasion were able to make any finer distinction.

Marxist Theory and Comparative Politics

It was left to M. N. Roy to discover the fascism in the ideology of Sun Yat-sen. There were others, of course, American and Chinese academics, who belatedly made something of the same discovery. Paul Linebarger, hardly a critic of Sun Yat-sen, suggested that Sun's Three Principles of the People, the *Sanmin zhuyi*, had "something in common with [Italian] Fascism."[5] Anthony Smith alluded to a family resemblance shared by fascism and Sun Yat-sen's revolutionary nationalism.[6]

In the final analysis, it was left to non-Marxist thinkers to make some sense of all that. What becomes clear, almost immediately, is the recognition that the Marxist-Leninist standard definition of fascism, which became available in the 1930s, was of almost no cognitive use whatever. Short of Roy, there was virtually no other Marxist who made a plausible case for identifying elements of a generic fascism in the Three Principles of the People. Roy's conviction that fascism provided the key to the early history of the Chinese revolution might well have represented nothing more than a personal intellectual idiosyncrasy. On the other hand, if Roy had succeeded in identifying something of significance, it is not at all evident what its significance might have been. Most Marxist theoreticians seemed to have missed it entirely.

The suggestion here will be that the Marxists' confusion resulted from a failure of "theory." Marxist theory, whatever else it might be, is a poor guide to the analysis of contemporary political developments. One of the principal reasons for its failure turns on the absence of a credible conception of "nationalism" among the ruminations of the founders of Marxism. Neither Marx nor Engels considered nationalism to be a matter of any serious theoretical consequence.

That has been recognized by Marxists themselves. Some time ago, Horace Davis acknowledged that "Marxism is not adapted to handling the problem of nationalism." Before "Marxism could cope seriously with the problem of nationalism," he maintained, it would have "to rework [that] part of Marx's theory completely."[7]

The issue is particularly interesting because some non-Marxists, better equipped with a theoretical sense of the role of nationalism in modern revolution, have isolated "fascist" elements in the thought of Sun Yat-sen. Those who have found such elements in Sun's *Sanmin zhuyi* are those who have taken the political role of nationalist sentiment seriously.

The similarities suggested by non-Marxist theoreticians turns on the reactive nationalism evident in both the thought of Sun and in that of the ideologues of Italian Fascism. It was their common reactive and developmental nationalism that suggested the association between Fascism and Sun's *Sanmin zhuyi*. Non-Marxists, unencumbered by inherited doctrine, could offer insight into the putative relationship where Marxists could not.

In fact, there is a loose collection of properties that suggests an affinity between the revolutionary nationalism of Sun and that of Italian Fascism. In the 1960s, Mary Matossian argued that some of the most significant revolutionary ideologies of the twentieth century might best be understood as common functional responses to determinate historic, social, and economic challenges. Some of the most important of those challenges arise when an industrially backward nation finds itself in sustained contact with those industrially advanced. The cultural, political, economic, and strategic disabilities associated with such contact produces a native intelligentsia increasingly sensitive to their nation's vulnerabilities. Afflicted with a painful sense of inadequacy, they become increasingly receptive to the conviction that their community requires large-scale industrialization and modernization if it is to regain control of its destiny.[8]

Matossian argued that the ideologies emerging out of such circumstances display certain similarities. Among those ideologies sharing a family resemblance, she identified Marxism-Leninism, Italian Fascism, Kemalism, Gandhism, the Indonesian Pantjasila, the Egyptian Philosophy of the Revolution, and Sun Yat-sen's *Sanmin zhuyi*. The suggestion was that Sun's ideology might best be understood in broad comparative context, since it shares certain defining properties with a number of other contemporary doctrines. The similarity of ideas that animate such ideologies are conceived more than the consequence of personal contacts and mimetism; they are a function of a common collective psychology born of common problems and shared socioeconomic influences. None of this appears in Marxist theory, neither in the Marxist theory of revolution nor in the standard Marxist interpretation of fascism.

Non-Marxist scholars, not burdened by the intellectual baggage of a doctrine more than a century old, have undertaken broad comparisons. China's revolution of 1911, for example, has been compared to nationalist and developmental revolutions that have taken place throughout the underdeveloped countries in general.[9] Such discussions suggest that Sun Yat-sen's original antidynastic ideological reflections might be construed as responses to an array of political, social, and economic problems more common than not to developing communities suffering delayed or thwarted industrialization.

In a clear sense, such comparative efforts share some methodological features with modern Marxism. Ideologies are understood to be a product of identifiable socioeconomic factors. Most of the shared properties are qualitative in character and serve to distinguish broad categories within a set of those more inclusive.

It will be argued here that in a broad sense a kinship did, in fact, exist between the revolutionary ideology of Sun and Italian Fascism, just as it exists among many ideologies of delayed or thwarted economic modernization. It will be further argued that standard Marxist theory missed most, if not all, of that. The Marxist theory of the Third International simply lapsed back into the traditional formulations of the standard version of fascism—conceiving of it as a passive "tool" of the most retrograde chauvinism of "finance capitalism." That characterization was almost entirely useless in the revolutionary circumstances of modern China.

Non-Marxist theoreticians have argued that both fascism and the Three Principles of the People contained elements that were complex ideational products that arise in economically backward communities when those communities find themselves in sustained contact with industrially advanced nations. It is argued, as well, that such a commonality must be qualified by a recognition that each ideology has its own peculiar character and that each incorporates a diversity of distinguishable political currents.

Reactive Developmental Nationalism

In the case of Italian Fascism, one of the most important political currents that was to shape doctrine was Italian Nationalism, a critical but distinctive component. It fused with several other intellectual elements to produce the mature ideology of Italian Fascism.

Italian Nationalism traced its origins to a prefascist ideological tradition that began to take form around the turn of the twentieth century and found fairly rigorous doctrinal expression among members of the Associazone Nazionalista Italiana between 1910 and 1912.[10] Among those generally recognized as the intellectual leaders of the prefascist Nationalist Association, Enrico Corradini and Alfredo Rocco are the most prominent. When Mussolini spoke of the ideologues of Italian Nationalism as having "given to Fascism the illumination of doctrine," he mentioned both Corradini and Rocco.[11] So prominent, in fact, was the influence of Italian Nationalism in the ultimate articulation of Fascism that Luigi Salvatorelli coined the expression *nazionalfascismo* to emphasize its decisive role.[12]

Whatever similarities M. N. Roy or Marxists and Western academics found between Italian Fascism and the revolutionary ideology of Sun Yat-sen derive almost exclusively from their shared reactive and developmental nationalism. But that nationalism was only one, if an extremely important, component of Italian Fascism.

In addition to nationalism, Italian Fascism incorporated the political style of F. T. Marinetti's futurism and much of the revolutionary syndicalism of Roberto Michels, Sergio Panunzio, and A. O. Olivetti.[13] For all that, nationalist ideas constituted so dominant a part of Italian Fascism's rationale that Karin Priester has argued that Alfredo Rocco, one of the foremost ideologues of Italian Nationalism, was the actual architect of Fascist doctrine.[14] For our purposes, it is significant that Italian Nationalism embodied a collection of ideas remarkably similar to those being put together at about the same time by Sun Yat-sen, half a world away. Sun, like the Italian Nationalists of the turn of the century, was searching for nationalist formulae with which he might regenerate China.

Whatever similarities obtain between Sun Yat-sen's ideology and that of Italian Fascism arise, in fact, out of their doctrinal nationalism. The similarities alluded to by Roy, Linebarger, Smith, and Matossian are not specifically fascist, but are characteristic of the reactive and developmental nationalism of communities suffering the disabilities that attend late industrialization and modernization in the modern world.

Nationalism has been, and remains, one of "the most successful political doctrines ever promoted." It has been identified as one of modern history's "most powerful of historical forces."[15] Even Marxists, originally averse to nationalism in principle, have been compelled to deal with it as a mass mobilizing phenomenon of significant consequence.[16] Some non-Marxist-Leninists have delivered themselves of reasonably sophisticated treatments of the subject,[17] but, in general, Marxists have failed to treat nationalism as a critical contemporary concern.

Karl Marx had assumed that the revolutions of the mid-nineteenth century would witness the "dissolution of all . . . nationalities,"[18] only to find that the following years were filled with the passion of nationalism. Whether or not Marx succeeded in accommodating his theories to the evident reality of nationalist sentiment among the populations of Europe, it was clear that nationalism would be a major factor in the revolutionary history of modern times.

Marx, in general, held nationalism to be a manipulative product of the bourgeoisie, interested in maintaining a unified and insulated domestic market for its commodities. In the last analysis, nationalism was, to the founders of Marxism, a derivate product of the class struggle.

Marxists have, more frequently than not, dealt with nationalism as an exclusively "bourgeois" concern. In terms of their own contemporary revolutionary responsibilities, they have, with some regularity, treated nationalism as a tactical issue but never as one having intrinsic merit. As a consequence, Marxists interpreted the nationalism of Sun Yat-sen and that of Italian Fascism as instrumental—of interest only as it might be marshaled to the service of proletarian revolution. In and of itself, nationalism was a matter of little theoretical concern for Marxists.

Actually, nationalism, both as a movement and an ideological system, has shown itself capable of serving as a powerful revolutionary force quite independent of any class interests. As a matter of theoretical interest, "nationalism" more frequently serves as an explanatory concept in any treatment of modern revolution than does "class." Even the most orthodox Marxists have recognized that peasants and workers have been inspired more frequently by nationalist enjoinments than they have been by invocations to "proletarian internationalism." In the contemporary world, nationalism counts as a major influence in explaining individual and collective revolutionary behavior.

Nationalism, like almost all concepts critical to understanding human political behavior, is "complex" and "impossibly fuzzy."[19] However imprecisely, commentators have characterized nationalism as rooted in the primordial psychological sense of community.[20] It has been spoken of as an expression of "supreme loyalty" to a community defined in terms of "a circumference within which the sympathy of [members] extends."[21] Whatever that community may have been in the past, since at least the eighteenth century, that natural association "within which the sympathy of members extends" has been a political entity identified as the nation-state.[22]

Among the members of the class of modern nationalisms, Italian Nationalists, at the turn of the twentieth century, identified one variant as "new." Italian Nationalists identified the new nationalism as reactive and developmental. In Italy, the "new nationalism" was a response to protracted national humiliation, and an immediate response to national military defeat in Africa in 1896. It was a reaction to a failure of national policy in the face of foreign power. It was a reaction to foreign control of the nation's culture and economy. It was a cry for "a place in the sun." It was a demand for economic and industrial development and national renewal in reaction to a lack of material and technological growth. It was a response to the perceived moral decadence and spiritual torpor of Italians in the face of foreign impostures.[23]

The evolution of nationalism in China followed a very similar course. Although the awakening of nationalism in China is usually traced to Western incursions during the first decades of the nineteenth century, it was China's defeat by Japan and the humiliation of the Treaty of Shimonoseki in 1896 that clearly marked the transition from a more traditional nationalism to the "new" reactive and developmental nationalism of the contemporary epoch.[24] By the end of the nineteenth century, it was clear that China had produced its own variant of reactive and developmental nationalism. The reformist thought of those like Kang Yuwei gradually gave way to the nationalism of Liang Qichao.[25] In Sun Yat-sen, the new nationalism attained full expression.

The new nationalism, distinct from the old, was less philosophical and "literary." The new nationalism was serious and practical. It was passionate and action oriented. In Italy, the thought of Giuseppe Mazzini gave way to the antisocialist, anti-internationalist, and developmental nationalism of Enrico Corradini and Alfredo Rocco.[26] In China, the literary and philosophical reformism of the nineteenth century gave way to the anti-Marxist, developmental nationalism of Sun Yat-sen.

The new nationalism distinguished itself from simple nationalism through its concern with the unbroken, classless integration of conationals. The new nationalism was informed by a passionate sense of historical mission. It was committed to the mobilization of human and material resources for a drive toward maximal national self-sufficiency and self-sustained economic growth and industrial development. All of that would involve a renovation and regeneration of the cultural and social fabric of the nation through substantial institutional and social changes.[27] In this general sense, Italian Nationalism and the revolutionary nationalism of Sun Yat-sen were related ideological species.

In Italy, Corradini and Rocco considered themselves heirs of the Risorgimento, which accomplished the nominal unification and independence of the Italian peninsula. On the other side of the globe, Sun Yat-sen, before the turn of the twentieth century, identified with the nationalistic impulse of the various anti-Manchu secret societies dedicated to the overthrow of the "foreign Tartars" and the restoration of the nation free of "foreign" domination.[28] Sun's founding of the Xing Zhong Hui (Society for the Regeneration of China) in 1894,[29] and the first appearance of Corradini's journals *Leonardo* and *Il Regno* in 1903–1904,[30] marked a qualitative change in the character of nationalism in both China and Italy.

As early as the manifesto of the Xing Zhong Hui, Sun argued that its revolutionary purposes extended beyond the simple overthrow of the foreign Qing dynasty. The goals of the society included the full integration of all Chinese into one sovereign nation bound together by a strong, centralized, and unified state.[31] Sun advanced the argument for a strong, centralized modern state with the conviction that it would be instrumental in transforming a "loose collection of sand" into a strong nation comparable to those of Europe and North America.[32]

Substantially the same ideas are found in the prose of the first Italian Nationalists. Although unified by 1871, Italy, according to Corradini, still lacked a sense of integral and collective unity. What the nation required, in his judgment, was a strong, centralized political apparatus that would effectively govern a united community in its competition with the already well-established powers. Only nationalism, in Corradini's assessment, could transform Italy's "servile disposition" into a firm resolve that might equip it to contend effectively with Germany, France, and Great Britain.[33]

Italy, at the turn of the twentieth century, shared all of the disabilities of a less-developed nation among nations that had already achieved economic development and substantial industrialization. Italy was among the poorer of the "civilized" nations.[34] It suffered the disdain of the major powers and was consigned, by almost universal judgment, to the role of a hewer of wood and a drawer of water for those more privileged. In an entirely comprehensible sense, Italy shared some of the psychological tensions that provoked the rise of reactive and developmental nationalism in China.

Italian Nationalists and the revolutionary nationalists of Sun Yat-sen were driven by a sense of the vulnerability of their respective nations. The sting of humiliation served to goad their respective intellectuals into putting together what they conceived to be a revolutionary ideology of national rebirth.[35] Given the vast differences in political circumstances, the particulars in each case varied in emphasis and specific content, but their similarities are unmistakable. Central to both ideologies was a preoccupation with economic growth and industrial modernization.

Beginning with the Opium War of 1840, a humiliating series of defeats at the hands of "barbarians" emphasized the efforts at substantive change in China. The self-strengthening movement in the nineteenth century, for example, clearly prefigured a concern with economic modernization and industrialization. Well before the end of the nineteenth century, a preoccupation with the manufacture of ordnance for national defense had emerged among the Chinese reformers. They envisioned a modernization of military education, the creation of an effective communications infrastructure for the nation, and the establishment of a steam-powered merchant fleet. Propelled by this momentum, it remained for Sun Yat-sen to formulate a comprehensive, distinctive, and revolutionary program of industrialization and economic development.

By 1920, Sun had developed a modernization program that later became an integral part of the revolutionary nationalism of the *Sanmin zhuyi*.[36] An elaborate plan for infrastructure development included the construction of railways and macadam roadways, telephone and telegraph systems, irrigation and transport waterways, and publishing facilities for mass communication. Sun's plans anticipated a vast program of hydroelectric power generation, fossil fuel extraction, harbor improvement, urban and agricultural modernization, resource management, conservation, and the development of basic and consumer goods industries, as well as state-of-the-art commodity distribution. Sun anticipated that the China that would emerge from such a program would be a strong nation capable of assuming, once again, its place at the world's "center."

Sun's developmental program was predicated on the joint involvement of private capital and state initiative. Sun was convinced that development required an economy governed, by and large, by market signals. Such an economy would be allowed a wide latitude for market incentives, always with the condition that market activities would not be undertaken to serve the exclusive interests of capitalism. In the final analysis, the state would control those activities that exceeded the capacity of private enterprise or upon which the security of the nation depended.[37]

This was the "socialism" of which Sun spoke in 1920. It was his idea to "make capitalists create socialism in China so that [those] two economic forces . . . [would] work side by side"[38] in what was clearly a form of state capitalism. The interventionist state would provide the indicative planning for Sun's program of the "unification and nationalization of industries"—modeled on the features of the war economy that characterized the Western powers under the productive exigencies of the First World War.[39]

The industrial base that Sun sought to create was expected to provide the arms necessary to protect the nation against real and potential predators. To enhance its ability to resist aggression, China would need not only an industrial base but political unity. Any form of class warfare or social division that threatened national unity was to be rejected. Sun spoke specifically of avoiding the "class struggle between capital and labor." Any such conflict would impair China's survival potential. As early as 1906, he emphasized the need to avert "social revolution" if

China was to survive in a threatening environment. Domestic conflict could only impair the unity he considered essential for national survival.

This was the doctrine that Lenin identified as "petty bourgeois" and Roy characterized as "casting the shadow of fascism" before itself. Lenin had entirely misunderstood its character, and Roy failed to recognize that what he had intuited was a broad category of modern political movements: reactive developmental nationalisms. The "shadow of fascism" he had seen in Sun's Three Principles of the People was, in fact, a developmental program of reactive nationalism.

Nazionalfascismo

While Sun was formulating his doctrine, Italian Nationalists put together a similar program for Italy for essentially the same reasons. By 1914, Alfredo Rocco recommended massive and regular increments of production as central to the concerns of Italian Nationalism.[40] An intensive and extensive "collaboration of industry and the state" was recommended to offset Italy's industrial and economic retardation.[41]

Like Sun, Italian Nationalists advocated a form of state capitalism in which there was a principled subordination of private initiative, private profit, and private ownership to the "superior interests of the nation, the fatherland."[42] Those superordinate interests would find expression in the "rational and perpetual organization of the state," for the state must necessarily be the ultimate agency of national organization and discipline.[43]

Rocco and Corradini spoke of this organization of labor and capital under the auspices of a strong central state as a "system of unitary, organic and integral collaboration."[44] What the peninsula required, in Rocco's judgment, was an antiliberal "organic [economic] plan" that included the construction of modern road, rail, telephone, and telegraph systems, and the expansion of hydroelectric generating plants that would provide the energy for such a program. Rocco went on to speak of the intensive development of heavy industry and the modernization of agriculture. What Italy required was "work, work, and more work, production, production, and more production."[45]

Rocco did not hesitate to identify this mixed system of private initiative and private ownership, subject to the regular tutelary control of the interventionist state, as a "socialism" for the nation.[46] It was a socialism that would provide the nation with a defense against the "superimperialism" of the predatory "plutocratic" powers of the Continent.[47] Italy had been humbled and humiliated too long.[48] It required a regime of discipline, solidarity, and sacrifice if it were to survive and prevail in the face of imposing force.

The implications were perfectly clear. Italian Nationalists, like their Chinese counterparts, deplored class warfare as inimical to national purpose.[49] They regarded classes as organic components in the "grand unity of forces" that must collaborate in the industrial development and economic modernization of the nation.[50] The Italian Nationalists, like Sun's revolutionaries, were animated by a conviction that their developmental program would provide sufficient benefits to produce a "solidarity of all classes with the state and a solidarity of all . . . with the nation."[51] Italy and China required nothing less than a rational, technically competent, and integral collaboration of classes if Italy and China were to rise above their "proletarian" status in a Darwinian world of group competition.[52]

At the turn of the century, both the Italian and the Chinese nationalists were convinced that their respective nations faced multiple threats, including external political, military, and economic aggression at the hands of nations industrially more advanced. Both argued that their respective nations were weakened by excessive individualism and regional and parochial loyalties. For Sun, only nationalism could unite the hundreds of millions of Chinese, "save the nation," and forestall "racial destruction."[53]

Like the Chinese, the Italian Nationalists argued that, in the incessant struggle that typifies the modern world, it would be necessary to evoke a sustained sense of national consciousness among citizens if the nation were to survive. Egoism, factionalism, class warfare, primitivism, underdevelopment, and the absence of civic virtue would condemn a nation to extinction. The advanced industrial and "plutocratic" powers had surrounded Italy on all sides, choked its waterways, and dominated its culture and its economy. "If the Italian race" was "not to perish," nationalism would have to steel it to economic and military combat.[54]

At the turn of the century, the term "race" did not carry with it all the negative implications with which it is presently burdened. In general, the term meant "members of the national community." Both Sun and the Italian Nationalists recognized the distinctions that marked the Han from the non-Han Chinese or the dark Sicilians from the fair Piedmontese. But there were few reactive nationalists prepared to discriminate against members of the national community because of skin pigment, religious affiliation, or class provenience.[55]

The new nationalists of the early twentieth century sought strength not only in disciplined unity but in numbers as well. Thus Sun argued that loyalty for the family, which had been traditional in China, should be extended to the nation. That strength in unity would be multiplied by numbers. Sun rejected Malthusian arguments for the limitation of China's reproductive rate.[56] Even though he granted that China already labored under the "pressure of population," he insisted that ways be found to in-

crease its rate of demographic growth.[57] The same argument appears in
the formulations of the most prominent Italian Nationalists. Numbers,
according to Rocco, constituted the "veritable force of the race," and any
limitation on the number of births would do irreparable damage to the
survival potential of the nation.[58]

For nationalists, the reluctance to reproduce, to ensure the continuity
of the "race," could only be explained by an impaired sense of national
responsibility. Decadence, preoccupation with personal comfort, or exaggerated egotism might cause individuals to fail in their responsibilities to
the national community. Both the Chinese and the Italian nationalists
sought to offset all of that. In particular, they all set their sights not only
on individualism but also on "universalism" as inimical to the well-being
and survival of the nation.

If universalism constituted a solvent of regenerative nationalism, individualism, in whatever guise, was considered equally pernicious. Sun
clearly rejected any contract theory of the state that sought to interpret
the nation as a voluntary association of individuals. Any such notion of
society or the state would reduce either or both to a fragile and insub-
stantial aggregate of contracting individuals.

The notion that individuals somehow came together to negotiate the
establishment of society or the state implied that individuals somehow
possessed rights antecedent to and prior to the establishment of the community and the state. Sun argued that such a conception of rights would
weaken the integrity of the "nation group," undermine its viability, and
leave the Chinese exposed to every threat.[59]

Sun argued that "just as each grain of sand must lose its freedom if
sand is to be solidified in cement, so the individual in China must also
give up his freedom if Chinese society is to become strongly organized."[60] In his judgment, China required organization, discipline, loyalty, and a disposition among its citizens to sacrifice unto death for the
national community.[61]

The same set of ideas is found in the literature of Italian Nationalism.
Italian Nationalists specifically rejected the contract theory of the state,
conceiving it as nothing more than a reflection of the enthusiasm for excessive individualism to be found among the bourgeois revolutionaries
of the eighteenth century.[62] They conceived society and the state as "organic" entities serving purposes that transcended those of the solitary individual. Any emphasis on individual rights and individual liberties
would impair the nation's prospects for survival and would contribute to
its disaggregation. "Individualism," Rocco insisted, "predicated on the
absence of social solidarity is the affirmation of individual egoism. It pul-
verizes society" and exposes the weakened nation to every foe. Nationalism, on the other hand, maintains that individual rights and liberties are

conditional grants by the state and society, redeemable only insofar as they contribute to the maintenance and perpetuation of the community.[63] In the judgment of Italian Nationalists, what the nation required was the cultivation of collectivist sentiments that would make the "sacrifice of individuals, even unto death," a natural response among Italians.[64]

Sun and his followers saw China as the victim of "imperialist" and "aggressor" nations; the Italian Nationalists conceived Italy a "proletarian" nation, subject to the exploitation of the "plutocratic" powers of the Continent.[65] Sun held China to be a "hypocolony" of foreign capitalism; Italian Nationalists saw Italy as a "dependency" and a "hostage" to foreign capital, foreign culture, and foreign political influence.[66] Italy, for all its nominal independence, was an "economic colony."[67]

The struggle for survival that characterized history, for both Sun and the Italian Nationalists, was not a conflict between individuals or classes, but a conflict between sovereign communities. In the twentieth century, it was a struggle between nations. "Class struggle" among members of the same community was "pathological," not natural. "Class struggle," Sun insisted, "is . . . a kind of social disease."[68] For both Sun and the Italian Nationalists, the social theories of Marxism were not only fundamentally wrong, but they threatened the survival of the nation.[69]

For both Chinese and Italian Nationalists, society was an organic unity, which, in order to survive, was composed not of opposing classes but of functionally integrated and mutually supportive elements. Should the relationships between the elements be disrupted, the entire organism would be threatened with dissolution. The invocation of the organic analogy carried in its train the image of an organization of parts, some subordinate and others superordinate, implying a "natural" inequality.

The parts of an organism must, of necessity, be different and perform different functions. The earliest Italian Nationalists insisted that society was composed of components having distinct and hierarchically arranged functions. There was talk of a "heroic" and "ingenious" minority that necessarily undertook the "directive function" in society while the majority subordinated itself to its strategic leadership.[70]

Sun, in turn, was convinced that people were not born equal[71] and that society was divided into three functionally distinct and interdependent elements: a cohort of "seers" or "geniuses"; a cohort composed of those who are "followers" and "doers"; and finally an "unthinking majority," which is led.[72] In Harold Schiffrin's judgment, the elitist strain in Sun's thinking was evident as early as 1905: "Sun's frequent references to the interventionist, spearheading role of 'men of determination' reflected his faith in a disciplined and enlightened elite."[73]

As a consequence of these convictions, both Sun and the Italian Nationalists entertained serious reservations about the effectiveness of

Western parliamentary government with its catalog of presuppositions concerning limited government and "inalienable" individual rights.[74] Although Sun remained convinced until the end of his life that some form of parliamentary democracy would be the ultimate political form a modern China would assume, between the antidynastic revolution of 1911 and 1924 Sun had witnessed the "decided failure" of a "venal" and "corrupt" representative government in China.[75] Whatever the ultimate political form of the modern China he anticipated, by the mid-1920s Sun was advocating an indeterminate interim of military and tutelary dictatorship for revolutionary China before the eventual advent of "constitutional government."[76]

Italian Nationalists expressed similar reservations concerning representative political institutions. "True Italian democracy" would be a democracy of efficiency and competence, not a democracy of corruption and parasitism like that of post-Risorgimento Italy.[77] Italy's future democracy would be government by representatives of interdependent functional bodies rather than representatives of geographic spaces or opposing classes. The future democracy would be a corporative government of "force and authority."[78]

For both Sun and the Italian Nationalists, the revolutionary outcomes they anticipated necessitated significant changes in the collective psychology of the nation. For Sun, it meant the recovery and renovation of traditional Chinese virtues, the most fundamental of which was loyalty. Loyalty to the nation was the linchpin of Sun's conception of a new China.

What Chinese renewal required was people prepared to sacrifice everything for the welfare of the nation. Sun maintained that the people must fulfill their duties to the revolutionary state; anyone who did not would forfeit all rights of citizenship. Such a person would become a "vagabond" and a "common enemy of the state." With such persons, Sun insisted, the state must deal harshly. They must be "compelled" to do their duty.[79]

For Italian Nationalists, "only a spiritual reformation could transform Italian life." It was the state's obligation to superintend and direct that reformation and rededication to the traditional civic and patriotic virtues of ancient Rome. Only such a "formation of true political consciousness among the masses" would make a new, true "Italian democracy" operable.[80]

Both Sun and the major Italian Nationalists considered these reforms a major part of the solution to the central problem besetting their respective "oppressed" and "proletarian" nations —the problem of economic, political, and cultural exploitation of retarded and industrially backward nations by those more advanced.

Reactive and Developmental Nationalism
in Comparative Perspective

Both Sun and the Italian Nationalists identified economic underdevelopment as one of the central problems afflicting their respective nations, rendering Marxist socialism, in their opinion, totally irrelevant to their revolutionary purposes. Both Sun and the Italian Nationalists understood Marxism to be a program of social revolution for industrially advanced nations—a guide to postindustrial revolution—and thus totally irrelevant to the problems of exploited less-developed communities.[81]

One of the reasons[82] Sun decided to allow his Kuomintang to pursue a connection with the Bolsheviks in the early 1920s turned on the conviction that the "Marxist" revolution in Russia had revealed itself to be anything but Marxist. He perceived the revolutionaries in Russia not as Marxists in any strict sense, but as advocates of revolutionary developmental nationalism. The realities of Russia's economic conditions had transformed Marxist utopian notions into Lenin's attempt at a sustainable developmental program through his New Economic Policy (NEP). Sun saw in some of the features of the NEP a compatibility with his own Three Principles of the People. He argued that in a perfectly comprehensible sense, Lenin had reshaped Bolshevism "into a *Sanmin zhuyi* revolution."[83] Bolshevism in Russia had been transformed by circumstances into an incoherent nationalist and developmental program in the effort to defend the new nation against foreign threats.

In substance, Sun anticipated by almost half a century an assessment now common in the professional literature. "Marxist" revolutions in the twentieth century, however else they might conceive themselves, are developmental nationalisms. Their real opponents are not domestic classes but foreign oppressors.[84] All of this had been lost on Marxist theoreticians and Roy, who alone among them sensed something of it all, failed to give it credible interpretation.

Like Sun, Italian Nationalists recognized some of the same features in the revised Marxism that made its appearance in Bolshevik Russia. Italian Nationalists early perceived that Marxism, in Bolshevik Russia, had been transformed into a kind of developmental dictatorship. In 1919, Dino Grandi, then a young Nationalist ideologue, insisted that the Russian revolution was an expression of national resistance to the impostures of foreign "plutocracies." Whatever "Marxism" there was in the Russian revolution was transmuted by the protracted crisis of the 1920s into an assertive nationalism. By the early 1920s, Grandi argued that whatever else it was, the "socialism" of the Soviet Union was a *national* socialism, more given to the rehabilitation of the nation than to international revolution.

Grandi maintained that events in Russia clearly indicated that the great conflicts of the twentieth century would involve nations rather than classes.[85] Only a grievous misassessment could induce Marxists to impair the developmental and defense capabilities of their nation by pursuing a class war when the historic situation demanded national economic development, discipline, sacrifice, and unanimity in the face of mortal challenge.

Thus, both Chinese and Italian nationalists rejected the notion that the twentieth century would be host to "class struggle." They saw no merit whatever in the conflict between the "proletarians" and the "bourgeoisie" of the same nation. Nationalists have always argued that the most fundamental interests of the individual citizen lie not in the revolutionary success of his class but in the survival and well-being of his national community.

Nationalists have never conceived their program, their leaders, or their membership to be "petty bourgeois" or "bourgeois" in origin. Like all reactive and developmental revolutionary nationalist movements of the twentieth century, their program, their leadership, and their membership derived from all classes in society.[86] The leaders and members of nationalist organizations were nationalists—not members of any specific class.

Those Marxists like M. N. Roy, who saw "fascism" in Sun's Three Principles of the People, were seeing, in fact, the elements of reactive and developmental nationalism to be found in great abundance in the revolutionary movements of the twentieth century. However perceptive some Marxists may have been, they had failed to understand the reality of what was transpiring. The "petty bourgeois" ideology of Sun was not a prefiguration of Italian Fascism. It was, in substantial part, an Asian variant of a developmental nationalism that was to become increasingly common among the less developed communities in the twentieth century. Sun's Three Principles of the People was an instantial case of a class of movements that were to define revolution in our time.

The class of reactive nationalist, developmental revolutions alluded to is very inclusive and, in the judgment of many, covers those revolutions that pretend to be "Marxist-Leninist" and "international" in original intention. For our purposes here, the similarities between Sun's nationalism and that of the Italian Nationalists identify the features that characterize them both as instantial cases of the class of movements under consideration.

Those similarities suggest features that characterize the range of political movements and regimes that fall under the general rubric "reactive and developmental nationalism." At the abstract level at which typologies generally commence, those similarities are difficult to deny.

As reactive nationalist systems accede to power and mature in control, the single, elitist, hegemonic party emerges to dominate the political environment. The party is generally led by a "charismatic" and "inerrant" leader—spokesman for a formal doctrine that legitimates minoritarian rule. At certain stages of their maturation, such systems mobilize masses through political theater—the employment of signs, symbols, and highly choreographed rituals.

Such systems exercise control through a variety of devices, including extensive, if not comprehensive, dominance of the economy. The general population is enrolled in a variety of organizations ranging over virtually all ages and all citizen activities. The military supplies the behavioral and normative model for all. At some stage in their development, all such systems are non- or antidemocratic in the sense that the industrialized democracies understand "democracy."

As reactive systems, these regimes tend to perceive themselves surrounded by real or potential enemies—traditional opponents such as "racial" antagonists, "imperialists," or privileged "plutocracies." Enduring threat generates the necessity for national defense, which in turn recommends extensive and intensive industrialization and economic growth.

Such systems seek their "place in the sun," a redistribution of the world's space and resources. They tend to be irredentist and sometimes expansive. They seek the restoration of "lost lands," the reincorporation of separated "conationals," and/or expansion into what is considered adequate "living space."

Some of these systems—certainly not all—have the potential of evolving into what social scientists have long identified as "totalitarianisms." It is uncertain what the initial properties must be that contribute to such an evolution in the case of members of the class, nor is it clear what environmental stimuli advance the process; it is just that the twentieth century has seen enough instances of such developments that the potential must be acknowledged.

The twentieth century has witnessed any number of such systems, displaying some or all of the defining features of the class. It has seen them arise, sometimes falter and fail, and sometimes mature in single-party dictatorships or totalitarianism. Social science has little cognitive purchase on such systems and their life cycle. Although they share sustained similarities, they differ in important respects, just as individuals share features of a class yet differ in substantial ways from their comembers.

Thus, what M. N. Roy identified in the political aspirations of Sun Yat-sen was not the long shadow of fascism but the outlines of a reactive and developmental nationalism. It was the same outline that Sun recognized in the reformed Marxism of V. I. Lenin's New Economic Policy of the early 1920s.

That there are differences between the members of the class of reactive and developmental nationalist systems is important. Sun's doctrine differed in a variety of ways from that of the Italian Nationalists, and by implication, Mussolini's Fascism.

Thus, although Sun argued that political authoritarianism would be required to shepherd less-developed nations along the trajectory of accelerated growth and industrialization for an indeterminate period of time, he always insisted that the process would conclude with "constitutional government." There is no doubt that his ultimate ideal was a government that shared the distinguishing features of those that currently govern the industrial democracies. That may not have been true of Italian Nationalists.[87]

More than that, Italian Nationalism was far more assertive and aggressive than the nationalism of Sun Yat-sen. Italian Nationalists, while adamantly opposed to the imperialism of the "sated" and "plutocratic" powers, anticipated and advocated territorial expansion for revolutionary Italy.[88] That sentiment passed without dilution in paradigmatic fascism.

Sun spoke of the future, when China would become strong and would easily win "first place in the council of nations." He even alluded to the possibility of reconstructing a new system of voluntary dependencies around a restored China—tributaries attracted by China's power.[89] Such expectations were predictable from a nationalist convinced that his nation's political thought was the most perfect in the world and that "Heaven" wished to use China "to foster the world's progress."[90] But there was remarkably little territorial expansionism and military aggressiveness anticipated in Sun's program for the restoration of China to its place in the world.

The tone and temper of the expansionism of Italian Nationalism, and subsequently Fascism, on the other hand, was transparently different. Italian Nationalists spoke frankly of the conquest of territories that had never been part of historic Italy or of historic Rome, for that matter. They were addressing the fact that European imperialism had extended itself throughout Africa and Asia, and Italy had been left without the colonies that might provide it the resource base and the market supplements that were critical, in their judgment, to survival in the world of the early twentieth century. Mature Fascism assumed essentially the same postures.

The differences between Chinese and Italian Nationalism seem to turn on the fact that although both advocated a maximally self-contained and self-sustaining economy of national development,[91] Italy enjoyed few of the prerequisites necessary for their attainment. Proper national defense, political autonomy, and international sovereignty required, in the judgment of both Chinese and Italian Nationalists, maximal economic independence. For that reason, both Sun and the Italian Nationalists advocated import substitution and domestic industry protection as part of a policy of autarkic national development. They sought inspiration and direction not in the free trade economic prescriptions of Adam Smith but in the national developmental program of Friedrich List.[92] All of that passed from the Italian Nationalists to Fascism without change.

Self-sufficiency and self-sustaining economic growth and development required, however, adequate resource and territorial potential. In this regard, in the view of Italian Nationalists, and the Fascists in turn, Italy was hopelessly malprovisioned. Italy lacked all the subsoil resources prerequisite to intensive industrialization or economic self-sufficiency. Furthermore, they argued, Italy possessed less arable soil, per capita, than any other nation in Europe.[93] As a consequence, Rocco insisted that "for Italy, a nation without raw materials, lacking in capital, but under enormous population pressure, only an expansive foreign policy [could] resolve the . . . fundamental problems of economic life."[94] Should there be no other alternative, "war and conquest [would] radically solve such problems."[95]

Sun Yat-sen, on the other hand, had every confidence that China's resources were more than adequate. "China," he told his audiences, "equals America in the vastness of territory and the richness of resources, and her agricultural and mineral wealth potentially is even greater than that of America." He was convinced that China possessed "unlimited supplies of raw materials and cheap labor."[96]

In effect, Italian Nationalism was an *exacerbated* reactive, revolutionary, and developmental nationalism, but Sun's nationalism was not. Whereas Sun could speculate on a time when the nations of the world might settle into an "ideal brotherhood," Italian Nationalists foresaw only a future in which the revolutionary Italian nation, having wrested its place in the sun from demographically stronger and resource-rich competitors, would remain forever threatened.

It was in this form that Italian Nationalism lent its doctrine to Mussolini's Fascism. And it was that, if nothing more, that decisively distinguished Sun's nationalism from fascism.

There were other features of both Sun's nationalism and that of Italian Nationalism that require some consideration. Until its coalescence into the ranks of Italian Fascism, for instance, Italian Nationalism largely remained an intellectual movement of literary luminaries and political thinkers. It was Fascism that gave Italian Nationalism a mass base and an armed political force.

Like Italian Nationalism, Sun's nationalism was originally a preoccupation of intellectuals. Whatever the involvement of Sun and his organization in China's antidynastic revolution, political events largely proceeded outside their control. There was little that could credibly pass as "mass mobilization" by Sun's clandestine revolutionary organizations. Only after the reorganization of the Kuomintang, following the rapprochement with the Soviet Union in the early 1920s, did Sun and his followers attempt to create a mass following and a political army.[97]

If the category of "reactive developmental nationalism" includes, whatever their differences, Italian Nationalism, Fascism, and Sun's Three Principles of the People, they must all be acknowledged to be varieties and subvarieties of the class. Although Italian Nationalism passed virtually intact into Italian Fascism, Fascism was, nonetheless, something more than Italian Nationalism. Some of the traits specifically identified with Mussolini's Fascism originated in the lucubrations and experience of other than Nationalist theoreticians so that what emerged was something other than the ideology of Italian Nationalism.

Marxist theoreticians never seemed to understand any of this. As a consequence, they never really understood the ideology or the political systems generated by the revolutionary activities of Sun Yat-sen, Italian Nationalism, or Mussolini's Fascism. What M. N. Roy identified as an anticipation of "fascism" in Sun's doctrines was, in fact, a confused recognition that The Three Principles of the People, Italian Nationalism, and Fascism were variants of a class of reactive, developmental nationalisms.

Whatever their differences, and however important those differences might be, all sought to secure their respective nations a place in the sun. For Marxists to see in all of that only the product of the "bourgeoisie's" effort to postpone the "inevitable" proletarian revolution is evidence of theoretical incompetence. To imagine that reactive nationalist movements were the passive instrument of "counterrevolution" underwritten by "finance capitalism" is a howling implausibility.

The theoreticians of the Comintern went into China with just such implausibilities as tools. They were unsure of the doctrines of Sun and how they were to be interpreted. They were hopelessly confused about what "fascism" might be. As a consequence, they brought ruin to the Chinese Communist party in 1927 and confused observers everywhere—including Mao Zedong and his followers.

Mao Zedong and his followers, confused by their mentors in Moscow, reorganized after the critical defeats of 1927 and 1928, and embarked upon their own revolution. In the course of that revolution they, like M. N. Roy, identified fascism once again in the ranks of the Kuomintang. If, for Mao's followers, Sun Yat-sen remained a "national patriot" and a revolutionary "anti-imperialist," by the early 1940s, Maoists conceived the Kuomintang to be China's "fascism."

In what measure Maoist theory, as a variant of Marxist theory, assists in understanding political events in China can be determined, at least in part, by considering what Maoists have had to say about fascism in China—particularly the fascism of the Kuomintang.

Notes

1. See, for example, A. I. Cherepanov, "Under Sun Yat-sen's Banner"; and R. A. Mirovitskaya, "Adviser to Revolutionary Kuomintang," in *Soviet Volunteers in China, 1925–1945,* ed. Y. V. Chudodeyev (Moscow: Progress, 1980), pp. 23–35, 36–49.

2. See the account of Madame Chiang Kai-shek, *Conversations with Mikhail Borodin* (Taipei: Li Ming Cultural Enterprises, n.d.).

3. See [Compilation Group for the History of Modern China Series] *The Revolution of 1911* (Beijing: Foreign Languages, 1976), chap. 2.

4. See Liu Danian, "Sun Yat-sen—A Great Patriot and Democrat"; Li Shu, "Reassessment of Some Questions Concerning the 1911 Revolution"; and Li Zongyi, "Chinese Bourgeois Revolutionaries and the Movement to Regain Economic Rights Towards the End of the Qing Dynasty," in *The 1911 Revolution,* ed. Hu Sheng and Liu Danian (Beijing: New World, 1983), pp. 26–66, 67–122, 147–169.

5. Paul M. A. Linebarger, *The Political Doctrines of Sun Yat-sen* (Westport, Conn.: Hyperion, 1973), p. 146.

6. At the same time, Smith argued that whatever their similarities, they constitute "separate doctrines and sociological phenomena." Anthony Smith, *Theories of Nationalism* (New York: Harper & Row, 1971), p. 260.

7. Horace B. Davis, *Nationalism and Socialism: Marxist and Labor Theories of Nationalism to 1917* (New York: Monthly Review Press, 1967), pp. ix, 9.

8. Mary Matossian, "Ideologies of Delayed Industrialization: Some Tensions and Ambiguities," in *Political Change in Underdeveloped Countries: Nationalism and Communism,* ed. John Kautsky (New York: John Wiley, 1966), pp. 252–253.

9. See the discussion in Mary C. Wright's introduction and Harold Z. Schiffrin's "The Enigma of Sun Yat-sen," in *China in Revolution: The First Phase, 1900–1913,* ed. Mary C. Wright (New Haven: Yale University, 1968), pp. 59–60, 474.

10. See Francesco Perfetti, introduction to *Il nazionalismo italiano,* ed. Francesco Perfetti (Rome: Borghese, 1969), pp. 17–34; Alexander J. DeGrand, *The Italian Nationalist Association and the Rise of Fascism in Italy* (Lincoln: University of Nebraska Press, 1978).

11. Benito Mussolini, "Pensieri Pontini e Sardi," in *Opera omnia* (Florence: La fenice, 1951–1964), 34:288.

12. See Luigi Salvatorelli, *Nazionalfascismo* (Turin: Gobetti, 1923), pp. 24–25.

13. See A. James Gregor, *Sergio Panunzio, sindacalismo e il fondamento razionale del fascismo* (Rome: Volpe, 1978); Gregor, *Roberto Michels e l'ideologia del fascismo* (Rome: Volpe, 1979); Gregor, *Young Mussolini and the Intellectual Origins of Fascism*

(Berkeley: University of California Press, 1979); Gregor, *Phoenix: Fascism in Our Time* (New Brunswick, N.J.: Transaction, 1999), chaps. 2–4.

14. Karin Priester, *Der italienische Faschismus* (Cologne: Pahl-Rugenstein, 1972), chap. 13; see also Tommaso Ascarelli, "La dottrina commercialista di Francesco Carnelutti," *La rivista delle societa* 1 (1960): 9.

15. Anthony H. Birch, *Nationalism and National Integration* (London: Unwin Hyman, 1989), p. 25; Louis L. Snyder, "The Meaning of Nationalism," in *The Dynamics of Nationalism: Readings in its Meaning and Development*, ed. Louis L. Snyder (Princeton: Van Nostrand, 1964), p. l.

16. See, for example, Davis, *Nationalism and Socialism*.

17. See the interesting work of Otto Bauer, *Die Nationalitaetenfrage und die Sozialdemokratie* (Vienna: Ignaz Brand, 1907).

18. Karl Marx and Friedrich Engels, *The German Ideology* (Moscow: Foreign Languages, 1964), p. 86.

19. See Eugene Kamenka, "Political Nationalism–The Evolution of the Idea," in *Nationalism: The Nature and Evolution of an Idea*, ed. Eugene Kamenka (Canberra: Australian National University, 1973), pp. 3, 19.

20. See Eugen Lemberg, *Nationalismus*, vol. 1 (Reinbek bei Hamburg: Rowohlt, 1964), chap. l.

21. See Hans Kohn, *The Idea of Nationalism: A Study in Its Origins and Background* (New York: Macmillan, 1944), p. 21.

22. Elie Kedourie, *Nationalism* (New York: Praeger, 1961), p. 9.

23. See the discussion in Giovanni Papini and Giuseppe Prezzolini, *Vecchio e nuovo nazionalismo* (Rome: Volpe, 1967); Romolo Ronzio, *La fusione del Nationalismo con il Fascismo* (Rome: Italiane, 1943), chap. l.

24. See Philip C. Huang, *Liang Ch'i-ch'ao and Modern Chinese Liberalism* (Seattle: University of Washington Press, 1972), p. 24; compare with Paola Maria Arcari, *Le elaborazioni della dottrina politica nazionale fra l'unità e l'intervento (1870–1914)* (Florence: Marzocco, 1934–1937), 1:5. Among Chinese reformers and revolutionaries the Manchu dynasty was charged with the responsibility of China's backwardness, but by the beginning of the twentieth century, imperialism was identified as the nation's principal enemy.

25. See the discussion in Hao Chang, *Liang Ch'i-ch'ao and Intellectual Transition in China, 1890–1907* (Cambridge: Harvard University Press, 1971); and Huang, *Liang Ch'i-ch'ao*.

26. See the discussion in Arcari, *Le elaborazioni*, particularly vol. l.

27. These traits are a paraphrase of those provided by Smith, *Theories*, p. 171. For a discussion of nationalist myths and missions, see Roberto Michels, *Der Patriotismus: Prolegomena zu seiner soziologischen Analyse* (Munich: Duncker & Humblot, 1929).

28. See Harold Z. Schiffrin, *Sun Yat-sen and the Origins of the Chinese Revolution* (Berkeley: University of California Press, 1968), chap. 1.

29. There is still some dispute concerning the founding date of the *Xing Zhong Hui*; see Hsueh Chun-tu, "Sun Yat-sen, Yang Ch'u-yun and the Early Revolutionary Movement in China," *Journal of Asian Studies* 19, no. 3 (1960): 309 n. 13.

30. See Scipio Sighele, introduction to *Il nazionalismo e i partiti politici* (Milan: Treves, 1911); and Arcari, *Le elaborazioni*, 1:3–18.

31. See Sun Yat-sen, *Guofu quanji* (The complete works of Sun Yat-sen) (Taipei: Party Historical Archives Committee, 1973), 1:A174–175. Hereafter *GQ*.

32. Ibid., p. A173. See also Lyon Sharman, *Sun Yat-sen: His Life and Its Meaning* (Stanford: Stanford University, 1968), pp. 74–79.

33. See Enrico Corradini, *Discorsi politici (1902–1923)* (Florence: Vallecchi, 1923), pp. 17, 36, 38, 41, 43, 47, 74, 87.

34. See A. James Gregor, *The Ideology of Fascism* (New York: Free Press, 1969), chap. 1.

35. No attempt will be made here to trace the evolution of their respective ideologies. For a reasonable account of the processes involved, see DeGrand, *Italian Nationalist Association;* and Martin Bernal, *Chinese Socialism to 1907* (Ithaca, N.Y.: Cornell University Press, 1976).

36. Sun Yat-sen, *International Development of China* (Shanghai: Commercial Press, 1920); and "The Strategy of National Reconstruction," in *GQ* 1:507–654.

37. "The industrial development of China should be carried out along two lines: (1) by private enterprise; and (2) by national undertaking. All matters that can be and are better carried out by private enterprise should be left to private hands which should be encouraged and fully protected by liberal laws." Sun, *International Development*, p. 9; see also pp. i–iii, 1–2, 137, 144–145, 147, 153–155, 159–160.

38. Ibid., p. 165.

39. Ibid., pp. 1–3, 147.

40. Alfredo Rocco, "Il problema economico italiano," in *Scritti e discorsi politici* (Milan: Giuffre, 1938), 1:15, 17–19, 21; and "Economia liberale, economia socialista ed economia nazionale," in ibid., pp. 54, 56.

41. Rocco, "Economia liberale," pp. 57, 62; see Enrico Corradini, *La marcia dei produttori* (Rome: L'Italiana, 1916), pp. viii, ix–xi, 6, 62.

42. Rocco, "Economia liberale," p. 76.

43. Rocco, "La resistenza civile," in *Scritti e discorsi politici*, 1:412–413; Rocco, "Il momento economico e sociale," in ibid., 2:586–587; see Corradini, "Sindacalismo, nazionalismo, imperialismo," in *Discorsi politici*, pp. 54, 60, 63.

44. See, for example, Corradini, "Il nazionalismo e i sindacati," in *Discorsi politici*, p. 423.

45. Rocco, "L'ora del nazionalismo," in *Scritti e discorsi politici*, 2:513–514; "Il programma politico dell'Associazione Nazionalista," in ibid., 2:477–481; and "Il programma nazionalista," in ibid., 1:502–504.

46. Rocco, "L'ora del nazionalismo," in *Scritti e discorsi politici*, 2:512.

47. Rocco, "Replica agli oratori," in *Scritti e discorsi politici*, 2:512; see Corradini, "Nazionalismo e socialismo," in *Discorsi politici*, pp. 227–228; and Corradini, "Stato liberale e stato nazionale," in ibid., p. 235.

48. Corradini, "L'emigrazione italiana nell'America del Sud," in *Discorsi politici*, pp. 74, 87; and Corradini, "Principii di nazionalismo," in ibid., pp. 92–93, 100.

49. See Sun, "Die Drei Prinzipien in der Manifests des Reorganisationsparteitages der Kuo Min Tang (1924)," in *Sun Yat-sen: Aufzeichnungen eines chinesischen Revolutionaeres*, ed. Karl Wittfogel (Berlin: Agis, 1928), p. 318.

50. Corradini, "Le nazioni proletarie e il nazionalismo," in *Discorsi politici*, pp. 107, 114; and Corradini, "Per la guerra d'Italia," in ibid., p. 272.

51. See Corradini, "La guerra e la lotta di classe," in *Discorsi politici*, p. 365. Sun's arguments were essentially the same.

52. See Corradini, "Politica ed economia della nazione e delle classi," in *Discorsi politici*, pp. 374–390; and Corradini, "Il nazionalismo e i sindacati," in ibid., pp. 421–425. For Sun's comments, see "The Disabilities Suffered by Chinese Workers Under the Unequal Treaties," *GQ*, 2:683–684; available as "Rede an die chinesischen Arbeiter," in Wittfogel, *Sun Yat-sen*, pp. 328–329.

53. Sun, *The Triple Demism of Sun Yat-sen* (1931; reprint, New York: AMS, 1974), pp. 85–86. Reprint of the 1931 Wuchang edition. See also Linebarger, *Political Doctrines*, pp. 62–63.

54. See Rocco, "Che cosa è il nazionalismo è che cosa vogliono i nazionalisti," in *Scritti e discorsi politici*, 1:69–89. The allusion to "race" in the writings of both Italian and Chinese nationalists is important insofar as "racism" is often conjured up as an issue in discussing nationalism. The issue will be more fully considered later in the discussion.

55. The discussion that surrounds the nature of Chinese nationalism, whether cultural, ethnic, or racial, need not detain us here. (See, in this context, Jonathan Unger, ed., *Chinese Nationalism* [Armonk, N.Y.: M. E. Sharpe, 1996].) Sun clearly entertained the notion of a Chinese "race" and feared "racial destruction" as emphatically as Italian Nationalists at that time feared the "destruction" of the Italian "race."

56. Sun, *Triple Demism*, pp. 78–84.

57. Ibid., pp. 178–179.

58. Rocco, "Che cosa è il nazionalismo," pp. 71, 83; see Rocco, "Il valore sociale del femminismo," in *Scritti e discorsi politici*, 1:62–63.

59. Sun, *Triple Demism*, pp. 271–273.

60. Ibid., pp. 291, 293, 295, 297. See also Sun, "Five Power Constitution," in *Fundamentals of National Reconstruction* (Taipei: Sino-American, 1953), pp. 35–36.

61. Sun, *Triple Demism*, pp. 175–180.

62. See Rocco, "Cause remote e possime della crisi dei partiti politici italiani," in *Scritti e discorsi politici*, 1:6; and Rocco, "Economia liberale," pp. 30–33, 42, 51.

63. Rocco, "Che cosa è il nazionalismo," p. 78; Rocco, "Esame di cosienza," in *Scritti e discorsi politici*, 1:98; and Rocco, "L'impero d'Italia," in ibid., p. 257.

64. Corradini, "La vita nazionale," in *Discorsi politici*, p. 46.

65. Sun, *Triple Demism*, p. 97; Rocco, "Il problema economico italiano," in *Scritti e discorsi politici*, 1:14; Corradini, "Principii di nazionalismo," pp. 92, 93, 100; and Corradini, "Nazionalismo e democrazia," in *Discorsi politici*, p. 161.

66. Sun, *Triple Demism*, p. 98; Corradini, "Le nazioni proletarie e il nazionalismo," in *Discorsi politici*, pp. 109, 111; and Corradini, *La marcia dei produttori*, pp. 4, 5, 16.

67. Corradini, *La marcia dei produttori*, pp. 6–7, 21.

68. Sun, *Triple Demism*, p. 430.

69. Ibid., p. 432; Rocco, "Economia liberale," pp. 35–36.

70. See Giovanni Papini, "Un programma nazionalista," in Papini and Prezzolini, *Vecchio e nuovo nazionalismo*, pp. 6, 14–15, 39, 42.

71. Sun, *Triple Demism*, pp. 278–279.

72. Ibid., pp. 301–302.

73. Harold Z. Schiffrin, "The Enigma of Sun Yat-sen," in *China in Revolution: The First Phase, 1900–1913*, ed. Mary C. Wright (New Haven: Yale University, 1968), p. 465.

74. See Franco Gaeta, *Nazionalismo Italiano* (Naples: ESI, 1965), pp. 136ff; Sun, "Five Power Constitution," pp. 20–38.

75. See Sun, *Triple Demism*, pp. 330–331.

76. See the discussion in Shu-ch'in Ts'ui, "Fundamentals of National Reconstruction: Introductory Note," in Sun, *Fundamentals*, pp. i-vii; and Sun, "Statement on Fundamentals of National Reconstruction," in ibid., pp. 1–2.

77. Corradini, "Sindacalismo, nazionalismo, imperialismo," in *Discorsi politici*, p. 63; see also Corradini, "Nazionalismo e democrazia," pp. 158–160, 162, 165.

78. Rocco, "Che cosa è il nazionalismo," p. 79; and Rocco, "Il programma politico dell'Associazione Nazionalista," in *Scritti e discorsi politici*, 2:475, 478.

79. Sun, *Triple Demism*, p. 538.

80. Rocco, "Ordine del giorno," in *Scritti e discorsi politici*, 2:491; and Rocco, "Che cosa è il nazionalismo," p. 79.

81. See the entire discussion in Sun, *Triple Demism*, pp. 422–443; Rocco, "L'ora del nazionalismo," in *Scritti e discorsi politici*, 2:515; and Rocco, "Economia liberale," p. 33.

82. There obviously were many reasons, not the least of which was the fact that the Bolsheviks were prepared to supply his forces with arms and support. Sun had made overtures to the industrial democracies but had been rebuffed. See the discussion in Shao Chuan Leng and Norman D. Palmer, *Sun Yat-sen and Communism* (New York: Praeger, 1960), chaps. 2–3.

83. Sun, "Statement on the Formation of National Government," in *Fundamentals*, p. 162.

84. See John Kautsky, "Neo-Maoism, Marxism and Leninism" and "From Proletarianism to Modernizing Movement," in *Communism and the Politics of Development* (New York: Wiley, 1968), pp. 42–102.

85. Dino Grandi, "La libertà communista" and "La cosienza nazionale," in *Giovani* (Bologna: Zanichelli, 1941), pp. 85–86, 94–96.

86. Marxists of all sorts have recognized that all revolutionary movements in the twentieth century—Marxist, nationalist and fascist alike—have been led by persons of petty bourgeois provenience. See Max Shachtman's comments in the forward to Trotsky's *Problems of the Chinese Revolution*, trans. Max Shachtman (New York: Paragon Book Reprint, 1966), p. vi. The fact is that membership in Marxist, nationalist, and fascist movements have been recruited from all classes. See Trotsky's comments in "Fascism," in *Fascism: What It Is and How to Fight It* (New York: Pioneer, 1944), pp. 11–12.

87. It is very difficult to make a definitive judgment concerning this issue. By 1923, the Italian Nationalists were swallowed up by Mussolini's Fascism and lost whatever ideological independence they had.

88. This theme is found throughout Italian Nationalist literature. See, for example, Corradini, *La marcia dei produttori*, pp. ii-iii, 27, 180–181, 184–199; see the entire discussion in Roberto Michels, *L'imperialismo Italiano* (Rome: Società Editrice Libraria, 1914).

89. Sun, *Triple Demism*, pp. 154–160, esp. p. 154.

90. Ibid., p. 138.

91. See, for example, Rocco, "Il problema economico Italiano," in *Scritti e discorsi politici*, 1:18–19; see also Rocco, "Economia liberale," p. 45.

92. See the discussion in Sun, *Triple Demism*, pp. 524–538; Rocco, "Economia liberale," pp. 40, 47.

93. Rocco, "Il problema economico Italiano"; "Economia liberale"; "Il programma politico dell'Associazione Nazionalista"; and "L'ora del nazionalismo," in *Scritti e discorsi politici*, 1:21, 56; 2:475, 477, 513.

94. Rocco, "Il programma nazionalista," in ibid., 2:496.

95. Rocco, "Economia liberale," p. 54.

96. Sun, "How to Develop Chinese Industry," in *Fundamentals*, p. 186; see also Sun, "International Development of China," in ibid., p. 173; and Sun, *International Development of China*, pp. ii, 47, 85, 135, 138.

97. See Leng and Palmer, *Sun Yat-sen and Communism*, pp. 68–83.

4
Marxism, Maoism, Fascism, and the Kuomintang

Whatever the pretensions of Marxism as a social science, both Soviet and Chinese Marxists found it difficult to make theoretical sense of what was transpiring in postdynastic China. Equipped as it was with its standard version of fascism, the Comintern and its agents nonetheless apparently failed to track, at the time, the emergence, trajectory, or endurance of what they later identified as fascism in China. Only sometime after the debacle of 1927–1928, which cost the Chinese Communist party much of its leadership and a good deal of its membership, did Soviet Marxists begin to characterize Chinese "counterrevolutionaries" as "fascists." Only years after the events did M. N. Roy, one of the Comintern's major representatives in China, trace Chinese fascism to its source in the revolutionary ideology of Sun Yat-sen.[1]

For their part, Chinese Marxists apparently never made the connection. Nowhere in Chinese Communist literature does one find a reference to Sun's Three Principles of the People, the *Sanmin zhuyi*, as "fascist," "protofascist," or containing "elements of fascism."

In fact, as late as 1940, Mao Zedong could still insist that "the Three Principles [of the People] . . . as interpreted by Dr. Sun Yat-sen in 1924 [were] basically similar to the communist political program for the stage of the democratic revolution in China."[2] At precisely the same time, however exculpatory his judgment concerning Sun, Mao intimated that in the years since 1924 the Kuomintang had become fascist—and that its "fascism" had found expression specifically in Chiang Kai-shek's doctrine of "Vitalism."[3] According to Mao, at some time between the death of Sun Yat-sen in 1925 and the appearance of vitalism in 1934, the Kuomintang had transformed itself into a vehicle for Chinese fascism.

At best, the notion that vitalism gave ideological expression to a form of Chinese fascism was curious. Vitalism, or the "New Life Movement" as it is generally identified in the West, was, in principle, an effort on the part of the nationalist government to instill a modern sense of discipline and conscientiousness among the citizenry of the republic.[4] Such efforts are common among reactive nationalist and developmental movements everywhere. Founded in early 1934, the New Life Movement was dedicated to "the social regeneration of China."[5]

The regenerative injunctions of the New Life Movement included everything from loyalty to the nation to respect for the flag, a readiness to sacrifice for the national community, and a reform of personal hygiene. The New Life Movement was singularly undistinguished. It sought to remedy collective defects by exhortation and evocative appeal.

Most nationalist and developmental movements in our time have embarked upon similar programs calculated to bring their populations into the twentieth century. Nationalists everywhere have sought to reawaken what have generally been considered the traditional virtues of self-sacrifice, frugality, loyalty, and discipline among conationals. That some have identified features of the Hitlerjugend or the Fascist Balilla in such efforts[6] only indicates that they have failed to appreciate how commonplace such regenerative efforts are. Many of the same features can be found in movements ranging from black nationalist movements in the United States to the Soviet or Cuban Young Pioneers.[7]

Such regenerative efforts commonly involve military or paramilitary training. Nationalist and developmental movements, more frequently than not, emerge in political environments of protracted crisis and perceived threat. Military training seems to recommend itself. In many cases, military training is part of the reactive "masculine protest" to real or fancied national humiliation.

In effect, there was nothing in the New Life Movement that was specifically fascist. Certainly, the Chinese Marxists did not so characterize it when it first manifested itself in early 1934. In fact, for a very long time Chinese Marxists did not identify "fascism" in the political activities of the Kuomintang, even though as early as 1928 they conceived its suppression of Communist activities in China as part of a program of "White Terror."[8] By 1934, Mao regularly reiterated that "the imperialists and the Kuomintang" had long conspired together to defeat the "proletarian revolution." According to China's Marxists, Chiang Kai-shek and the Kuomintang had enlisted themselves in the service of the "evil gentry," "big bureaucrats," and the Chinese "compradors"—all of whom were under the ultimate direction of international imperialism.[9] The devastation of the Chinese Communist party in 1927–1928 was understood to have been a consequence of the fact that "the imperialists" had ordered its "lackeys," the landlord and comprador classes, to direct a compliant Chiang Kai-shek and a submissive Kuomintang to "betray" the Chinese revolution.[10]

For China's Marxist-Leninists, the political behaviors of the Kuomintang were to be understood in the standard terms of "class warfare." Neither Chiang Kai-shek nor his party could be independent actors on the China scene. They had to be unreflecting tools of the bourgeoisie and, ultimately, of "international imperialism."

However familiar, none of that, apparently, was sufficient to identify either Chiang Kai-shek or the Kuomintang as fascist. Whatever the Comintern or M. N. Roy may have thought at the time, the intellectual leadership of Marxism-Leninism in China failed to see fascism in either the doctrines of Sun Yat-sen or the class-driven activities of the Kuomintang. Even though possessed of the Kremlin's standard version of fascism as the compliant "instrument" of international finance capitalism, the Marxists of China still failed to recognize fascism in its Chinese incarnation until the early 1940s.

Even though Mao insisted that the "big bourgeoisie" and the "landlord class" directed all Kuomintang policy, he was reluctant to identify either Chiang Kai-shek or the Kuomintang as "fascist" until as late as 1941.[11] As already indicated, until the mid-1940s, Mao continued to insist that Chinese Marxists should labor for the implementation of the Kuomintang's Three Principles of the People.[12]

Whatever fascism the Chinese Marxists were to later discover in the New Life Movement of the mid-1930s seems not to have been recognized as such at the time. Only in 1943 did Mao begin to speak about a "Kuomintang comprador-feudal fascist dictatorship" predicated on "one party, one doctrine, and one leader."[13]

That the theoreticians of Communist China traced fascism to the New Life Movement—however belatedly—is interesting for a number of reasons. The New Life Movement itself was largely a product of the enterprise of a small but aggressive minority among the members of the Kuomintang. Often identified as the Blue Shirt Society, that minority was composed of revolutionaries committed to the regeneration of a faltering China, threatened from within by moral and political decay, and facing invasion by a determined external enemy.[14]

The Chinese Blue Shirt Society

In early 1932, the Blue Shirt Society was founded in Nanjing. Composed of fervent nationalists, it was dedicated to the mobilization of masses and the inculcation of nationalist virtues among them. By the end of 1932, the Blue Shirts had established branches in almost every provincial capital of the republic. By 1934, they had organizational offices in every major city, sections in each county capital, and cells in a variety of institutions, including local Kuomintang party committees, military units, newspaper offices, radio stations, and educational establishments. Members were drawn from every social and economic provenance. They included workers, small capitalists, students, and intellectuals.

By 1938, the Blue Shirts listed more than 100,000 members in its Chinese Renaissance Society, one of the public organizations it sponsored as part of its program of national regeneration. The Renaissance Society was only one of its undertakings.

The Blue Shirts were the sponsors of at least four mass campaigns during the 1930s, among which the New Life Movement was one of the less important. The National Voluntary Labor, the National Economic Reconstruction, and the Military Education Movements exceeded the New Life Movement in importance. The Voluntary Labor Movement mobilized tens of thousands of citizens for public economic and defense projects. In 1937, 60,000 citizens were mobilized to clear and dredge rivers and streams and 20,000 more were employed in the construction of a line of defensive entrenchments, more than 100 miles long, in the doomed effort to defend Nanjing from Japanese attack.

All of this must be understood within the context of revolution in post-dynastic China. In the early 1920s, when there was every reason to believe that Sun Yat-sen already had intimations of early demise, an effort was made to reorganize the Kuomintang. Under the influence of Soviet advisers, Sun sought the overhaul and restructuring of his revolutionary party. Long a loosely structured clandestine organization of intellectuals and revolutionary adventurers, after the collapse of the dynasty, Sun recognized that the Kuomintang required a mass base if it was to free itself from dependency on a mercenary military and succeed in its programs.[15]

The 1924 reorganization of the Kuomintang sought to create a highly centralized party structure, animated by an articulate ideology and characterized by tight discipline. The party was to create its own political army charged with its defense, as well as a collateral propaganda apparatus calculated to attract and effectively harness a mass following.[16] Sun was to serve as the party's leader (*Tsungli*), with the power to direct and control the conduct of party functionaries.

The party constitution of 1924 contained six articles devoted to the powers and responsibilities of the *Tsungli*. All party members were enjoined to "obey the *Tsungli's* leadership and exert themselves in the implementation of [the party's] principles." The *Tsungli* was to serve as chairman of both the National Party Congress and the party's Central Executive Committee.

The reorganization of the Kuomintang in 1924 was the product of a variety of influences. After the collapse of the Qing dynasty in 1912, China disintegrated into regional enclaves. When Sun Yat-sen resigned as the leader of the military government in Canton in May 1918, his prospects were few. He was discouraged and disillusioned. He found little support among the hapless masses of southern China, and the loyalty of followers resulted more from personal attachment than ideological conviction.

Clearly, what the revolution required was a modern political party that was capable of mobilizing masses in the service of national economic and military development. The decisions that resulted in the reorganization of the Kuomintang in 1924 arose out of that recognition, and out of Sun's appreciation of some of the contemporary European social science literature available to him.

His conviction that the Chinese revolution required determined leaders who would employ executive powers to direct a truly centralized and disciplined mass-mobilizing revolutionary party arose out of his own experience, a familiarity with theoretical works such as those provided by Roberto Michels,[17] and the urging of Soviet advisers who had made their appearance in revolutionary China in those years.

Sun's decision to embark on the reorganization of the Kuomintang was more than a response to his Soviet advisers. It was shaped by Michels's judgment that even revolutions inspired by ultimate democratic principles must employ "military discipline" in the protracted period of transition from the old to the new order.[18] It was Michels, together with those European theorists who conceived governance to be forever characterized by the presence of dominant elites, who convinced Sun that revolutionary leaders served as the nonsubstitutable catalysts of successful revolution.

Thus, before his death Sun Yat-sen was convinced of both the special role of elites in revolutionary situations and the efficacy of modern revolutionary parties. The reorganization of the Kuomintang followed in 1924. The reorganization was designed to produce a mass-mobilizing, leader- and elite-dominant, hierarchically structured revolutionary party committed to the Three Principles of the People. In institutional form and political character, the 1924 party charter of the Kuomintang shared features that would be found in many nationalist and developmental revolutionary parties then and since.

The confusion following Sun's death in 1925, and the subsequent struggle for political control in a fractious environment, left the Kuomintang itself disorganized and uncertain. The dissolution of the "united front" with the Chinese Communists in 1927–1928, the Kuomintang's military effort to reunite China, and the attempts to deflect the increasing aggression of the Japanese all compromised the Kuomintang's efforts at economic development and political reorganization.

Whatever the efforts at reorganization, the years between 1925 and 1930 found the Kuomintang wracked by divided loyalties.[19] The mobilization of the masses remained irregular and, in considerable measure, unsatisfactory at least in part because of the competitive intervention of the Chinese Communist party.[20] As a consequence, by the beginning of the 1930s, the most desperate members of the Kuomintang organized themselves into the Blue Shirt Society, dedicated to the realization of the goals of the original reorganization of the party undertaken almost a decade earlier.

Why the Blue Shirts or the New Life Movement were singled out as representatives of "Chinese fascism" is very difficult to understand. They entertained neither ideological convictions, strategic orientations, nor tactical postures that distinguished them from the reorganized Kuomintang that Sun Yat-sen authorized in 1924. What they were was more desperate. By the early 1930s, republican China was threatened with extinction. What the Blue Shirts sought, in response, was a leader "like Mussolini or Stalin" who could energize a flaccid China. They sought a disciplined party that could mobilize revolutionaries who might, through obedience and personal sacrifice, restore China's dignity in the face of internal and external threat.[21]

That Fascist Italy, in a dozen years, had taken a "broken and divided Italy" and, through the agency of a disciplined mass mobilizing party, had produced in its stead a "leading power" was cited as demonstrative evidence of China's need of just such a truly revolutionary political organization. Thus, when Chiang Kai-shek addressed China's need to rigorously control consumption, systematically inculcate the work-and-sacrifice ethic, and cultivate the civic virtues of loyalty and obedience among the nation's citizenry, he cited Fascist Italy and National Socialist Germany as instructive instances of success,[22] just as Sun, before him, had cited the Soviet Union as just such an exemplary case.[23]

It was not Italian Fascism or German National Socialism, per se, that Chiang Kai-shek or the Blue Shirts recommended to the revolutionaries of China. What the Blue Shirts found admirable in Italian Fascism and German National Socialism was the same thing they, and Sun Yat-sen, found attractive in Bolshevism. All these movements had succeeded in restoring dignity to their respective national communities. Fascist Italy, National Socialist Germany, and the Soviet Union had all succeeded in overcoming domestic disabilities, internal dissension, economic constraints, and international threat through the agency of a "dedicated revolutionary party under the leadership of men of integrity."

They had all accomplished that by dint of revolutionary elan, organizational integrity, political discipline, nationalist enthusiasm, and moral rectitude. In the judgment of the Blue Shirts, China required nothing less.

In making their case, the Blue Shirts were saying nothing more, nor anything less, than Sun Yat-sen had said a decade before. In the preambulatory discussions on the reorganization of the Kuomintang in 1924,

Sun had acknowledged that his party needed the ideological integrity and the organizational discipline of the Bolsheviks. That was not in any way to suggest that Sun anticipated that the Kuomintang would abandon the Three Principles of the People for Leninism.[24] Similarly, the Blue Shirts never recommended the abandonment of the Three Principles of the People for a fascist alternative.

That Western scholars, following the intimations of Chinese Marxists, identified "Chinese fascism" with the Blue Shirts remains a source of considerable puzzlement.[25] That Marxist theoreticians have sought to support the thesis is more easily understood, but no more persuasive.[26]

The Blue Shirts, like Chiang Kai-shek and the Kuomintang, remained resolutely committed to the doctrines of Sun Yat-sen. They were developmental nationalists, absorbed in the economic development and the military defense of the national community. In the service of that development and that defense, they sought the regeneration of China through the disciplined auspices of the New Life Movement.

It would be entirely unrealistic to attempt to suggest the intricacies of the relationship between the Chinese Communist party and the Nationalist government as they participated in yet another "united front," at that time during the long struggle against the Japanese invaders, but part of the reason the Blue Shirts were singled out as "fascists" was to provide China's Marxist theoreticians an issue with which to divide, and weaken, the Kuomintang.[27] The Chinese Communist party always anticipated a time when the Kuomintang would have to be directly defeated.

In those circumstances, the issue of "capitulationism" was regularly raised, with the intimation that the "right wing" of the Kuomintang—the Blue Shirts or their equivalent—was prepared to surrender to imperialism and betray the nation. China's Marxist theoreticians were to exploit the prospect of capitulation to imperialism by a "Chinese fascism."

Since "fascism" had been defined by the Comintern as the tool of finance capital and imperialism, fascists in China would be expected to be entirely susceptible to their importunings. Through a series of entailments, resting on premises provided by the standard Marxist-Leninist interpretation of fascism, it was maintained that the Blue Shirts were employed exclusively in the suppression of Chinese Communism, rather than a defense of the homeland from imperialism, because they were the agents of foreign interests. Only the anti-imperialism of the Chinese Communist party could be trusted to defend the nation. Anything less would be a concession to defeat.

These were the arguments used by the Chinese Communist party to attack the Kuomintang by indirection. All the implications were evident. Whatever could be said of the "fascist right wing" or the "fascist Blue Shirts" could be said of the Kuomintang.

Thus, according to Mao Zedong, Chiang Kai-shek and the Kuomintang were not only the "representatives" of the "big bourgeoisie," but they undertook political activities at the "instigation" of "imperialists."[28] They were captives of international finance capitalism, and international finance provided the direction and substance of imperialism.

This entire line of argument was a product of the original Marxist-Leninist interpretation of fascism. It was not only predicated on the false premise that fascism was the creature of finance capitalism, but it entirely misunderstood the anti-imperialism of Sun Yat-sen and the Kuomintang. The theoretical failures of Marxism-Leninism in general, and those of the Chinese Marxists in particular, compounded revolutionary China's problems during the time of the Japanese invasion and the civil war that followed.

Marxist-Leninists never seemed to understand Sun's recommended policies concerning comprehensive national development, foreign imperialism, and the defense of China's territorial and political sovereignty. In not understanding Sun, they failed to understand the Kuomintang and the Blue Shirts as well.

Sun Yat-sen, Marxism, and Imperialism

Sun Yat-sen's doctrinal position was well-established by the time he entered into rapprochement with the Soviet Union in 1924. Whatever tactical reasons Sun Yat-sen may have had for entering into that rapprochement, he made very clear that whatever the relationship between the Soviet Union and Nationalist China, Marxism had absolutely no place in the revolutionary program of the Kuomintang.[29] That rejection included the prevalent Marxist-Leninist notions concerning uprisings on the periphery of world imperialism in order to support and foster world revolution.

In his final lectures on the Three Principles of the People, Sun characterized Marxism, with its anticapitalism and its commitment to unremitting domestic and international class warfare, as "pathological."[30] The fact was that Sun unequivocally rejected all the central tenets of Marxism as Marxism found expression in the revolutionary creed of Marxism-Leninism. Although Sun was pleased to refer to his social policies as "socialism," his socialism was predicated on the cultivation of Chinese industrial capitalism—and to that end, on systematic collaboration with all domestic and international forces capable of providing assistance.[31]

Characteristic of revolutionary developmental nationalism, Sun's doctrine did not emphasize domestic "class struggle" but collaboration in pursuit of economic growth and development.[32] Increasing agricultural yield and accelerated industrial growth were the central preoccupations of his system and might require calculated collaboration with advanced industrial nations.[33]

As early as 1904, Sun argued that the economic development and industrial modernization of China not only required the protection of the "lives and property of all persons"[34] but, more than that, collaboration with the major foreign powers. Sun recognized that China was capital poor and consequently required major financial investments from the industrially advanced nations of the West. But foreign investments could not be obtained without the security of capital and assurance of the repatriation of profit.[35]

Sun argued that China would "not be able to promote . . . industries by [its] own knowledge and experience [or its own] capital; we cannot," he went on, "but depend upon the already created capital of other countries. If we wait until we ourselves have enough capital before we start to promote industry, the process of development will be exceedingly slow. . . . So we shall certainly have to borrow foreign capital to develop our . . . facilities, and foreign brains and experience to manage them."[36]

Sun anticipated extensive collaboration with the advanced industrial democracies. They would supply capital and allow the transfer of technology in exchange for access to the vast Chinese market. For Sun, all of China "would be open to foreign trade . . . and a grand field hitherto undreamed of would be opened to the social and economic activities of the civilized world."[37]

With its low-cost labor and its seemingly boundless resources, China "would create an unlimited market for the whole world."[38] The advanced industrial powers would supply the capital and would collaborate with China in "joint action" to provide investment opportunities for international financial institutions, commodity markets for foreign industry, and offshore assembly and production facilities for commodity production.[39]

The general failure of Marxist theoreticians to appreciate the fact that Sun Yat-sen had a reasonably sophisticated understanding of international trade and investment, as well as programmatic convictions about national development, led them to imagine that his programs were nothing more than simple concessions to "imperialism."[40] Even some Western scholars have repeated the notion that Sun never managed to effectively come to grips with imperialistic threats to China's sovereignty and developmental potential.[41]

The failure to understand Sun's views concerning imperialism led Marxists to imagine that he, the Kuomintang, and the Blue Shirts were "subservient" to foreigners and to their "comprador" and "big capitalist" agents in China. The fact was that Sun, and those animated by the convictions of the *Sanmin zhuyi*, entertained a sophisticated and nuanced conception of the relationship between economically backward China and imperialism.

Sun developed his views concerning imperialism by reading Western theorists. One of the most influential of those was J. A. Hobson, whose *Imperialism* worked its influence not only on many of Sun's contemporaries[42] but, as we have seen, on V. I. Lenin as well.

Hobson cataloged all the abuses of imperialism long familiar to Chinese revolutionaries and then went on to argue that commodity and investment capital surpluses in the advanced economies drove the "great controllers of industry" to transfer technology and finances to less-developed countries. He argued that capitalists of the advanced nations would be compelled to draw the less-developed nations into trade and would be driven to the "making of railways, development of mines, [and] the improvement of agriculture" in the less-developed economies, all in the effort to profitably empty their inventories and profitably invest their capital.[43] Lenin had chosen to make nothing of that. The argument that imperialism might underwrite the development of economies on the periphery of capitalism was a thesis that had no place in his plans for international revolution.

Hobson argued that "as one nation after another enters the machine economy and adopts advanced industrial methods, it becomes more difficult for its manufacturers, merchants and financiers to dispose profitably of their economic resources," and they seek vent for their "excess of goods and capital" in economically less-developed environs. The "endeavor of the great controllers of industry to broaden the channel for the flow of their surplus wealth by seeking foreign markets and foreign investments to take off the goods and capital they cannot sell or use at home," Hobson maintained, is the "taproot of imperialism."[44]

Given the argument, it was clear that Hobson conceived of imperialism as the result of an ever tightening cycle of economic development and overdevelopment. In a fashion reminiscent of Karl Marx and Friedrich Engels, Hobson maintained that industrial capitalism was compelled to exceed any of its domestic or regional markets and would be driven to seek foreign outlets for both its commodities and its surplus capital—to create on its boundaries its own competition.[45]

Hobson, like Marx and Engels, argued that the expansion of the capitalist powers throughout the world created the preconditions for the economic development of backward regions.[46] Like Marx and Engels, Hobson recognized that the advanced industrial powers, in their pursuit of their own interests, would be compelled to impose a modern economy on those communities less developed. The economic development that would irresistibly follow from their penetration into the less-developed region would just as predictably be accompanied by exploitation and abuse.

Sun was acutely aware of all the implications of Hobson's argument. Thus, although he was convinced that commercial exchange with the advanced industrial powers would leave a legacy of concrete economic benefits for retrograde China, he fully realized that the "imperialist powers" would employ every stratagem to strengthen their bargaining power and ensure their advantage. He argued that neither Germany nor the United States could have succeeded in their economic growth and industrial development without the intercession of capital and technology flows from the more materially advanced economies, but he acknowledged that prudence required that China, as a less-developed nation without the material means and military ordnance necessary for its own defense, would have to marshal all its political resources to protect itself.

Sun and those around him were sufficiently sophisticated to appreciate that putting together the political and military resources necessary to protect their community from exploitation would be extremely difficult. They were fully apprised of the complex mechanisms available to the imperialist powers in their relationships with less well-developed countries. Among Sun's collaborators were those who wrote extensively on the ability of the Western powers to tailor the terms of trade to favor themselves and stipulate the conditions of investment to serve their own interests.[47] Resisting such depredations required major *political* influence in shaping the processes.

More than that, the Chinese revolutionary movement was fully aware of the economic consequences of the "unequal treaties" that resulted from foreign military incursions into China. With the loss of territory and critical elements of sovereignty, the Chinese lost control of their inland and territorial waters, their maritime customs, and their salt revenues.

By the end of the nineteenth century, the Qing dynasty had surrendered consular jurisdiction to foreigners. The regime had lost control over tariff regulations and the imposition of customs duties on exports and imports. The right of foreign warships to cruise and anchor along China's coasts and in her inland ports led to foreign dominance of her waterways.

By the turn of the century, foreigners administered China's entire customs and tariff system. Tariff rates were determined by foreign powers and tariff revenues were appropriated by foreigners. The International Protocol of 1901 allowed foreign powers to fix tariff levels on export goods and imports. To assure the payment of the indemnity imposed on imperial China after the Boxer Rebellion, foreigners assumed all but absolute control over some of the most vital revenue-generating functions of the nation. As Sun was to emphasize, the protocol was a significant

factor in the determination of the terms of trade that would largely fore-
close the possibility that China could accumulate the capital necessary to
embark upon, and sustain, rapid economic growth and development.
Sun argued that escape from these circumstances could only be achieved
by a strong and politically unified China. Only a united China could escape the trammels of those unequal treaties that threatened its economic,
political, and military survival. Only an assertive, self-confident China
could impose conditions on the inflow of capital, the repatriation of profits by foreign investors, and the tariff arrangements governing the nation's trade.[48] An aggressive and popular nationalism was required to
support both the policies and the state prepared to impose them. Led by
a strong, popular government, a determined population could escalate
the costs incurred by foreigners as they attempted to evade the nation's
sovereign legislation or violate its territory.[49]

More than that, a strong government, enjoying the nationalist support
of the general population, could impose controls on tariff and currency
regulations and monitor international exchange and investment.[50] That
would allow China to accumulate the capital so essential to its program
of comprehensive economic development and modernization.

Throughout his life, unlike the Marxist-Leninists of the Comintern,
Sun continued to maintain that international economic relations were
not, in and of themselves, exploitative. He argued that in a world of self-
seeking sovereign states it was natural for international actors to attempt
to maximize their own advantages. Where any one community was
demonstrably weak (as was the Manchu dynasty), others could be expected to exploit opportunities to increase their gains.[51]

The principle governing relations between strong and weak states, in
Sun's judgment, was that as long as nations were "strong enough to carry
out acts of injustice" at acceptable cost, one could hardly expect "respect
for justice."[52] As long as China remained politically disorganized and
militarily weak, it faced the prospect of unremitting economic exploitation. It would remain forever in a "state of serfdom, so that a profitable
trade [could] be carried on forever by the ruling country . . . [and China
would] always be a market for [its] industrial products."[53] Under such
constraints, China would have enormous difficulty in extracting itself
from economic underdevelopment.

For Sun, imperialism was the "policy of aggression upon other countries by means of political force." In the pursuit of security and advantage, the "strong states" impose their will on "smaller and weaker peoples,"[54] for without political and military dominance over subject
peoples, exploitative economic relations could not be effectively maintained. For Sun, economic exploitation was a function of political and

military variables and not the result of some inherent necessities of the commercial and financial dynamics of industrial capitalism.[55]

As a country facing the arduous task of rapid economic growth and development, China, according to Sun, would have to insulate itself within a strong state—as the Japanese and the Germans had done at a similar stage in their evolution.[56] Such a state would not only regulate the conditions governing international trade and financial transactions but would also seek out temporary or enduring security alliances with one or another of the advanced nations in order to ensure that the industrial powers could not move against China in concert.[57]

Sun's argument was that given the existence of a strong state—enjoying popular consensus and receiving collateral support from an advanced industrial nation with which it shared some commercial and/or strategic interests—China could embark on a program of rapid economic growth and industrial development that would redound to everyone's advantage. Potentially exploitative relations with imperialist powers could be transformed into relations of interdependency and mutual advantage. Under those circumstances, China could open its markets to international commerce, welcoming those foreigners who would underwrite industry and develop the infrastructure necessary for the nation's development, as well as provide the skills and experience requisite to the process.[58]

This was the concept of imperialism to which Sun committed both himself and his revolutionary movement. Its clear implications were that revolutionary China would enter into alliances with any nation prepared to negotiate with China as an equal but would be prepared to resist, with force, any attempts at armed aggression.

This policy was pursued by the Kuomintang—and, by implication, the Blue Shirts—throughout the 1930s. Relationships with the advanced industrial democracies were cultivated as long as such relationships worked to China's advantage. Resistance to Japanese territorial pretensions in no way contradicted Sun's programmatic recommendations.

For Sun, and the Kuomintang, imperialism was not all of a piece. When Marxist theorists lamented that Sun betrayed his anti-imperialism by continuing negotiations with the industrial democracies even while in a special relationship with the Soviet Union, they revealed their ignorance of his reasonably well articulated convictions about relations between less-developed and industrially mature economies. As early as 1919, Sun and the theoreticians of the Kuomintang had formulated a policy intended to allow China to profit from traffic in international trade, the inflow of capital, and the transfer of technology. Nothing in the relationship Sun's China enjoyed with the Soviet Union militated against

China's continued relationship with the industrial democracies. Sun was neither an enemy of the industrial West nor an advocate of Marxist-Leninist international "proletarian revolution."

At the same time, it was eminently clear that the ideology of the Kuomintang made resistance to armed aggression an unqualified obligation. Before his death, Sun had argued that a coherent and assertive nationalism could control any negative effects of political, economic, and military relations between an economically retrograde China and more advanced nations. In the years that followed, Sun more fully articulated that programmatic policy. By the time he delivered his final lectures on the Three Principles of the People, he reiterated China's unalterable need for foreign capital and foreign skills[59] and, by express implication, the necessity to continue to cultivate the capital-rich countries of the industrialized West.

But whatever the policies, China required absolute sovereign control over its territory and its external relations. Without that sovereign control, the Kuomintang would have not only violated its sacred obligation to protect the integrity of the nation, but China would find itself invariably subject to unequal conditions of trade, suffering every disadvantage in the sale of its exports and compelled to purchase foreign producer goods and technology at elevated prices. The trade deficits that would necessarily result, would leave China without the resources to pay for the ongoing purchase of critical imports or the capital to fuel growth and development.[60]

Sun Yat-sen, Imperialism, and the Doctrines of Friedrich List

This was the anti-imperialism that constituted a critical part of the ideology Sun bequeathed to the Kuomintang. It was a policy that shared some features with traditional Marxism (as formulated in Hobson's *Imperialism*) but contradicted the Leninist substance of the anti-imperialism of the Third International. In no wise did it compromise the obligation to resist the armed aggression of military imperialism.

Like many of the reactive, developmental nationalisms we will consider, Sun's anti-imperialism bears striking resemblance to the national economic policies of Friedrich List, who outlined a policy of national growth and industrialization for nations languishing in underdevelopment.[61] List, as we have seen, recognized the advantages enjoyed by those nations that had early succeeded to extensive and intensive industrialization compared with those that remained at the level of primary—extractive and agrarian—production.[62]

As early as the 1840s, at a time when Karl Marx was writing his first speculations about world revolution, List warned that nations locked into agrarian economies would suffer every economic and military disadvantage in international relations. He warned that the advanced industrial powers were capable of controlling not only the security environment in which agrarian nations were required to survive but also the very conditions of international trade. The result could only be massive disadvantage to the less-developed nations.

While Marxists called upon the proletariat to prepare for universal socialism, List warned that for the foreseeable future nations would have to contend for space, resources, and security in an environment of intense competition. List argued that throughout the phase of accelerated development, only an insistent sense of threat, capable of mobilizing public sentiment, might begin to create the necessary national unity, the potential for political resistance, that could, under the best circumstances, begin to protect the economically less developed nations from those industrially more mature.

List argued that breaking out of the restraints of an agrarian economy with a program of rapid development required that each nation control, to the best of its ability, the flow of trade, capital, and technology that penetrated its sovereign space—as well as that sovereign space itself. It was evident to List that national development required the accumulation of capital in capital-poor circumstances if any effort was to be made to underwrite the economic and industrial growth that would ultimately provide the military capabilities necessary to insulate the evolving nation from physical threat.

The export of goods, increased domestic savings, and reduced domestic expenditures would contribute to the accumulation of capital. All of this necessitated national leverage over the prevailing terms of trade—which, in turn, rested on "the unity and power of the nation."[63] List argued that each nation, faced with the task of domestic economic growth and development, was compelled to invest in its own "powers of production."[64] Prudence recommended that each nation develop its own forces of production if it were to survive in a highly competitive international economic environment.[65]

In the course of economic and industrial development, each nation traverses the stage at which primary agricultural and extractive goods are produced to that in which an increasing segment of the nation's gross national product is composed of machine production. In the course of its transition, each nation must face, on the international level, those nations that have already succeeded to industrial maturation.[66] Agricultural nations, in those competitive circumstances, are always at a disadvantage. Unless they could mobilize effective resistance, agrarian nations would find it difficult, if not impossible, to undertake self-sustaining economic development. The people of agrarian nations would remain condemned "to mere raw agriculture, dullness of mind, awkwardness of body, obstinate adherence to old notions, customs, methods, and processes, want of culture, of prosperity, and of liberty."[67] They would be overwhelmed by the culture, if not the raw power, of the more industrially developed communities, and thus consigned to play a secondary role in the modern world. They would inevitably fall victim to nations equipped with the power projection capabilities that are the products of industrialization and technological sophistication.

Everyone is capable, List argued, "of distinguishing between the lofty position which is occupied by a manufacturing nation of the first rank, and the inferior position of a country which merely exports corn and timber. . . . Who has not learned from . . . example . . . how greatly the existence, the independence, and the power of the nation depends on its possession of a manufacturing power of its own, developed in all its branches."[68]

The policy of the industrially advanced countries, unimpeded by any countervailing force, would be to render the less-developed nations repositories of agrarian and raw materials reserves. In violating their territorial and political sovereignty, imposing prejudicial terms of trade on less-developed nations, the advanced nations would force those less-developed to serve as their market adjuncts and investment outlets.[69] To avoid the humiliation that inevitably followed from their circumstances, List advocated a program of national economic expansion and development for agrarian states. Comprehensive development would not only assure equity in the international arena but would provide the wherewithal for institutional development capable of responding to citizen concerns, on the one hand, and fostering liberty, self-confidence, and civilization on the other.[70]

Because of the parlous circumstances in which less-developed communities found themselves, List advocated policies that required, in his judgment, the political unity and assertiveness of those preparing for rapid economic growth and development. A community in the course of development required the creation of a strong, centralized, and interventionist state. It required a system of domestic and international commercial legislation that allowed the inflow of foreign investment capital at controlled exchange rates and under conditions of repatriation that would allow for reciprocal benefits. The state would create and sustain a market-governed economy that would foster technology transfers from the advanced industrial nations.

The state would provide the tariff constraints and the protective insulation that would defend domestic infant industries. A policy of import substitution, underwritten in part by the state, would favor the growth of local manufacturing enterprises.[71]

Implicit in all of this was the developing nation's capacity to defend its sovereignty as well as control the terms of trade governing its multilateral relations with more advanced industrial powers. A nation making the transition from an agricultural to an industrial economy required a state-governed "system of protection" that would allow infant industries to establish themselves and a communications and transportation infrastructure to emerge that would unite the nation into an organic economic unity.[72] In effect, each nation, embarking on a trajectory of industrial development, must necessarily pursue a sovereign and independent program of internal infrastructural and infant industries development as well as seek control of its external trade policies in order to maintain a favorable balance of trade.[73]

List argued that such conditions governed the phased economic evolution of many, if not all, nations. In his discussion of the economic and political development of Italy, for example, List rehearsed the catalog of requirements necessary to husband that community through the phases of "slavery and serfdom, of barbarism and superstition, of national disunity and of caste privileges" to national unity, the prevalence of collective interests over those the individual, until the clear onset of development. List foresaw the possibility that the process might involve periods of authoritarian rule. Of indeterminate duration, those periods of authoritarian rule would provide the stability and order, the security of property, and efficiency of institutions requisite to rapid economic growth and industrial development.[74]

"Nations," List argued, "like individuals, if they at first only permit themselves to be ill-treated by one, soon become scorned by all, and finally become an object of derision."[75] Unless prepared to embark upon the onerous task of rapid economic growth and development, less-developed nations would forever suffer humiliation and deprivation at the hands of those industrially more advanced.

These were the policies with which we have become familiar. They were the policies advocated by Sun Yat-sen and they were the policies the Kuomintang and the Blue Shirts defended. They represented an anti-imperialism more coherent and certainly as persuasive as any advanced by Lenin's and Stalin's Comintern—all of which seemed lost on Marxist theoreticians. They were never really able to deal with reactive and developmental nationalism in the form in which it manifested itself most forthrightly in the twentieth century.

Karl Marx and Friedrich List

In the 1840s Karl Marx summarily dismissed the ideas of Friedrich List. For Marx, List's entire program for national economic and industrial development was "irrelevant" to any serious end. By the mid-1840s, Marx imagined that the world was on the threshold of international socialism and, as a consequence, nations were destined, in short order, to disappear.[76] For both Marx and Engels the universal dissolution of nations was imminent. The "international proletarian movement" would overwhelm them. Somehow or other, the revolution of the proletariat in the advanced industrial states would draw all the peripheral peoples of the world into the new cosmopolitan world order.

For Marx, that new order would know nothing of markets or wages. There would be none of the international trade in commodities, investment capital, or talent envisioned by List. List's entire vision of development being undertaken in a competitive international system of exchange, investment, and profit between nation-states was meaningless for Marx.[77]

Marxists never seemed able to extract themselves from such notions. As a consequence, they never understood the "anti-imperialism" of reactive, developmental nationalism. They not only misunderstood the anti-imperialism of Italian Fascism but entirely misinterpreted the anti-imperialism of Sun Yat-sen and, by implication, that of the Kuomintang and the Blue Shirts as well.

Neither Fascism nor nationalist China was "subservient" to international finance capitalism or imperialism. Both resisted imperialism in their own fashion. Sun's followers were prepared to collaborate, politically, strategically, and economically, with the advanced industrial democracies as long as collaboration was mutually beneficial. Fascists early assumed a truculence that ultimately matured into a demand for developmental autarchy—complete economic independence from the industrially advanced "plutocracies."

Neither Chiang Kai-shek, the Kuomintang nor the Blue Shirts ever committed themselves to the autarchy that would have made China the enemy of the advanced industrial democracies. In assuming any such posture, not only would China have lost the potential assistance of the industrialized nations in its effort at development, but it would have been entirely helpless in its war of resistance against Japanese military aggression.

Fascist Italy ultimately assumed something like the "anti-imperialist" posture recommended to the Kuomintang and the Blue Shirts by the ideologues of the Comintern. It grew out of the cynicism and aggressiveness that originally distinguished Italian Nationalism from the developmental nationalism of Sun. It was to mature into the bitter anti-imperialism of Fascist Italy that drove it into a fatal anti-Western military pact with imperial Japan and National Socialist Germany.

Although Italian Nationalists had taken their inspiration from Friedrich List,[78] the policies he advocated had taken on a singular intensity in their interpretation. List's ideas constituted the core of the redemptive doctrine of the Italian Nationalists, but they anticipated more threat than collaboration in the relationship of Italy, as a "proletarian nation," to the industrialized "plutocracies."[79]

The growth policies of Italian Nationalism, Fascism, and the Kuomintang were all unmistakably "anti-imperialist" in the sense that they all found their origins in the ideas of Friedrich List. By the time Sun Yat-sen delivered his final lectures on the Three Principles of the People, List's recommendations had become relatively commonplace among nations that had already begun their trajectory of independent growth and development. What distinguished the programmatic policies of Italian Nationalism and Fascism from those of the Kuomintang was their "anti-imperialist" intransigence—an intransigence very much like that recommended by the Comintern.

Once again, all that proved unfathomable to China's Marxists. Although they insisted that Marxist theory guided their revolutionary activity,[80] they consistently failed to understand the political and economic realities of revolutionary China. They pretended to see "fascism" in the political, social, and economic activities of the Kuomintang. They imagined they saw the hand of "imperialist finance capital" in the behavior of Chiang Kai-shek and his entourage.

The reactive nationalism and developmentalism that informed the program of Chiang Kai-shek and the Kuomintang during the 1930s was that of Sun Yat-sen's Three Principles of the People.[81] That Chen Boda discovered "fascism" in the thought of Chiang Kai-shek[82] and in the political activities of the Kuomintang[83] was the consequence of an inability to understand the logic of economic development undertaken by a weak nation in an environment of risk. The Kuomintang's interaction with the advanced industrial nations did not constitute "submission to imperialism." Loans procured from the capitalist nations of the West did not demonstrate the Kuomintang's "subservience" to finance capitalism. That the economy of republican China responded, in general, to market signals did not constitute evidence of "control" by the bourgeoisie or the compradors or the petty bourgeoisie.

That the Kuomintang refused to pursue class warfare was the consequence of its conviction that only a united China could resist the immediate threat of Japanese invasion, and the long-term danger of being overpowered in the inevitable competition of international trade and investment. All of that reflected not only common sense but the prescriptions of developmental theorists like List.

To this, the Blue Shirts sought to impose absolute commitment and everything that absolute commitment implied. They sought neither to abandon the doctrines of Sun nor to take up those of European fascism. The overt institutional and doctrinal features they displayed were those of a desperate nationalism, compelled to defend its survival while attempting extensive and intensive economic growth. The effort clearly involved what could only be conceived as a long and demanding struggle between a weak and disunited people and vastly superior opponents.

In some sense, Mao Zedong, never a competent Marxist, dimly perceived the merits of developmental nationalism and the doctrinal commitments of the Kuomintang. Through all the Marxist obfuscation, he recognized that China's principal task in the twentieth century was rapid economic development. As a consequence, he could never quite bring himself to reject Sun's programmatic Three Principles of the People.

However much he may have been advised that the doctrines of the Kuomintang and the Blue Shirts were "fascist," Mao nonetheless continued to insist that Sun's program for the accelerated development of China was the "minimum program" of the Chinese Communist party.[84] Whatever else he was, and whatever else he was to become, Mao Zedong recognized that if China were to prevail in the modern world, it would have to develop its industry, expand its economic potential, and arm itself against all enemies.

Mao intuitively appreciated the fact that revolution in the twentieth century had a great deal to do with economically backward nations struggling to obtain and secure a place in the sun. Sun Yat-sen had recognized as much when he identified Lenin's efforts at a "new economic policy" as a developmental nationalism having little, if anything, to do with Marxism. Subsequently, the leadership of the Kuomintang was to recognize that Bolshevism, Italian Fascism, and German National Socialism shared critical similarities, born of their common efforts to make whole their "broken nations."

Chiang Kai-shek and the leadership of the Kuomintang acknowledged their kinship with the major revolutionary movements of the 1930s. In their judgment, that meant nothing more sinister than that all those movements were essentially developmental in intention and reactive nationalist in inspiration. Although a great deal separated them, they all shared ideological and programmatic affinities with the revolutionary doctrines of Sun Yat-sen. That was the "fascism" faintly perceived by M. N. Roy and Chen Boda.[85] After the collapse of the united front, the Communist party undertook a struggle against those they considered the "running dogs of imperialism" and the "lackeys of the big bourgeoisie."[86] That, given the quaint lexicon of Marxism-Leninism, could only mean that "fascism" had come to China.

In the privative Comintern interpretation, "fascism" was identified as nothing other than a political movement animated by "petty bourgeois nationalism," "controlled and directed by imperialists, international financiers, and the big bourgeoisie," marshaled to defend capitalism against the world revolution of the proletariat.[87] Burdened by this kind of analysis and incapable of comprehending the coherence of the developmental nationalism of the Kuomintang, Marxists simply subsumed all the complexities of the 1930s and 1940s under an omnibus "fascism."

As we have seen, the subsumption was done with misgivings and a singular lack of timeliness. The "fascism" of Sun Yat-sen and the Kuomintang was only clearly recognized as such by Marxists after almost two decades of familiarity. The Comintern had advised the Communist party of China to join the ranks of the Kuomintang, acknowledging Sun Yat-sen and Chiang Kai-shek as the "true leaders" of revolutionary China. All of this must have left the leadership of Chinese Marxism very confused, at best. The fact was that Marxists were incapable of distinguishing fascism from the generic developmental nationalism of economically retrograde nations.[88] Marxists refused to recognize the ultimate democratic intention of the Three Principles of the People, just as they failed to appreciate the differences between the exacerbated and aggressive nationalism of fascism and the remarkably affable nationalism of Sun.

The implications of the failure of Marxists, Marxist-Leninists, and Maoists to appreciate all of this led to the misfortunes that were to settle on China for a quarter of a century after the end of the Second World War. Marxists and Maoists totally misunderstood revolution in the twentieth century. Time was to confirm that they understood very little, if anything, of reactive nationalism, paradigmatic Fascism, generic fascism, or Sun Yat-sen's aspirations for a revolutionary China.

Notes

1. Karl Wittfogel, who wrote a biography of Sun Yat-sen around 1928 and considered himself, at the time, a Marxist theoretician, made no reference to "fascism" in the thought of the founder of the Kuomintang. See K. A. Wittfogel, *Sun Yat-sen: Aufzeichnungen eines chinesischen Revolutionaers* (Vienna: Agis, n.d. [probably 1928 or 1929]). In fact, years after the advent of the Chinese Communists to power, Soviet theoreticians failed to identify Sun with fascism. The identification of the Kuomintang as "fascist" was more common but by no means consistent. In 1932, Moscow sought to normalize diplomatic relations with the Nationalist government of China. In 1937, Moscow succeeded in signing a nonaggression pact with Nationalist China. In 1938 and 1939, the Soviet Union advanced credits to China with which Chiang Kai-shek purchased arms and essential raw materials. Soviet volunteers served in Nationalist Chinese units against the Japanese until the early 1940s. See the accounts provided by Soviet volunteers in China through-

out the entire period in *Soviet Volunteers in China, 1925–1945* (Moscow: Progress, 1980).

2. Mao Zedong, "On New Democracy," in *Selected Works* (Beijing: Foreign Languages, 1967), 2:362.

3. In "On New Democracy," Mao spoke of "fascism" and "vitalism" as two doctrines. Years later, the editors of his works clarified his allusion to vitalism as a reference to the ideology of "Kuomintang fascism" (pp. 362, 383 n. 13).

4. See the discussion in Robert Payne, *Chiang Kai-shek* (New York: Weybright & Talley, 1969), pp. 160–165; Keiji Furuya, *Chiang Kai-shek: His Life and Times* (New York: St. John's University, 1981), pp. 434–436; Robert Berkov, *Strong Man of China: The Story of Chiang Kai-shek* (Freeport: Books for Libraries, 1938), chap. 28.

5. All the subsequent references will be to Chiang Kai-shek, *Outline of the New Life Movement* (Nanchang: Association for the Promotion of the New Life Movement, n.d.).

6. See Payne, *Chiang Kai-shek*, p. 163.

7. Chiang Kai-shek seems to have understood as much. He spoke of communities in crisis having to restore private and public virtues if they were to survive. He cited the ancient kingdoms of China as illustrative instances—together with Italy and Germany of the early 1930s. See Chiang, *Outline*, p. 12.

8. Mao, "The Struggle in the Chingkang Mountains," in *Selected Works*, 1:88.

9. Mao, "On Tactics Against Japanese Imperialism," in *Selected Works*, 1:155, 160.

10. Ibid., p. 166.

11. Mao, "The Situation After the Repulse of the Second Anti-Communist Onslaught," in ibid., 2:460; and "Conclusions on the Repulse of the Second Anti-Communist Onslaught," in ibid., p. 464.

12. Mao, "Current Problems of Tactics in the Anti-Japanese United Front," in ibid., p. 429.

13. Mao, "A Comment on the Sessions of the Kuomintang Central Executive Committee and of the People's Political Council," in ibid., 3:138.

14. Much of the following discussion follows Maria Hsia Chang, *The Chinese Blue Shirt Society: Fascism and Developmental Nationalism* (Berkeley: University of California, 1985).

15. See the discussion in Eugene W. Wu, "The Politics of Coalition: An Analysis of the 1924 Kuomintang Constitution," in *Proceedings of Conference on Eighty Years History of the Republic of China, 1912–1991* (Taipei: Committee on Kuomintang Party History, 1993), 1:71–87.

16. See the discussion in F. Gilbert Chan, "Sun Yat-sen and the Origins of the Kuomintang Reorganization," in *China in the 1920s: Nationalism and Revolution*, ed. F. Gilbert Chan and Thomas H. Etzold (New York: New Viewpoints, 1976), pp. 15–37.

17. We know that Sun read Michels, *Political Parties*, at the time of its appearance and was significantly influenced. Michels was a major influence on the thought of Italian Nationalists and Italian Revolutionary Syndicalists prior to the First World War. He later became a prominent member of the Partito Nazionale Fascista. In this context, see Francesco Perfetti, "La sociologica di Roberto

Michels," in *Elite e/o democrazia*, ed. Francesco Perfetti (Rome: Volpe, 1972); and A. James Gregor, "R. Michels, la tradizione rivoluzionaria di sinistra ed il fascismo," *Intervento* 40 (November-December 1979): 37–44.

18. See Edward Friedman, *Backward Toward Revolution: The Chinese Revolutionary Party* (Berkeley: University of California Press, 1974), chap. 3.

19. Richard B. Landis, "Training and Indoctrination at the Whampoa Academy," in Chan and Etzold, *China in the 1920s*, pp. 77f.

20. See Donald A. Jordan, *The Northern Expedition: China's National Revolution of 1926–1928* (Honolulu: University of Hawaii, 1976), chap. 18.

21. See the discussion in Chang, *Chinese Blue Shirt Society*, pp. 17f., n. 15.

22. Chiang, *Outline*, p. 12.

23. See Shao Chuan Leng and Norman D. Palmer, *Sun Yat-sen and Communism* (New York: Praeger, 1960), pp. 75f.

24. See ibid., pp. 83–95.

25. Hung-mao Tien and Micheal R. Godley both single out the Blue Shirts as representatives of "Chinese fascism." See Hung-mao Tien, *Government and Politics in Kuomintang China, 1927–1937* (Stanford: Stanford University Press, 1972); and Michael R. Godley, "Fascismo e nazionalismo cinese: 1931–1938. Note preliminari allo studio dei rapporti italocinesi durante il periodo fascista," *Storia contemporanea* 4, no. 4 (1973): 739–777.

26. See W. F. Elkins, "'Fascism' in China: The Blue Shirts Society, 1932–1937," *Science and Society* 33, no. 4 (1969): 426–433.

27. The primary materials contained in Warren Kuo, *Analytical History of the Chinese Communist Party* (Taipei: Institute of International Relations, 1971), book 4, are particularly relevant.

28. Mao, "Conclusions on the Repulse of the Second Anti-Communist Onslaught" and "On New Democracy," in *Selected Works*, 2:376, 464.

29. At the time of the Sino-Soviet alliance, Sun arranged for a formal agreement to be crafted that specified the general conditions of cooperation between the Nationalists and the Marxists. In the joint statement issued on 26 January 1923, it was affirmed that "the communistic order or even the Soviet system cannot actually be introduced into China, because there do not exist . . . the conditions for the successful establishment of either Communism or Sovietism." As cited, Leng and Palmer, *Sun Yat-sen*, p. 63.

30. Sun Yat-sen, *The Triple Demism of Sun Yat-sen* (1931; reprint, New York: AMS, 1974), p. 433. This Wuchang translation is the best unabridged version of Sun's final lectures.

31. Ibid., pp. 432f., 438f. Sun was very explicit in his qualified use of the term "socialist." He made it clear that he was not associating his doctrine with Marxism. See ibid., p. 411.

32. See the discussion in ibid., pp. 423–430.

33. See ibid., p. 424. In this context, Sun cited the volume by Maurice William, *The Social Interpretation of History: A Refutation of the Marxian Economic Interpretation of History* (New York: 1921), as confirmation of his views. Sun's views were firm long before he read William's book. It was cited solely as a confirmation of the views held. There is an exaggerated assessment of William's influence on Sun in Maurice Zolotow, *Maurice William and Sun Yat-sen* (London: Robert Hale, 1948).

34. Sun, "The True Solution of the Chinese Question," in *Guofu quanji* [The complete works of Sun Yat-sen; hereafter referred to as *GQ*] (Taipei: Kuomintang Party History Committee, 1973), 5:86–87.

35. See the discussion in A. James Gregor, "Sun Yat-sen, the Kuomintang and Modern China," in *Proceedings of Conference on Eighty years History of the Republic of China, 1912–1991* (Taipei: Committee on Kuomintang Party History, n.d.), 4:4f.

36. Sun, *Triple Demism*, pp. 474–475. The translation that appears in Sun, *Sanmin chui* (Taipei: China Publishing, n.d.), pp. 182–183, is used here.

37. Sun, "True Solution," pp. 116–117.

38. Sun, "International Development of China," in *GQ*, 5:129.

39. Ibid., pp. 130, 133.

40. See the discussion in Wittfogel, *Sun Yat-sen*, pp. 92–93, 98; and M. N. Roy, *Revolution and Counter-Revolution in China* (Calcutta: Renaissance, 1946), p. 253.

41. Harold Z. Schiffrin, *Sun Yat-sen: Reluctant Revolutionary* (Boston: Little, Brown), p. 120. See the somewhat similar judgment in Jeffry G. Barlow, *Sun Yat-sen and the French, 1900–1908* (Berkeley: Center for Chinese Studies, 1979), p. 90.

42. J. A. Hobson, *Imperialism: A Study* (Ann Arbor: University of Michigan Press, 1965).

43. See ibid., pp. 49, 80–81, 308.

44. Ibid., chap. 6.

45. See "The Communist Manifesto," in *Collected Works*, by Karl Marx and Friedrich Engels (New York: International, 1976), 8:486–488.

46. These notions were commonplace among Marxists at the turn of the twentieth century. They are to be found in the works of Rudolf Hilferding (*Das Finanzkapital* [Berlin: Dietz, 1955]), Rosa Luxemburg (*The Accumulation of Capital* [London: Routledge & Kegan Paul, 1951]), and Nikolai Bukharin (*Imperialism and World Economy* [New York: Howard Fertig, 1966]). Even Lenin was convinced of Hobson's thesis: "The export of capital influences can greatly accelerate the development of capitalism in those countries to which it is exported." As a consequence, countries importing capital from more highly industrialized countries would undergo "extraordinarily rapid" development. V. I. Lenin, "Imperialism: The Highest Stage of Capitalism," in *Collected Works* (Moscow: Progress, 1964), 22:242–243.

47. Lai T'ing, "The Paris Peace Conference and the Financial Situation of Nations," *Jianshe* (Reconstruction) 2, no. 4 (1920): 659–675; *Jianshe* 2, no. 5 (1920): 851–875.

48. Sun, "The Cause and Effect of the Creation of the Republic and the Duties of the Citizen," in *GQ*, 2:315. Speech of 26 October 1912 to the military academy at Nanjing.

49. Chu Chih-hsin, "Public Opinion and Agitation," *Jianshe* 1, no. 1 (1919): 177.

50. See Liao Chung-k'ai, "Currency Reform and Reconstruction," *Jianshe* 1, no. 3 (1919): 473–485; *Jianshe* 1, no. 4 (1919): 789–798.

51. Sun, "The Problem of Foreign Relations Requires an Open Door Policy," in *GQ*, 2:264.

52. Sun, *The Vital Problem of China* (Taipei: China Cultural Service, 1953), pp. 8–10.

53. Ibid., p. 96.

54. Sun, *Triple Demism*, pp. 142–143; see the discussion on pp. 70ff., 90, 92, 96f.

55. In this regard, see Hsu Yu-chu, "The Regulation of Private Capital and Equalization of Wealth and Income," *China Forum* 3, no. 2 (1976): 69; and the discussion in Benjamin J. Cohen, *The Question of Imperialism* (New York: Basic, 1973), pp. 231–245.

56. See, in this regard, Sun, "Promote National Socialism," in *GQ*, 2:261; and Sun, *Triple Demism*, pp. 72–73.

57. Sun, *Vital Problem*, pp. 124–125.

58. Ibid., p. 135; Sun, "The Chinese Republic," *Independent* (New York), 9 September 1912, reproduced in *China Forum* 4, no. 2 (1977): 341–342.

59. Sun, *Triple Demism*, pp. 475f.

60. Ibid., pp. 528–531.

61. See Roman Szporluk, *Communism and Nationalism: Karl Marx versus Friedrich List* (New York: Oxford, 1988).

62. See J. Shield Nicholson, introductory essay to *The National System of Political Economy*, ed. Friedrich List (London: Longmans, Green, 1916), pp. xiii–xxvii.

63. Ibid., p. 87.

64. Ibid., pp. 108f.

65. Ibid., pp. 136f.

66. Ibid., pp. 144f.

67. Ibid., p. 159.

68. Ibid., p. 320.

69. Ibid., pp. 322f.

70. Ibid., p. 164.

71. See the account in Margaret E. Hirst, *Life of Friedrich List and Selections from His Writings* (New York: Scribners, 1909), pp. 128f. As early as 1819, List had outlined his policy recommendations in his "Petition on Behalf of the Handelverein to the Federal Assembly, April, 1819." See ibid., pp. 137–144.

72. List, *National System*, pp. 177, 183.

73. Ibid., pp. 247–252.

74. Ibid., pp. 266f.

75. Ibid., p. 312.

76. For a more extensive discussion of Marx's relationship to List, see A. James Gregor, *Marxism, China and Development* (New Brunswick, N.J.: Transaction, 1995), chap. 5; and Szporluk, *Communism and Nationalism*, pts. 1–2.

77. See Karl Marx, "Draft of an Article on Friedrich List's Book *Das Nationale System der Politischen Oekonomie*," in *Collected Works*, by Karl Marx and Friedrich Engels (New York: International, 1976), 4:266, 279, 281–284.

78. Alfredo Rocco, "Il problema economico italiano," in *Scritti e discorsi politici* (Milan: Giuffre, 1938), 1:40, 47.

79. Scipio Sighele, *Il nazionalismo e i partiti politici* (Milan: Treves, 1911), pp. 42f.

80. See Mao, "On Practice," in *Selected Works*, 1:296f.; "Preface and Postscript to Rural Surveys," in ibid., p. 13; and "Appendix: Resolution on Certain Questions in the History of Our Party," in ibid., p. 211.

81. See A. James Gregor and Maria Hsia Chang, "Chiang Kai-shek, China, and the Concept of Economic Development," in *Proceedings of Conference on Chiang Kai-shek and Modern China* (Taipei: Compilation Committee, 1987), 3:614–635.

82. See Chen Boda, "Critique of *China's Destiny*" (mimeograph).

83. Chen Boda, *Stalin and the Chinese Revolution* (Beijing: Foreign Languages, 1953), pp. 7–9.

84. See Mao, "On New Democracy," in *Selected Works*, 2:362–363; Mao, "Current Problems of Tactics in the Anti-Japanese United Front," in ibid., p. 429.

85. Chen, *Stalin*, p. 9.

86. Mao, "On Tactics Against Japanese Imperialism," pp. 155, 160, 166.

87. M. N. Roy identified the Kuomintang as the "agent" of the "big bourgeoisie," the "bankers, the industrialists and the compradors." As a consequence, Chiang Kai-shek and the Kuomintang were "fascists." See Roy, *Revolution*, chap. 21.

88. In this context see the discussion in Denis Goulet, *The Cruel Choice: A New Concept in the Theory of Development* (New York: Atheneum, 1973); and John H. Kautsky, *The Political Consequences of Modernization* (New York: John Wiley, 1972). Although there is considerable confusion concerning "fascism" and "developmental nationalism" in these discussions, they are insightful.

5
Maoism, the Ideology of Sun Yat-sen, and Fascism

From the vantage point of the end of the twentieth century, a persuasive case can be made that the success of the Chinese Communist party (CCP) in the civil war against the Kuomintang turned on its ability to mobilize the rural population of China with an appeal to anti-Japanese nationalist sentiment.[1] Until the Japanese invasion of China, and the subsequent dislocation of peasants, the CCP experienced a series of signal failures, beginning with the debacle of 1927–1928. It would seem that the Japanese invasion created the necessary conditions for Chinese Communist recruitment successes in the rural areas that ultimately culminated in their victory in 1949.

For our purposes, one of the more interesting features of the Communist party's successes in rural China was the fact that it was accomplished by utilizing the political slogans of Sun Yat-sen's Three Principles of the People. By late 1939 and early 1940, the chief of staff of the Japanese Imperial Army occupying northeastern China reported that Chinese Communist recruitment successes were accomplished under the "plagiarized slogans of [Sun Yat-sen's] Three Principles of the People."[2]

The fact was that as early as the first years of the 1920s, the CCP had agreed that the party would never "cast any aspersions" against Sun's Three Principles, recognizing Sun's ideology as reflecting the interests of the Chinese people.[3] Soviet representatives in China had already agreed that Marxism-Leninism had no place in China's "bourgeois nationalist revolution" and had agreed that Sun's ideology would be employed in mobilizing the Chinese people to revolution. The adherence to Sun's principles of nationalism, democracy, and "livelihood" became part of the CCP's permanent propaganda armarium throughout the interwar years.

The CCP strategy, as early as 1926, was to consider China's revolution to be essentially multiclass in character, bringing together "revolutionary intellectuals, middle-class national capitalists in industry and commerce, petty bourgeois handicraftsmen and small merchants, peasants, and workers" in an inclusive enterprise that would free the nation from backwardness and the impostures of foreigners.[4] At that point in time, there was no disagreement that Sun's principles, nationalism foremost among them, were "doubtless what the Chinese revolution required."

What was evident was that the imperative animating the CCP in the 1920s and 1930s was the "national interests of China." Even when the party spoke of the ultimate victory of the "proletarian revolution," the fundamental purpose was "the total liberation of China from the oppression of foreign capital" and the "liquidation of all feudalist remnants that are detrimental to China's development."[5]

In effect, the interwar ideology of China's Communists had always been nationalistic and developmental. In that sense, Sun's Three Principles constituted the party's "minimum program." The party's "maximum program," on the other hand, anticipated the transformation of the "bourgeois national" into a "socialist revolution." It was the emphasis on the one, at one time, and on the other, at another time, that gave the CCP the appearance of political deception and exploitation of the masses through amoral subterfuge. As the circumstances changed, the party would pursue one strategy at the seeming expense of the other—only to subsequently alter strategy and tactics.

For present purposes, it is important to recognize that Mao Zedong regularly appealed to Sun's principles in his political rationale for China's revolution. Under his explicit instruction, in September 1937, the Central Committee of the Communist Party of China issued a formal declaration that "solemnly declared" that "Dr. Sun Yat-sen's Three People's Principles being what China needs today, our Party is ready to fight for their complete realization." In October 1943, Mao reiterated that "solemn declaration" and held that CCP recruitment activities in the war zones in the rural areas were compatible, in their entirety, with the principles of Sun.[6]

In 1945, Mao reaffirmed his position without equivocation. He lamented that "some people suspect that the Chinese Communists are opposed to the development of individual initiative, the growth of private capital, and the protection of private property, but they are mistaken. It is foreign oppression and feudal oppression that cruelly fetter the development of the individual initiative of the Chinese People, hamper the growth of private capital and destroy the property of the people." Mao insisted that the policies of the Chinese Communist party recognized all that. These policies were inspired by, and gave expression to, "Dr. Sun's principles and the experience of the Chinese revolution."[7]

Mao regularly reaffirmed his commitment to Sun's principles and insisted that CCP policy would be one of "adjusting the interests of labor and capital" so that there would be a "guarantee [of] legitimate profits to properly managed state, private and cooperative enterprises—so that . . . both labor and capital will work together to develop industrial production."[8] He had informed his audiences that the party's program included a nationalization of "all the big enterprises and capital of the imperialists, traitors and reactionaries, and the distribution among peasants of the land held by the landlords," but that was not to be taken to mean that the Communist revolution would do anything other than "preserve private capitalist enterprise in general and not eliminate the rich peasant economy. Thus," he went on to assert, "the new type of democratic revolution clears the way for capitalism on the one hand and creates the prerequisites for socialism on the other. . . . The new democratic revolution . . . differs from a socialist revolution in that it overthrows the rule of the imperialists, traitors and reactionaries in China but does not destroy any section of capitalism which is capable of contributing to the anti-imperialist, anti-feudal struggle."[9] All of that was seen as fundamentally compatible with the views of Sun Yat-sen.

In 1945, Mao told the Chinese people that the imminent victory of the CCP would deliver itself of a "new democracy" that would exhibit the traits that distinguished Sun's revolutionary program from "communism"—and that such a "general program" would "remain unchanged throughout the stage of the bourgeois-democratic revolution, that is, for several decades."[10] According to Mao's "solemn declaration," the accession of the CCP to power would bring with it the realization of Sun Yat-sen's program for the nationalist development of retrograde China.

Mao clarified that point by reminding his followers that the revolution was calculated to offset the circumstances that left the nation to "suffer the oppression of imperialism." The revolution would address the reality that Chinese "industry was not developed and [Chinese] scientific and technical level was low." He went on to remind his conationals that "we had been slaves far too long and felt inferior to others in every respect—too much so. We could not hold up our heads in the presence of foreigners."[11]

All of this is familiar to anyone knowledgeable about the reactive and developmental nationalism of our time. The sense of humiliation born of imperialist affront and the reactive nationalist demand for rapid economic growth and industrial development are only partially obscured by Mao's use of the vocabulary of Marxism and Marxism-Leninism.

Prior to his accession to power in 1949, Mao very clearly identified not capitalism but imperialism and feudalism as the "chief targets or enemies" of the Chinese revolution. "Imperialism" and "feudalism" were the primary obstacles to the rebirth and redemption of China. Mao, like Sun, saw both of them conspiring to keep China subordinate to the advanced industrial powers. For Mao, like Sun, it was imperialism and feudalism that were the "chief oppressors, the chief obstacles to the progress of Chinese society."[12] It was not domestic capitalism that inspired revolution—it was the spontaneous nationalist reaction to international imperialism and the retrograde state of China.

The Characterization of Mao's Revolution

In retrospect, it is easy to recognize the confusion that attended the accession of Mao's Communist party to power in China. Some would see the Communist enterprise as one devoted to "agrarian reform," which had been critical to Sun's program for Chinese economic development.

Others saw the new regime as essentially antidemocratic, ideocratic, and elitist—informed by a "leadership principle" that envisioned ultimate control emanating from a charismatic individual. It was seen as a mass-mobilizing system that was emphatically anti-individualistic and voluntaristic, with an appeal to personal self-sacrifice, obedience, and commitment to the nation.[13] Together with its nationalism, anti-imperialism and developmentalism, Mao's China had taken on some of the major species traits of paradigmatic Fascism as those traits had been identified by the political folk wisdom of the period.[14]

That notion quickly dissipated when Mao embarked on the "socialization" of the Chinese economy. Contrary to everything to which he had committed himself before 1949, Mao, thereafter, undertook the total abolition of private property and the elimination of the market exchange of goods and services in the Chinese economy. By 1952, China's private banking system had been entirely abolished by orders from the Communist party. There was a precipitous decline in the number of privately held enterprises—and a corresponding collapse in their contribution to the gross national product of the nation. By 1956—contrary to everything Mao had promised before the Communist seizure of power—private enterprise and the market exchange of goods and services had disappeared from mainland China.[15]

Sun Yat-sen had opposed the abolition of private property and private enterprise. Although he advocated state management of those undertakings that exceeded the capacity of private enterprise, he insisted on the legal protection of property and the exercise of private initiative as essential to the rapid economic growth and industrialization of China.[16] He argued that only together could the revolutionary state and private individuals succeed in the modernization of retrograde China.

Mao, almost immediately upon succeeding to power, abandoned all the enjoinments that had been at the center of Sun's plans for the modernization of China. Not only did Mao proceed to the abolition of private property, but he became responsible for initiating the "class struggle" in

China that, over the next quarter century, was to consume millions of lives and untold resources. Maoism had finally distinguished itself from Sun's Three Principles.

Given its "socialization" of the economy and the invocation of "class struggle," Maoism could no longer be considered a simple reactive and developmental nationalism. It was no longer a variant of Sun Yat-senism and within the decade, by the end of the 1950s, it could not plausibly be classified as a form of Stalinism.

With the victory of Chinese Communist arms, Mao, upon coming to power, had "leaned to one side"—he had committed China to an affiliation with the Soviet Union of Josef Stalin. The consequence was that the economy of the "new China" was not to follow the programmatic suggestions of Sun but the Soviet Union.[17] Nonetheless, by the end of the 1950s, Mao chose to depart from economic Stalinism to embark on strategies of his own.[18]

By 1958, Mao had driven China into the "Great Leap Forward"—an effort to surpass the productive capabilities of some of the most advanced industrial nations by marshaling raw peasant labor to fabricate pig iron and steel in primitive "backyard furnaces." Capital poor, Mao expected simple labor power to achieve the results normally purchased by capital-intensive, sophisticated machine production. Neither Sunist nor Stalinist, the result was a disaster of biblical proportions. With millions of peasants tending primitive furnaces, agriculture was neglected. That, together with adverse weather conditions, produced a shortfall in agricultural production that condemned millions of Chinese to starvation.

As though dissatisfied with the catastrophe he had created, Mao drove China from the "Great Leap Forward" to the "Great Proletarian Cultural Revolution" that saw "class struggle" exacerbated until further millions were swept into turmoil that cost an untold number of innocent lives. By 1966, Mao had convinced himself that the major part of the leadership of the CCP had defected to "antisocialism" and threatened to change the "color" of the revolution.[19] Mao was convinced that those who resisted his economic programs were "bourgeois capitalist roaders" who had insinuated themselves into every level of party organization. They advocated an alternative to the Maoism that had revealed itself after 1949. The "capitalist roaders" were everywhere and Mao conceived them threatening to undo his saving revolution, restore capitalism, and capitulate to imperialism.

By the time the Great Proletarian Cultural Revolution had run its course, China's economy had been significantly impaired, much of the leadership of the CCP had been sacrificed, and the People's Republic of China found itself threatened from the West and the North by the Soviet Union, and from the East and Southeast by the United States.[20] By what-

ever measure one chose to employ, "Communist China" under Mao Zedong had been a resounding failure. After abandoning Sun Yat-senism, it
had been neither a consistent reactive nationalist developmental system
nor a "proletarian dictatorship." It had been part Stalinist, part fascist,[21]
and, ultimately, almost entirely idiosyncratic.

The Soviet Interpretation of Maoism

For many reasons, after the death of Stalin in 1954, Mao's China began to
loom large as a potential enemy of the Soviet Union. By the time of the
Great Proletarian Cultural Revolution in 1966, Beijing had identified the
Soviet Union as one of its principal enemies, a form of "social imperialism" that, like the imperialism of the industrialized democracies, sought
to "contain," and exercise "hegemony" over, China.

Mao Zedong had discovered that "bourgeois elements" in the Soviet
Union had betrayed Marxism-Leninism and had introduced "revisionism": a system of ideological betrayal that sought to establish enterprise
profit as a measure of efficiency, wages as an incentive to increase labor
productivity, and the market as a means for establishing something of a
rational price structure that would govern costs and the distribution of
goods. Mao saw the post-Stalinist reforms in the Soviet Union as an attempt to "reestablish capitalism."[22]

Mao's call for a "cultural revolution" in China was calculated to isolate
and destroy similar "bourgeois elements" in the People's Republic who
sought to accomplish the same ends. By 1966, Mao's conflict with some
of the major leaders of the CCP had exploded into charges that they were
pursuing a "capitalist road" and sought to betray the revolution through
Soviet-style "revisionism." Mao's commitment to the struggle resulted in
years of internecine violence that left hundreds of thousands dead.

The first response by Soviet commentators was to argue that Mao's
self-destructive policies were simply the result of paranoid delusion, the
diseased consequence of Mao's ignorance and his petty bourgeois con-
ceit. The Great Proletarian Cultural Revolution, during which the Soviet
Union was excoriated as a "revisionist" and "social imperialist" power,
was understood to be the result of politically induced mass hysteria—the
consequence of a great wave of stupidity and destructiveness conjured
up by the leaders of China in the course of a protracted and violent in-
traparty struggle for power.[23] By the end of the 1960s, however, that
seemed hardly sufficient to explain what was transpiring.

Soviet theoreticians began to speak of Maoism as an anti-Marxist, militaristic, and chauvinistic "petty bourgeois nationalism," animated by
voluntarism and an appeal to violence.[24] To Soviet analysts, Maoism was
a personalist dictatorship, supported by a form of antisocialist ideological "infantilism" and an action-oriented "primitivism," born of the anti-

intellectualism of Mao's petty-bourgeois background.[25] Soviet analysts
went on to argue that in his effort to delude the masses, Mao had created
a "cult of personality" with few parallels in the history of modern political systems. He had given himself over to autocratic rule, elitism, and
voluntarism, and to the conviction that will and "heroic" violence could
resolve problems of whatever magnitude.

Whatever Soviet Marxist-Leninists objected to in Maoist policies was
immediately identified as "petty bourgeois." Thus, if Maoists were
"Great-Han hegemonists" and "racists," it was because the Chinese population consisted of "petty artisans, traders, and nonproletarian elements." The hegemonism, nationalism, chauvinism, and racism of Maoism "was ultimately due to the fact that most of the members of the
Communist Party of China were of peasant origin."[26] Attributing everything to the fact that the leadership and membership of the CCP was of
peasant provenance was a quaint product of "Marxist theory." How such
an assertion might be confirmed independently of the speculative theses
of "Marxist theory" was never explained.

Nonetheless, by the beginning of the 1970s it had become evident in
the judgment of Soviet scholars that Maoism had degenerated into a
form of political perversity that had cost China millions of lives and had
resulted in impairments that significantly reduced its rate of real growth.
Maoism was no longer considered a form of Marxist-Leninist revolution.
Its anti-Marxist, militaristic, and chauvinistic "petty bourgeois nationalism" animated by an "idealistic" voluntarism and an appeal to violence
characterized it, in the judgment of Soviet analysts, as a variant of European fascism.

Soviet commentators began to speak of Maoism as sharing the "hare-
brained assumptions of Mussolini."[27] It was identified with an "aggressive
Han chauvinism,"[28] intent upon provoking a third world war from which
China would emerge as world hegemon.[29] Even more damning, perhaps,
was the Soviet judgment that the "class struggle" imposed upon China by
Mao was nothing other than a subterfuge employed to destroy any and all
political opposition. The "socialist" command economy was designed
more to impose Mao's will on a supine population than to develop China's
productive activity.[30] Maoism, for Soviet academicians of the 1970s and
early 1980s, was nothing other than a caricature of European fascism.

The Chinese Communist Critique of Maoism

Whatever others thought of Mao and Maoism was largely a matter of in-
difference to Chinese intellectuals, who had to face the devastation
wrought by Mao's policies.

In China, the catastrophe produced by the Great Proletarian Cultural
Revolution provoked a response on the part of the most convinced

Marxist-Leninists. Even before the death of Mao, the discussion surrounding the Great Proletarian Cultural Revolution was abundant. That literature, originating among "leftists" and those who were subsequently to be identified as advocates for democracy, containing an argument that, for our purposes, is instructive.

A select number of intellectuals began to oppose the entire rationale for the series of tragedies that Mao's call for "Cultural Revolution" brought in its train. Thus, in 1973, three years before Mao's death, three young men—Li Zhengtian, Chen Yiyang, and Wang Xizhe—affixed a poster to a wall in downtown Guangzhou. It was entitled "On Socialist Democracy and the Legal System" and was a long and reasonably sophisticated analysis of issues that had been raised during the protracted years of the Cultural Revolution. Written by nonparty Marxists, the "big character poster" sent shock waves through the local party leadership.

The authors of "On Socialist Democracy" embarked upon their analyses employing some of the same arguments provided by Maoists critical of the "revisionist" Soviet Union. If socialist systems could produce "bourgeois elements" prepared to take the "capitalist road" even after the abolition of private property and the establishment of socialism, there could be no security for any socialist system. If "capitalist roaders" could surface in socialist systems at any time, the danger that threatened Chinese socialism was not the simple consequence of the malfeasance, misfeasance, and personal character flaws of renegade individual "Party members in authority taking the capitalist road." The threat, they argued, arose out of the system itself. In their judgment, the "antisocialist" betrayals of Liu Shaoqi and Lin Biao represented not personal character flaws but the symptoms of a systemic disorder.[31]

The fact that the Chinese Communist party regularly produced "demons," "monsters," and "freaks" suggested that the threat of revisionism could not be simply attributed to the shortcomings of morally indigent individuals. The failure of individuals was a function of the system itself.

The authors of "On Socialist Democracy" argued that the attacks against "capitalist roaders" was misplaced. It was, in their judgment, a mistake to attack individuals like Liu Shaoqi, Deng Xiaoping, Lin Biao, or Chen Boda. It was not the failure of individuals that threatened socialism. Rather, it was the system that seemed to produce such men with regularity. The authors of "On Socialist Democracy" were drawing out the implications of the Maoist "class analysis" developed during the long years of the Cultural Revolution.[32]

The argument was that the party's "capitalist roaders" represented an entrenched and privileged stratum that had collected around the institutions of what was called the "dictatorship of the proletariat." With the abolition of private property, the authors of "On Socialist Democracy" argued, all property becomes, presumptively, the property of all. However much that property belonged to all, it would have to be managed by some. However much the economic system was the property of all, planning for that system could only be conducted by some. The putative property of all would have to be administered by some. Those who manage, plan, and administer the property of all exercise real, and potentially absolute, control over those who neither manage, plan, nor administer. They become the members of a "newborn bourgeoisie." They profit from their particular relationship to the means of production. Without legal ownership, this "emergent new class" displays all the properties of a dominant class in capitalist society.[33] Thus the authors of "On Socialist Democracy" applied the Maoist analysis of Soviet "revisionism" and "social imperialism" to the People's Republic of China.

In a perfectly clear sense, the nonparty Marxists of China maintained that the first stage of socialist society bears many features of the society it has overthrown.[34] Although the revolution overthrew a bourgeois dictatorship, a new class of bureaucrats and party cadre substituted themselves for the traditional owners of the means of production and created a "proletarian dictatorship"—a new class dictatorship.

In the new class system, lesser administrators and party cadre profit less than those who occupy positions at the apex, but all profit from the exploitation that would seem to be intrinsic to political and economic arrangements of the first stage of socialism. Given the inevitable inequities of the system, those who profit seek to defend and perpetuate their privileges. Unless there are institutionalized safeguards against the excesses of this privileged stratum, the authors argued, revolutionary socialism becomes simply a dictatorship of state monopoly capitalism. The nonparty Marxists argued that where there were no institutional checks on arbitrary rule in the system, the system would inevitably devolve into a variant of fascism. They maintained that the history of other socialist regimes taught nothing less. They insisted that even Mao, in his criticism of the Soviet Union, had recognized the merit of their argument but could not (or would not) change the prevailing system of entrenched privilege.

The critics argued that "socialism" in China had revealed itself to be incapable of self-correction. Without established mechanisms to ensure responsiveness to constituencies, no change in the allocation of power and welfare benefits could be expected in the system. Given the system's intrinsic properties, change could only come if the party itself spontaneously chose reform. It was evident, however, that the "new bourgoisie" in the party had little incentive to attempt that.

If there was little prospect that the Communist party in and of itself would undertake fundamental reform, it was equally clear that the party had created an environment in which change could not be expected to originate from without. Any persons or group of persons outside the party who advocated reform were immediately suspect. Whatever initiatives for political or economic change there might have been were summarily suppressed by the party and its agents. Given such circumstances, the nonparty Marxists anticipated that "for the next several hundred years, generation after generation of the new bourgeoisie will inevitably emerge regardless of the will of the people."[35] They argued that without massive political reform that would institutionalize substantial civil and political rights to all persons, allowing effective popular control of the Communist party, socialist China was destined to suffer permanent dictatorial rule.

The authors argued that removing individual party members in authority who were "capitalist-roaders" would be pointless if nothing was done to change the system that spawned them. The problem was that the system had effectively insulated itself from challenge. The general population had few resources and little opportunity to articulate interests and express special needs. They were mass mobilized into rituals of loyalty and obedience with the "religious chanting" of excerpts from the thought of Mao Zedong. All of public life became the object of "empty politics," "ritual performances. . . . smeared with an intensely religious coloring and aura,"[36] calculated to produce conformist behavior and abject obedience in the masses.

The fact that no one could produce a clear and convincing list of traits that would unequivocally identify "capitalist roaders," "counterrevolutionaries," "revisionists," or "monsters" left everyone with an abiding sense of free-floating anxiety. Anyone could be charged with being a "freak" or a "ghost" for failing to comport themselves in some indeterminate fashion or other. The population lived in perpetual fear of party sanction.

The authors of "On Socialist Democracy" were particularly emphatic about the issue. They argued that no one seemed capable of identifying the worst offenders in the socialist system. Those who held the highest ranks in the party, even those most revered for their service to socialism, were all found, at one time or another, to be wanting. Some were purged or punished, only later to be restored when the "decisions were reversed." In all of this, the general population was compelled to wait until instructed by the party on how to obey. Without explicit instructions, the "revolutionaries" of today might well be the "counterrevolutionaries" of tomorrow. The socialism of today, the fascism of tomorrow. The consequence was all but universal political confusion and institutionalized anxiety. There was no sure guide to political propriety. The people were inertly dependent on "instructions" that emanated from whoever happened to possess the power to issue them. Since those who occupied positions of privilege in the system had no reason to want to change it—and those who sought change had neither the organization nor the resources to undertake it—the system was rigid and unalterable.

In the judgment of the authors of "On Socialist Democracy," the system they described was best typified as a "despotic socialist-fascism" that exploited the "feudalistic" disposition of the Chinese people to simply obey those in authority.[37] The overt political properties of "socialist-fascism" included the notion that only a "genius" could lead the party and direct the entire historical process from the overthrow of capitalism to the advent of communism. According to the prevailing political convictions in Communist China, a world-historical genius was decisive to the entire historical process in which the Chinese people found themselves. That genius possessed the will and charismatic authority to inspire the masses to fulfill their tasks.

Among those tasks was the redemption of territories lost to China through unequal treaties and aggression. What was sought was the restoration of China's place in the world. In the judgment of the authors of "On Socialist Democracy," the genius of Chinese socialism inspired a foreign policy of "big-nation chauvinism."[38]

What Li, Chen, and Wang had produced was yet another variant of the Marxist interpretation of fascism. Familiar in many ways, the new variant included several elements that are instructive. There was a recognition that a "socialist-fascist" or "social-fascist" dictatorship was the product of revolution in an environment of delayed or retarded economic development. In those circumstances, as both Karl Marx and Friedrich Engels had argued,[39] an elite could impose itself on a population and, by choreographing a work and sacrifice ethic, could extract from the masses low-cost labor and from a managerial and bureaucratic stratum, enterprise and planning services at correspondingly low wages.[40]

What the authors of "On Socialist Democracy" had outlined was a nondemocratic, elite-dominant strategy for the accelerated growth and development of delayed or retarded economies. Within that system, they recognized the functional role of ritual and charismatic leadership. What they did not recognize was that the system they described was a perverse and incoherent variant of reactive and developmental nationalism.

As democratic socialists, they deplored the Maoist system. They recognized its potential for human rights violation, and they acknowledged that those within the system could not mount any meaningful opposition. As the nonparty Marxists made the case, in such a system there would be no way to mitigate the oppression. The absence of institutional protections against abuse by the "privileged stratum" and the "genius" who ruled the system in its entirety rendered the population defenseless against a dictatorship that was assured indeterminate tenure.

Ultimately, at least in part as a consequence of their analysis, the authors of "On Socialist Democracy" were to abandon "Marxism-Leninism Mao Zedong Thought" to become advocates of "bourgeois" political democracy. They left a legacy of some notions of generic fascism that are interesting—notions that grew out of the Marxism they knew.

At about the same time that Li Zhengtian, Wang Xizhe, and Chen Yiyang were posting their analysis of "socialist democracy," a young worker of peasant origin, Chen Erjin, was completing his own assessment of socialism in China.[41] About three months before the death of Mao Zedong in 1976, Chen completed his task. Two years later, in early 1978, he submitted his manuscript, "China: Crossroads Socialism," to the appropriate government agencies for possible publication. He was immediately arrested by the authorities for advocating political subversion.

Like the authors of "On Socialist Democracy," Chen was a Marxist-Leninist and a Maoist of conviction. He, like them, had been a member of the Red Guard conjured up by Mao Zedong and the leadership of the Chinese Communist party during the Great Proletarian Cultural Revolution. He was convinced that his analysis was Marxist in both spirit and letter.

Chen began his account by identifying the economic base of the "predatory new system of exploitation" that threatened to overwhelm socialist China. Since socialism is predicated on the abolition of private property, the state system that follows Marxist-Leninist revolution is one that monopolizes all property into its own hands.

Those who administer state property become a "new class." That newly emergent class—"the bureaucrat-monopoly privileged class"—arrogates to itself "the twin powers of political leadership and economic control." Like the authors of "On Socialist Democracy," Chen argued that the new privileged elite of the first stage of socialism tends to construct a "bureaucratic-military machine" that resonates with the sound of "the gongs and drums of narrow-minded patriotism and nationalism." The masses are distracted by war and preparation for war. Confused by "deceitful propaganda," seduced by the promise of material rewards, labor is domesticated to the system. What emerges out of the socialist revolution is a "fascist dictatorship."[42]

Chen argued, with perhaps more coherence than those who preceded him, that the "root cause" of the emergence of fascism in a socialist state is to be located in the contradiction that rests at the very foundation of the new mode of production. That a small minority concentrates all coercive power in its hands, while controlling the highly organized means of social production, results in the creation of a hierarchical system potentially more despotic than the state monopoly capitalism of which it is an analog.

The concentration of political power in the hands of the "new class" allows totalitarian "monopoly to be exerted over all spheres" of society.[43] The major overt features of the system are (1) nonelective appointments to positions of power at the discretion and pleasure of the party and its leader; (2) the hierarchical arrangement of authority; (3) the complete separation of state organs from any responsibility to the general population; and (4) the "sanctification of the party."[44]

Chen argued that the prevailing circumstances ultimately require people "to prostrate themselves in adulation before the Party. . . . First of all, it is the Party leader who is canonized and idolized, and then eventually every level and each individual member of the Party organization." No opposition could prevail against such a "charismatic" system. "Proletarian dictatorship" is transformed into "social-fascist dictatorship by the bureaucrat-monopoly privileged class."[45]

That Chen Erjin and the other dissidents in post-Maoist China spoke in generic terms and insisted that they were all perfervid Maoists did not mollify the political authorities in general or the censors in particular. All of the major dissidents were compelled to endure organized public criticism, political abuse, and eventual imprisonment. By the end of 1980, when the People's Republic had entered into its long period of economic reform, many of the dissidents no longer spoke the Aesopian language they had earlier employed to conceal their true intent. By that time, Wang Xizhe had written his "Mao Zedong and the Cultural Revolution" in which he attributed all the enormities of the Cultural Revolution to Mao himself.

Once again, it was the state monopoly of the means of production and the attendant bureaucratic control over property, wages, profits, and the allocations of benefits that allowed the Party to exercise almost seamless political control over people.[46] By the end of 1980 there no longer was talk of the the "revisionist system," the "system of Lin Biao," or that of the Gang of Four, or of Liu Shaoqi. Mao Zedong was identified with the "socialist-fascist system" that had grown out of the dictatorship of the proletariat. It was Mao who had captained the passage from the one to the other. Mao had created the system that shared features with the one crafted by Benito Mussolini, who, Wang Xizhe reminded us, had himself been a leader of the Italian Socialist party before he became the Duce of Fascism.[47]

Maoism, Anti-Maoism, and "Social-Fascism"

In fact, Wang Xizhe suggested that Maoism shared species traits with Stalinism, Italian Fascism, and Hitler's National Socialism.[48] What Wang alluded to were the familiar properties shared by all these systems. "Marxist" systems were distinguished from those traditionally called "fascist" by their insistence on the abolition of private property and its monopolization by the state,[49] together with the insistence on the significance and perpetuity of class warfare. "Stalinism," Wang argued, was an appropriate designation for "Marxist" socialist-fascism, while "fascism" covered all similar non-Marxist systems. By 1980, the "revisionists" of post-Maoist China had begun to identify all these systems as species variants of the same genus. According to Wang Xizhe, Maoism was a perverse form of Stalinism. Where Stalinism had been content to bureaucratize the system, Maoism sought direct and immediate control of the masses through interminable "campaigns" and "struggles." Mao was even prepared to attack his own party in order to impose his will directly on everyone. Out of the ruins of the Chinese Communist party, largely destroyed in the long struggle of the Great Proletarian Cultural Revolution, Mao created what Wang chose to call "a Mao Zedong Fascist party."[50] As will be suggested, China had some distance to travel before it would experience the emergence of a "Chinese fascism."

The Soviet and Anti-Maoist
Interpretation of Fascism

However quaint some of the arguments, beneath the fury of polemics lie select elements that are intrinsically interesting and particularly relevant to the present general discussion. Both the Soviet and the anti-Maoist Chinese authors we have here considered have all maintained that there could be no possibility of creating a humane and democratic Marxist socialism in conditions of economic retardation and technological backwardness—and used that conviction to explain the advent of "fascism" in Maoist China.[51]

In their own time, Fascist theoreticians had consistently made very much the same argument. Mussolini himself reminded the first Bolsheviks that every socialist from Karl Marx forward had insisted that the goals of the salvific "proletarian" revolution were predicated on the availability of a mature industrial base. "Socialists have always maintained," Mussolini informed his audience, "that socialism was attainable only under determinate, objective conditions. . . . The advent of socialism presupposes a capitalism that has achieved the final stage of its development." Only a fully developed industrial base, he went on, could provide both the material well-being necessary for a classless socialism, as well as the "class conscious" and competent proletarian majority upon whom responsibility would fall in the new postrevolutionary arrangement.[52]

In effect, Fascist theoreticians consistently argued that a primitive economic system could not generate the necessary preconditions for the advent of a Marxian socialism.[53] Revolutions in societies suffering retarded economic development and retrograde industrialization could not host socialist revolutions. Fascists argued that revolutions in such environments might pretend to socialist outcomes, but in reality they could produce only their caricature.

The major Fascist theoreticians contended that revolutions that manifested themselves in backward economic circumstances would necessarily be largely "petite bourgeois" in character, nationalist in inspiration, developmental in intention, mass mobilizing of necessity, and authoritarian in disposition. Fascist theoreticians anticipated the development of an entire class of reactive nationalist and developmental dictatorships in the twentieth century, with distinctions between class members turning on some one or another structural feature, the absence or persistence of private property, a commodities market, or some differences in their respective eschatologies. The class to which they alluded included systems as different as that of National Socialist Germany, Kuomintang China, and the Soviet Union of Josef Stalin.[54] Fascist "theory" was to prove far more credible than anything produced by Marxists, Marxist-Leninists, or Maoists in the twentieth century.

Fascist theoreticians maintained that in the Soviet Union, the "Marxist" and "socialist" revolution had devolved into a system dominated by a *Vozhd*—an inerrant leader—to be ruled by a hegemonic single party composed largely of petty bourgeois functionaries whose labors were informed by a formal ideology and whose enterprise was calculated to create a modern industrial system out of what had been an essentially agrarian economy.[55] For Fascists, Stalin had adopted and adapted the political principles of Fascism in order to pursue an enterprise totally unanticipated by the founders of Marxism.

For their part, Soviet theoreticians seemingly recognized the merits of just those Fascist arguments. As we have seen, when they addressed themselves to Maoist China, they identified the system as the product of China's overwhelming industrial backwardness and the predominance of petty bourgeois elements among both the leadership and the membership of the Communist party. Maoist China was "fascist" because there could be no socialism in so austere an economic environment.

Since at the time of Mao's accession to power China was economically primitive, the necessity of accelerated economic growth and industrial modernization was self-evident if there was to be any prospect of the revolution surviving in the manifestly threatening circumstances of the time. More than that, the "masses" of China were politically primitive and required disciplined marshaling to developmental purposes. There were no "class-conscious proletarians" in the China of the 1940s. Mao became the charismatic "never-setting red sun" who "inscribed the most precious words" on the "blank" peasant population of China.[56] Given the circumstances, only a relatively protracted period of single-party dictatorship could secure and sustain the new revolutionary system in the uncertainties of economic backwardness.

The system Mao produced was neither Marxist nor socialist. It shared some of the major species traits of Mussolini's Fascism[57]—just as Soviet and Chinese non-Maoist Marxists had argued. It was a reactive nationalist, developmental dictatorship conducted under single-party auspices. It was an elitist system that had demonstrated its readiness to employ anti-intellectualism, emotive suasion, and massive violence in the service of its "cause"—under the direction of an indispensable "chairman." Maoist China was a variant of the reactive and developmental nationalism of our time—a variant that was singularly savage and incompetent.

However Maoist China is identified at Mao's death in September 1976, it was left suffering "economic collapse and police state terror."[58] Whatever name is attached to the system he fabricated, Mao had failed to create a viable and self-sustaining economy for revolutionary China. Those Chinese Marxist-Leninist theorists who were not Maoists attempted to make some sense of the devastation that had overwhelmed China between 1949 and 1976. In the course of their efforts, they advanced a "theory" of socialist-fascism composed of a loosely jointed collection of propositions that identified the bureaucratic strata of socialist communities as functional surrogates for the various subclasses of the bourgeoisie in capitalist society. Those bourgeois elements were considered the operational equivalents of the "big capitalists" and "finance capitalists" who were understood to dominate historic "fascist" systems.

During the final years of his tenure, some Chinese Marxists had undertaken a searching criticism of socialist rule as it had manifested itself under Mao Zedong. In the course of that criticism, many things had become evident. The "socialism" that manifested itself in primitive economic conditions was clearly different from any socialism anticipated by the founders of classical Marxism.

In all of this, it became very evident that the categories that afforded apparent substance to the original Marxist analysis of socioeconomic and political systems were, at best, ill-defined. For Maoists, "classes" could be understood to refer to many different real or fancied aggregates—all ill-defined. Classes could function in systems in which no private property existed. Classes were defined either in terms of exploitation, through coercive state control in the absence of private property, or subjectively, in terms of personal ideological commitments. All the complex lucubrations of Karl Marx and Friedrich Engels had collapsed into tactical simplisms.

Beyond that, by the first quarter of the century, many Marxists concluded that any effort at accelerated industrial development and economic growth in a primitive environment required authoritarian rule. A less-developed community that sought to survive and prevail in the modern world required a broad and deep industrial base. To transform the essentially labor-intensive agrarian systems of the past into the revolutionary, developmental enterprises of the present required an indeterminate period of minority control.[59]

That period was variously identified. For some, in circumstances in which private property is abolished and the productive and distributive system is governed by command, that period was called the "dictatorship of the most advanced vanguard of the proletariat." It was a "proletarian" party dictatorship where there were few, if any, proletarians. For others, in a system that tolerated private property and an economy governed largely by market signals, the period was identified with generic fascism. Whether "proletarian" or "fascist," the systems were variants of the reactive and developmental dictatorships that typify the twentieth century.

What Marxist theory, in one or another of its forms, managed to produce during the years between the Sino-Soviet dispute and the death of Mao Zedong in 1976 was a reformulation of its inherited notions about fascism. Fascism was no longer understood simply as the pathological product of the final crisis of industrial capitalism. Fascism, for Soviet commentators, during the years of the Sino-Soviet dispute, was one form of developmental dictatorship and could arise whenever an exiguous minority controlled and administered the property of a community. In such a system, class, in and of itself, was no longer a significant social, political, or economic determinant. In fact, class was a derivative product of a monopoly of political control. It was politics, not class, that determined the major features of the system—whether "socialist" or "fascist."[60]

Such a system characteristically manifests itself in retrograde economic circumstances—in communities suffering retarded industrial development. The "socialism" of such a system is not the reflection of an economic base but the product of political decision by a hegemonic single party and its "charismatic" leader.

All of these assessments were taking place at the close of the Maoist era and at the commencement of the transition to the rule of Deng Xiaoping. Chinese Marxists themselves were attempting to understand their own revolution. Out of all the confusion, a number of very critical questions would emerge. They would have some significance during the entire period of reform entrained by Deng Xiaoping's accession to power as "Paramount Leader" of China.

The Chinese Communist Party Critique
of Mao Zedong Thought

By the time of Mao Zedong's death in 1976, the political leadership in the People's Republic of China had decided that he had been responsible for the "most severe setback and the heaviest losses suffered by the Party, the state and the people since the founding of the People's Republic."[61] Between the time of Mao's death in 1976 and the Third Plenary Session of the Eleventh Central Committee of the CCP in December 1978, the Communist leadership of the People's Republic had decided that the nation had been brought to the brink of catastrophe because of the prevalence of "left errors" among the leadership of regime.[62] In June 1981, all of that found expression in a "Resolution on Certain Questions in the History of our Party Since the Founding of the People's Republic of China," adopted by the Sixth Plenary Session of the Eleventh Central Committee of the CCP. In the resolution, the Communist leadership of China subjected Mao and Maoism to sustained and penetrating criticism.

In the resolution, China's revolution was characterized as a national effort to "overthrow, once and for all, the reactionary rule of imperialism and feudalism." For the new leaders of Communist China, the enemies of the nation were not "class enemies" but imperialist oppression and economic and cultural backwardness. The resolution contained little talk of universal proletarian revolution, and there was no talk of the unified "socialist camp." Rather, there was talk about China and its place in the modern world.

That victory in 1949 was won "under the guidance of Marxism-Leninism," and the "great system of Mao Zedong Thought" was affirmed. Affirmed as well was the recognition that Mao, however meritorious his qualities as a revolutionary, had made egregious errors after 1949.

Very conspicuous in the text is the post-Maoist leadership's commitment to an inclusive conception of the "revolutionary people" of "socialist China." In several places, the resolution identifies the "people" of China as all "working people" and "all patriots who support socialism" as well as those "patriots who stand for the unification of the motherland."[63] In effect, the authors of the Resolution of 1981 crafted an inclusive vision of the Chinese "people" in which "all patriots," without real or fancied class distinctions, were united in resistance to, and resolution of, "imperialism and feudalism"—insulating China from foreign impostures and offsetting those social and economic impediments that obstructed its rapid economic growth and industrialization.

For the authors of the resolution, one of the gravest errors made by the party under the guidance of Mao was "enlarging the scope of class struggle," together with the excessive haste "in pressing on with agricultural cooperation and the transformation of private handicraft and commercial establishments." The changes identified at the time of their enactment as "socialization" "were too fast."[64]

In the short space of time between 1949 and 1956, all private establishments on the Chinese mainland had been socialized, and the Eighth National Congress of the CCP had declared that the socialist system had been established in the People's Republic. As a consequence of the abolition of private property, the authors of the resolution argued, there was no longer a foundation for any "contradiction" between classes in "socialist" China. There were no conceivable grounds for "class struggle" in a "socialist" China. The "real contradiction," in China after 1956, they insisted, was that which represented the distance between the "demand of the people for rapid economic . . . development" and the backward state of the nation's productive system. The basic task of the party after 1956, in the judgment of the authors of the Resolution of 1981, was not "class struggle" but the development of revolutionary China's "productive forces."[65] Failing to understand that, Mao Zedong had led China into political turmoil and economic misadventure for more than two decades.

The principal failure of the party after 1956 was the increase in "the scope" of class struggle and the consequent increase in the number of its victims—which included an untold number of "patriotic people"—all with "unfortunate consequences." All those failures were laid at the door of Mao Zedong. He was "chiefly responsible" for them all. Under his direction, a clutch of "entirely wrong" policies had been enacted.

Mao had "widened and absolutized the class struggle" in an effort to solve what he thought to be a variety of social, political, and economic problems. Mao's errors, the resolution continued, were the consequence of his failure to understand Marxism and China's reality. Mao was convinced that his policies were Marxist, we were told, but they were not. The resolution went on to maintain that Mao's policies "conformed neither to Marxism-Leninism nor to Chinese reality." In fact, many of the things Mao "denounced as revisionist or capitalist during the 'cultural revolution' were actually Marxist and socialist principles."[66]

The "Marxist and socialist principles" to which the authors of the resolution alluded were those that found expression in the policies of Liu Shaoqi, Deng Xiaoping, and the other "capitalist roaders" disgraced during Mao's Great Proletarian Cultural Revolution. The general sense of the resolution was that Mao had failed to understand that. Instead, he gave expression to "left errors" upon which "counterrevolutionary cliques" capitalized. The compounded errors that resulted led to "domestic turmoil and brought catastrophe to the Party, the state and the whole people."

While leading the nation into those leftist errors that would bring the People's Republic to the very brink of disaster, Mao "repeatedly urged the whole Party to study the works of Marx, Engels and Lenin conscientiously and imagined that his theory and practice were Marxist." That, for the leaders of the post-Maoist CCP, was the central "tragedy" of Mao's rule from the early 1950s until his death a quarter of a century later.[67]

By 1981, the Chinese Communist party announced that, under Mao Zedong, it had not been fully prepared to undertake the rapid industrial development of continental China. The party, under the leadership of Mao, had misunderstood or "dogmatically interpreted . . . the writings of Marx, Engels, Lenin and Stalin." Those writings did not provide "ready-made answers" to the many, many problems faced by the revolutionary CCP in assuming responsibility for the redemption of a backward nation. The inexperience of the party had allowed Mao Zedong to lead it and the nation into "gross error" and "leftist" deviation that was to exact incalculable cost from China and the people of China.

December 1978 marked a crucial change in the revolutionary policies of the CCP. "It firmly discarded the slogan 'Take class struggle as the key link,'" which was "unsuitable in a socialist society, and made the strategic decision to shift the focus of work to socialist modernization." The Resolution of 1981 formalized a fundamental change in the goals of the revolution. Class struggle, income equality, and "international proletarian revolution" disappeared into a nationalist program of rapid economic and industrial development. Communist China committed itself to Deng Xiaoping's "theory of the unique importance of productive forces," which saw the "central task" of the revolution to be "economic construction," not class warfare or international proletarian revolution.[68]

The program of accelerated growth and industrialization Deng proposed would be distinguished from Maoism by the fact that the national economy would be governed, in part, by the "supplementary, regulatory role of the market"—something traditional Marxists had always identified as a betrayal of Marxism. Indifferent to such criticism, the resolution insisted that the task was to "create those specific forms of the relations of production that correspond to the needs of the growing productive forces and facilitate their continued advance."[69]

Traditional Marxists had always argued that the "relations of production" had to "conform" to the "material forces of production" that characterized the productive system. Marx had consistently argued that in the course of production human beings entered into relations of production that necessarily corresponded to a definite stage of development of their material productive forces.[70] One could not simply fabricate relations of production to satisfy one's political, social, or economic choosing. Marx and Engels had made very clear that socialist relations of production, the distribution of benefits, and the unlimited satisfaction of needs would be an exclusive function of an advanced industrial productive system. They regularly denied that "advanced relations of production" could be imposed on a primitive economic base.[71]

The readiness of the authors of the resolution to understand that elementary notion of classical Marxist theory had important implications. As long as China's economy remained "primitive" and in the "first stage of socialism," it was evident that the prevailing "relations of production" would have to be revised to conform to the requirements of the economic base.

The immediate consequence was to legitimize Deng Xiaoping's economic "reforms." Mao's experiment with agricultural communes was abandoned and "responsibility rights," with all their qualified property rights, were extended to peasant families. Peasants were permitted to farm their own land and sell any surplus that exceeded the requirements of sale to the state in a "free" and "competitive" market. Elements of private property rights reappeared in a system in which they had been banished since 1956. In some sectors of the economy competitive markets for the sale of commodities, in general, reappeared.[72]

The general economic reforms that quickly followed were as revolutionary as those specifically undertaken in the agrarian sector. The People's Republic rapidly opened itself to the industrialized democracies in order to elicit transfers of capital and technology.[73]

What the authors of the Resolution of 1981 implicitly recognized, and some may have recognized since the founding of the People's Republic, was that economically backward China was not ready for socialism, however socialism was understood. Socialist relations of production could not simply be imposed on a retrograde productive base. Like Sun Yat-sen before them, the leadership of the CCP acknowledged that classical Marxism really had little relevance to their enterprise. The "socialism with Chinese characteristics" that emerged after the death of Mao was to share features with Sun's Three Principles and with the reactive nationalist and developmental ideologies of others found almost everywhere in the less-developed and revolutionary communities of the twentieth century.

Notes

1. See Chalmers A. Johnson, *Peasant Nationalism and Communist Power: The Emergence of Revolutionary China, 1937–1945* (Stanford: Stanford University Press, 1962).

2. Ibid., p. 41.

3. See the discussion in Warren Kuo, *Analytical History of the Chinese Communist Party* (Taipei: Institute of International Relations, 1968), 1:236–237.

4. Ibid., pp. 253–257; see the Comintern Resolution of December 1926 in ibid., pp. 268–269.

5. "Resolution on the Political Task and Policy of the Chinese Communist Party," *Circular No. 2*, 23 August 1927, in ibid., p. 440.

6. Mao Zedong, "A Comment on the Sessions of the Kuomintang Central Executive Committee and the People's Political Council," in *Selected Works* (Beijing: Foreign Languages, 1965), 3:147.

7. Mao, "On Coalition Government," in ibid., p. 281.

8. Ibid., pp. 283, 304.

9. Mao, "The Chinese Revolution and the Chinese Communist Party," in ibid., 2:327.

10. Mao, "On Coalition Government," p. 285.

11. Mao, "On the Ten Great Relationships," in *Chairman Mao Talks to the People* (New York: Pantheon, 1974), p. 82.

12. Mao, "The Chinese Revolution and the Chinese Communist Party," in *Selected Works*, 2:315.

13. See the account given in Richard L. Walker, *China Under Communism: The First Five Years* (New Haven: Yale University Press, 1955), chap. 2.

14. See the characteristic species traits of fascism as presented by Michael T. Florinsky, *Fascism and National Socialism* (New York: Macmillan, 1936), chap. 3.

15. See Chu-yuan Cheng, *China's Economic Development: Growth and Structural Change* (Boulder: Westview, 1982), chap. 5.

16. See Sun's affirmations in Sun Yat-sen, *The International Development of China* (Taipei: China Cultural Service, 1953), p. 9. See the discussion in A. James Gregor, Maria Hsia Chang, and Andrew B. Zimmerman, *Ideology and Development: Sun Yat-sen and the Economic History of Taiwan* (Berkeley: Center for Chinese Studies, 1981), chap. 1.

17. See Liu Suinian and Wu Qungan, *China's Socialist Economy: An Outline History (1949–1984)* (Beijing: Beijing Review, 1986), pts. 1–2; see pp. 172–173.

18. See Mao Zedong, *A Critique of Soviet Economics* (New York: Monthly Review Press, 1977).

19. Of the twenty-three members of the politburo of the CCP before the Proletarian Cultural Revolution, only nine retained membership. Approximately two-thirds of the members of the CCP Central Committee elected in 1956 were purged. A large majority of the leaders of the CCP who had exercised leadership during the first two decades of Mao's rule were publicly disgraced, including his heir apparent, Liu Shaoqi.

20. Different factions in the party emphasized different threats. Lin Biao had identified the United States as China's principal antagonist and apparently sought realignment with the Soviet Union to offset the threat.

21. See the discussion in A. James Gregor, *The Fascist Persuasion in Radical Politics* (Princeton: Princeton University, 1974), chap. 6.

22. The Chinese press during the Great Proletarian Cultural Revolution was filled with these charges. An easily available English-language rendering is found in Martin Nicolaus, *Restoration of Capitalism in the USSR* (Chicago: Liberator, 1975).

23. See the discussion in A. Zelochovtsev, *La Rivoluzione Culturale vista da un sovietico* (Milan: Rusconi, 1971).

24. See Boris Leibson, *Petty-Bourgeois Revolutionism (Anarchism, Trotskyism and Maoism)* (Moscow: Progress, 1970); V. Krivtsov, ed., *Maoism Through the Eyes of Communists* (Moscow: Progress, 1970).

25. O. E. Vladimirov, ed., *Maoism As It Really Is* (Moscow: Progress, 1981), pp. 7, 9–11, 24, 28, 30–31, 34, 38.

26. V. A. Krivtsov and V. Y. Sidikhmenov, *A Critique of Mao Tse-tung's Theoretical Conceptions* (Moscow: Progress, 1972), pp. 64, 66.

27. A. Kruchinin and V. Olgin, eds., *Territorial Claims of Mao Tse-tung: History and Modern Times* (Moscow: Novosti, n.d.), p. 33.

28. *A Destructive Policy* (Moscow: Novosti, 1972), p. 30.

29. See the discussion in G. Apalin and U. Mityayev, *Militarism in Peking's Policies* (Moscow: Progress, 1980), chap. 3.

30. See the discussion in Fedor Burlatsky, *Mao Tse-tung: An Ideological and Psychological Portrait* (Moscow: Progress, 1980), pt. 1.

31. The following synoptic account is taken from the English translation available in *On Socialist Democracy and the Chinese Legal System*, ed. Anita Chan, Stanley Rosen, and Jonathan Unger (Armonk, N.Y.: M. E. Sharpe, 1985), pp. 31–85.

32. By that time, the ideas contained in Djilas's *The New Class* were broadcast among Chinese intellectuals.

33. See, in this regard, the insightful discussion in Chen Erjin, *China: Crossroads Socialism* (London: Verso, 1985), chap. 11.

34. See the discussion in Wang Xizhe, "Strive for the Class Dictatorship of the Proletariat," in Chan, Rosen, and Unger, *Socialist Democracy*, pp. 138–139.

35. Ibid., p. 37.

36. Ibid., p. 40.

37. Ibid., pp. 43, 58, 61–69, 73, 75, 81, 82f.

38. Ibid., p. 65.

39. See the discussion in Gregor, *Fascist Persuasion*, p. 117.

40. See ibid., pp. 82f.

41. For an insightful biographical account of Chen Erjin, see Robin Munro, "Introduction: Chen Erjin and the Chinese Democracy Movement," in Chen, *China*, pp. 1–68.

42. Ibid., pp. 72f.

43. Ibid., pp. 91–93. Wang Xizhe speaks specifically of "totalitarian" controls. See Wang Xizhe, "Mao Zedong and the Cultural Revolution," in Chan, Rosen, and Unger, *Socialist Democracy*, p. 185.

44. Ibid., pp. 98–109.

45. Ibid., p. 106. "Proletarian dictatorship? Nothing of the sort! On the contrary, this is out-and-out social-fascist dictatorship, out-and-out dictatorship by the bureaucrat class, out-and-out dictatorship *over* the proletariat." Ibid., p. 199.

46. Wang Xizhe, "Mao Zedong and the Cultural Revolution," in Chan, Rosen, and Unger, *Socialist Democracy*, p. 209.

47. Ibid., p. 180.

48. Ibid.

49. "As Marx and Engels said . . . the theory of the Communists may be summed up in the single sentence: Abolition of private property'." Chen, *China*, p. 191.

50. Wang Xizhe, "Mao Zedong and the Cultural Revolution," in Chan, Rosen, and Unger, *Socialist Democracy*, p. 206.

51. Ibid., pp. 186–187; and Wang Xizhe, "Strive for the Class Dictatorship of the Proletariat," in ibid., pp. 136–137.

52. Benito Mussolini, "Divagazione," in *Opera omnia* (Florence: La fenice, 1954–1963), 11:341.

53. See the discussion in A. James Gregor, *Young Mussolini and the Intellectual Origins of Fascism* (Berkeley: University of California Press, 1979), chaps. 9–10.

54. The discussion follows closely on the analysis of Sergio Panunzio, one of Fascism's foremost theoreticians. See Sergio Panunzio, *Teoria generale dello stato fascista* (Padua: CEDAM, 1939), pt. 5, chaps. 1–3; and "Teoria generale della dittatura," in *Gerarchia* 4 (April 1936): 228–236; *Gerarchia* 5 (May 1936): 303–316.

55. See A. James Gregor, *Phoenix: Fascism in Our Time* (New Brunswick, N.J.: Transaction, 1999), chap. 6.

56. See the Soviet commentary, V. A. Krivtsov and V. Y. Sidikhmenov, eds., *A Critique of Mao Tse-tung's Theoretical Conceptions* (Moscow: Progress, 1972), pp. 57–58.

57. See the discussion in Walter Laqueur, *Fascism: Past, Present, Future* (New York: Oxford University, 1996), pt. 1. The critical role of the charismatic leader, the presence of the hegemonic party, the appeals of revanchist nationalism, the mass-mobilizing features, the invocation of force to maintain compliance, the notion of a "popular democracy" as legitimating party rule, all reflect the standard features of paradigmatic Fascism recognized by scholarship.

58. Wang Xizhe, "Mao Zedong and the Cultural Revolution," in Chan, Rosen, and Unger, *Socialist Democracy*, p. 237.

59. Ibid., pp. 140–141, 152–153. See the discussion of the "historic necessity" of dictatorship at the commencement of socialist rule in Chen, *China*, pp. 96–97.

60. See the discussion in A. James Gregor, *The Faces of Janus: Marxism and Fascism in the Twentieth Century* (New Haven: Yale University Press, 2000), chap. 3.

61. *Resolution on CPC History (1949–81)* (Beijing: Foreign Languages, 1981), p. 32.

62. Ibid., pp. 49–50.

63. Ibid., p. 13.

64. Ibid., pp. 17, 21

65. Ibid., p. 23.

66. Ibid., pp. 27–29, 32–33, 34.

67. Ibid., pp. 36–37, 41.

68. Ibid., pp. 50, 76–77.

69. Ibid., pp. 78.

70. See the more ample discussion in A. James Gregor, *A Survey of Marxism: Problems in Philosophy and the Theory of History* (New York: Random House, 1965), pp. 158–159.

71. See the discussion in Karl Marx and Friedrich Engels, *The German Ideology* (Moscow: Progress, 1964), pp. 457f.; and Friedrich Engels, *Anti-Duehring* (Moscow: Foreign Languages, 1962), pp. 386 ff.

72. See Henry K. H. Woo, *Effective Reform in China: An Agenda* (New York: Praeger, 1991), pp. 193–200; Cheng, *China's Economic Development*, pp. 404–408.

73. See Samuel P. S. Ho and Ralph W. Huenenmann, *China's Open Door Policy: The Quest for Foreign Technology and Capital* (Vancouver: University of British Columbia, 1984); Jonathan R. Woetzel, *China's Economic Opening to the Outside World: The Politics of Empowerment* (New York: Praeger, 1989).

6
Post-Maoist China, Sun Yat-sen, and Fascism

Before Deng Xiaoping acceded to paramountcy in Communist China, Madame Mao—Jiang Qing—identified him as a "fascist dwarf," a "counterrevolutionary" who would "change everything" should he come to a position of authority.[1] Jiang Qing was convinced that Deng, and those around him, were "revisionists" who, like those who had transformed the Soviet Union, would "change the color of the socialist revolution," to introduce fascism into revolutionary China. She was not alone in that judgment.

Non-Chinese Maoists observed the advent of Deng to power in post-Maoist China with similar misgivings. In the United States, Charles Bettelheim saw Deng's projected policies as an explicit repudiation not only of Maoism but of Marxism in general. He warned that the direction in which Deng sought to guide China could only result in the "restoration of capitalism" and transform the Chinese Communist party into a "counterrevolutionary fascist party."[2]

In Canada, Michel Chossudovsky warned that the policies of Deng Xiaoping were not only anti-Maoist and "bourgeois" in essence but threatened a "restoration of capitalism" as well as a fallback to the policies of the reactionary Kuomintang.[3] Among Maoists, the proposed post-Maoist reforms carried with them the threat of a restored capitalism as well as the potential for a "Chinese fascism." A review of Deng's reforms will explain why they appeared so ominous to domestic and foreign Maoists.

Marxism and the Reforms of Deng Xiaoping

Given the extent of post-Maoist reforms, identifying in just what sense Deng's China remains "Marxist" has become a very significant taxonomic issue. It sets the stage for a corollary consideration of whether "fascism," as a historic and analytic concept, has any relevance for attempts to understand what is transpiring in the China of Deng Xiaoping and Jiang Zemin. But first, we will consider a brief catalog of the changes introduced by Deng since 1978.

Deng Xiaoping's reforms transformed Communist China so extensively that the emerging system now shares programmatic features with some of the major non-Marxist developmental programs advanced in a variety of less-developed nations at the very turn of the century. If nothing else, that fact prompts a synoptic rehearsal of the history of radical thought in the twentieth century—and how "the thought of Deng Xiaoping" enters into that history.

Before Deng Xiaoping could undertake the changes that would transform Communist China, an intense political struggle between factions within the Communist party had to resolve itself.[4] By the beginning of the 1980s, the struggle had concluded. Briefly dominated by Hua Guofeng—Mao's chosen heir—political control of the People's Republic passed into the hands of Deng Xiaoping. Identified by Maoist enthusiasts as an incorrigible "capitalist roader"[5] throughout the long years of the Great Proletarian Cultural Revolution, by 1981 Deng was sufficiently secure as "paramount leader" of Communist China to commission his followers to embark upon a studied and critical review of the history of the Communist party and of Chairman Mao Zedong's role in that history.

Everything suggests that such a review was intended to settle accounts, once and for all, with the late chairman.[6] It seems clear that the official "Resolution on Certain Questions in the History of our Party"[7] of 1981 was calculated to establish Deng Xiaoping's legitimacy as China's leader. Long considered a renegade by Maoists,[8] after his succession, it was felt that the issue of Deng's revolutionary credibility could only be settled by a public assessment of the role of Mao Zedong in the Chinese revolution.

All that has been recognized by Sinologists. What has not been so readily perceived are the complex issues joined by the party's critical review of Mao's place in China's long revolution. One of the more insistent, if implicit, questions raised by the resolution was that which dealt with the relationship of Leninism, Stalinism, Maoism, or any of its variants, to the original doctrine of Karl Marx and Friedrich Engels.

Between the time of Friedrich Engels's death in 1895 and Mao's succession to power in China in 1949, what might count as Marxist orthodoxy had become exceedingly uncertain. In the course of the twentieth century, classical Marxism was transfigured by a tide of self-serving and conflicting interpretations by Stalinists and Maoists. Only in the transmogrified form that emerged after decades of "creative dialectic development" did enthusiasts find it possible to employ Marxism as a putative guide for revolution in the least Marxist of places and by the least Marxist of people.

Given its curious history in the twentieth century, by the time the Communist Party acceded to power in China in 1949, it was uncertain what Marxism was expected to accomplish through successful revolution. As long as Mao ruled China, that issue could hardly be addressed. Whatever Mao did was, by definition, Marxist. In the final analysis, Mao Zedong had made himself the final arbiter of what Marxism was.

All that changed with his passing. Whatever the intended purpose of the Resolution of 1981, the most fundamental issue it raised turned on the question of what Marxism was supposed to accomplish by making revolution in an economically backward environment.[9] As has been suggested, the resolution, by insisting as it did that Mao Zedong had made grievous mistakes since his very assumption of power, implied either that he had not understood the nature and responsibilities of Marxist revolution or that he could not or would not fulfill them.

As indicated earlier, according to the resolution, Mao had obstructed the rapid economic growth and industrial development of China by uncritically emphasizing class conflict and ideological struggle.[10] The turmoil generated by "mass struggles," the violence against intellectuals, the suppression of expertise, and the insistence on absolute conformity to the "party line," impaired the entire productive process. Mao Zedong, the resolution revealed, had been too much of a "leftist." His errors infected not only "economic work" but "the spheres of politics, ideology and culture"[11]—all to the detriment of the developmental goals of the revolution. The express judgment was that Mao had not only misunderstood Marxism but also failed the revolution.

Even while Mao was still alive, Deng Xiaoping had insisted that "the productive forces . . . and the economic base" were the critical foundation of "Chinese socialism."[12] Unlike Mao, Deng emphasized that accelerating economic development—promoting the output growth and technological sophistication of the "forces of production"—was the core responsibility of revolutionaries.

Deng insisted, without qualification, on the primacy of economic development. Prior to the death of Mao, that insistence suggested to Maoists a "revisionist" neglect of the "class struggle." Maoists insisted that the express emphasis on economic growth and development, through the variety of material incentives urged by Deng, would result in the growth of class differences, the eclipse of socialism, and the possibility of fulsome "capitalist restoration."

Before the passing of Mao, Maoists argued that the preoccupation with growth and technological development implied an infatuation with foreign industrial systems and generated an abiding admiration for "all things foreign" among the people of China.[13] Until Mao's death, Deng's "theory of the productive forces" was identified as a "venomous weed"—a treasonous abandonment of Marxism.[14]

In substance, what Deng had done in formulating his "theory of the productive forces" was to raise the central question of what the Marxist revolution in China was expected to accomplish. If Mao had failed the revolution,[15] it was important to know why.

The question reopened the long and tortured dispute that turned on the issue of what the "socialist" revolution was all about. The Resolution of 1981 elliptically addressed the question of what Marxism—traditionally understood—had to do with the Chinese revolution. This question had been addressed by some of the foremost Chinese revolutionaries at the turn of the twentieth century but was largely neglected thereafter.

During the long years when "Marxist theory" served as a tool of Stalinists and Maoists, it was never quite clear what "Marxists" making revolution in politically and economically backward environments imagined their responsibilities to be. The Dengist Resolution of 1981, intentionally or unintentionally, reopened that question for Chinese intellectuals.

Was Marxist revolution charged with the responsibility of lifting the burden of oppression from the shoulders of the working class, the liberation of humankind from all the inequities of modern capitalism, the establishment of universal harmony, the complete abolition of war, and the creation of a social order in which all individuals might fully realize their fullest potential without the constraints of material want? Was the Marxist revolution expected to bring with it the abundance that would release human beings from the obligation of work—to participate only because labor provided creative release?

It is very doubtful that the long Chinese revolution—commencing in the middle of the nineteenth century before the advent of organized Marxism—was inspired by any of that. In China, calls for systemic reform and revolutionary initiatives commenced with the incursions of Western imperialism into politically and economically primitive Asia.[16] Neither the first Chinese revolutionaries nor Karl Marx himself believed that Marxism, in and of itself, would have any influence on the unfolding Chinese circumstances. The Chinese revolution that Marx had anticipated in the 1850s was to be "bourgeois" in inspiration, a necessary consequence of China's economic backwardness.[17]

Everyone seemed convinced of the circumstances. As has been suggested, at the turn of the century, Chinese reformers and revolutionaries were not pursuing Marxist utopias but attempting to formulate policies that would ensure the survival and revitalization of their nation.[18] In the quarter century that followed, those efforts matured into several candidate revolutionary creeds that each claimed to more effectively address the challenges that faced China.

Whatever the creed, what seems to have ultimately become obvious to everyone was the recognition that economic growth and industrial modernization were the responsibility of reform and revolution in China. Almost every politically and intellectually active person during the last days of the Qing dynasty recognized the necessity of modernizing and industrializing the nation. What separated them was how all that might be accomplished.

Deng Xiaoping, however much of a Marxist he may have conceived himself, was born into that tradition and was imbued with those convictions. This led biographers to assert that whatever ancillary goals Deng pursued during his long career, none was more emphatic or persistent than strengthening the Chinese nation-state. Deng had always been a nationalist committed to the restoration of China's wealth, power, and prestige. Whatever his Marxism, his quest was not unlike that of previous Chinese reformers and revolutionaries, ranging from those of the late Qing to Sun Yat-sen.[19]

Like all of them, Deng sought "the creation of a modern industrial base [for his oppressed nation]. . . . Driven by a demand for reclaimed national independence, dignity, and freedom of manoeuvre in foreign relations [he sought] a strong national defence and maintenance of territorial integrity . . . and [he committed himself to] the attainment of great power status [for China]."[20] Whatever else he was, Deng Xiaoping had always been a reactive developmental nationalist. Out of that emerged Deng's "theory of the primacy of the productive forces."

Given that recognition, the essence of the criticism contained in the Communist party's Resolution of 1981 immediately reveals itself. In that document, the role played by Mao Zedong in the course of the Chinese "socialist revolution" was very carefully considered. The measure of success or failure of his revolutionary efforts was calculated against criteria that, if not anti-Marxist, were essentially non-Marxist.

In the resolution, as we have seen, the "salvation of China" necessarily required the "overthrow" of both "imperialism and feudalism." That, according to the text of the resolution, entailed the recognition that "industrialization" constituted "an indispensable prerequisite" for China's national "independence and prosperity."[21] Feudalism and imperialism could be defeated only by fully industrializing China. Only a modernized and industrialized China could put together, sustain, and foster capabilities necessary to overcome domestic social anachronisms and resist external economic and military threat. There was precious little Marxism in any of that.

In the Resolution of 1981, the apologists for Deng Xiaoping argued that Mao Zedong had failed to understand the "unique importance of productive forces" in strengthening a retrograde China threatened by the economic and military pretenses of world imperialism.[22] Instead of committing all of China's resources to accelerated economic growth and industrial development, Mao had dissipated the nation's energies in "class struggle."[23]

In the eyes of his detractors, Mao had failed to fully recognize the imperatives that drove the Chinese revolution. If he did recognize them, he served them badly. According to the assessment made in the resolution, instead of pursuing the goal of extensive and intensive economic growth and development, Mao obstructed their pace and extent by involving the nation in frenzied class conflict and factional strife.[24] Class struggle wasted the time and resources of the Chinese people and succeeded in alienating those most essential to national development.[25]

In fact, Mao had failed to adequately invest in agriculture, sustain the extensive and intensive growth of heavy industry, or initiate and foster small and intermediate industries. He failed to plan and finance the collateral articulation of the nation's infrastructure. He failed to allow the market to generate a rational price structure for the system or influence resource allocation. The result was the escalation of capital costs and the accumulation of multiple failures throughout the system. He closed China to the inflow of foreign capital and technology. He had, in almost every way, impaired the growth and technological maturation of the nation's economy.

Mao Zedong never seemed to fully understand the implications of making revolution in a backward economic environment. Once securely in power, he imposed a ramshackle command economy on the fragility of what was basically an agrarian productive base. Afflicted by an irrational pricing system and dominated by an ignorant and ill-informed cadre, the Chinese economy gradually spiraled down into system-wide dysfunction—with unsold inventory, wasted investment capital, gross intersectoral imbalances, and steadily declining factor productivity.[26]

Mao chose not to address the most fundamental problems that beset the primitive Chinese economy. Instead, he imagined that ideological conformity and class conflict would somehow bring about their resolution. With his passing, Mao left behind him a seriously handicapped productive system. In the judgment of many, Mao had failed, as a consequence, not only as a revolutionary but as a Marxist thinker as well.[27] By the early 1980s, it had become evident that the revolutionaries who succeeded Mao believed that he had failed, in substantial part, to satisfy the most fundamental imperatives of the Chinese revolution. In the judgment of Deng Xiaoping and those who collected around him, the Chinese revolution was basically about the modernization and industrialization of the national economy.[28]

There could no longer be any confusion. Whatever the long pretense might have been, the Chinese revolution was not about international revolution, personal fulfillment, political democracy, individual liberty, the abolition of poverty, income equality, or class struggle.[29] For all the talk in all the political pamphlets, the revolution was not about international proletarian solidarity. It was about the rebirth of the Chinese people, the renaissance of the Chinese nation, and the restoration of China's central place in the world through the rapid development of the nation's "productive forces." It was nationalistic and developmental in both inspiration and intention. Once that is understood, in what sense can the long Chinese revolution be considered Marxist?

At its origin, the Chinese revolution had been a reaction to the economic retardation and the competitive vulnerability of the nation. As a consequence, the revolution was about creating an industrial base that would offset those vulnerabilities. The obligation of the revolution was to modernize China. Only modernization could provide the material foundation for a modern society and an effective and deterrent military. Industrialization alone could equip the nation not only to survive but to prevail in a threatening international environment. The Chinese revolution was about the defeat of imperialism and the restoration of China's sovereignty. In essence, the Chinese revolution had always been about the "liberation of [the] nation"[30]—and that liberation required not "proletarian internationalism," "world socialist revolution," class warfare, the abolition of the market economy, or the suppression of private property, but rapid economic development.

Throughout the long years of the Chinese Communist revolution, Deng Xiaoping recognized all that. He consistently argued against the "leftism" and the "ultraleftism" of party enthusiasts.[31] In the years before the Communist seizure of power on the mainland, Deng spoke of mobilizing "all strata of the population" and "all social forces."[32] Deng urged that agrarian reforms proceed slowly and prudently to avoid alienating any substantial elements of the population. Deng urged that property that had been seized from landlords be returned. Similarly, he demanded that the practice of "settling very old accounts with landlords . . . be ended" and that landlords be allowed to "make a living and enjoy a certain economic status and that their legitimate right of property [be] safeguarded." Communists were urged to resolutely reject the "destructive theory of agricultural socialism."[33] In substance, the party's policy, as Deng understood it, was to give "consideration to the interests of workers and peasants, on the one hand, and those of the landlords and capitalists, on the other."[34] He insisted that the "ultraleft mistakes" that sought to penalize everyone but the workers and peasants would render "the middle sections of society . . . displeased with us."[35] That would alienate them from the revolution itself—and in Deng's judgment, the revolution could not be successful without them.

All of this must be understood in the context of Deng's conviction that the revolution was all about the rapid modernization and industrialization of retrograde China. The party's policy, as he understood it, was to win the support of the vast majority of the population, necessary for the accelerated growth and sophistication of the "material productive forces" without which there could be no "salvation for the nation."[36]

Deng Xiaoping understood perfectly well what all that meant. "These policies," he told the members of the Chinese Communist party, "are all designed to promote development of the economy. . . . This is the path that Dr. Sun Yat-sen pointed out to us."[37] He urged all party members to always "act in conformity with [Sun Yat-sen's] Three People's Principles."[38]

In this light, Deng Xiaoping's criticisms of Mao take on a special significance. Deng had always remained true to the central convictions of Sun Yat-sen. After Mao's death, explicitly and without apology, Deng changed the order of priorities for revolutionary China. "Class struggle" was no longer considered the "key link" in the set of obligations that faced Chinese revolutionaries.[39] For Deng, it had never been. The "four modernizations" and the advocacy of economic incentives, professional rather than "red" management of enterprises, profit as a measure of efficiency, and opening China to the industrialized democracies, took its place.

Deng Xiaoping had always been a loyal Communist party member. He had diligently served the party throughout its long struggle to political power. In spite of, or because of, his loyalty, Deng continually advocated pragmatic and surprisingly moderate economic policies in those areas "liberated" by Communist forces before the final seizure of power in 1949.

Against "leftists,"[40] Deng recommended that revolutionaries "support private industry and commerce beneficial to the national economy and the people's livelihood, encouraging private enterprises' enthusiasm for production."[41] For Deng, *that* was the true "Marxist" responsibility.

Deng's conception of Marxist obligations included the establishment and furtherance of regulations "between the workers and their employers to benefit both of them." Deng clearly imagined that such class collaboration would "facilitate the development of the productive forces."[42]

It seems evident that for substantial periods of time during his long service to the revolution, Deng Xiaoping did not distinguish Marxism from developmental nationalism. At critical junctures, he expressed productivistic and class collaborationist convictions that shared unmistakable affinities with the nationalist and developmental doctrines of Sun Yat-sen.[43]

In fact, Deng clearly recognized substantial compatibilities between Mao's "new democracy" of the 1940s and the anti-Marxist developmental convictions of Sun.[44] None of this was considered unusual by the Chinese Marxists of the period because of the peculiar history of the relationship between the Communist party of China and the nationalism of Sun's followers.

At its very inception Chinese Marxism had unmistakable affinities with developmental nationalism in general and the nationalist doctrines of Sun in particular. For decades, the Chinese Communist party had advertised itself as the true exponent of Sun's doctrines.[45]

Only after his accession to power did Mao Zedong abandon any pretense of being guided by Sun's revolutionary doctrines. It was in response to the changes flowing from that decision that the first resistance to "capitalist roaders" mounted. The economic damage that resulted when Mao abandoned Sun's developmental strategies in the 1950s created a gulf between him and some of the major leaders of the party. In the context of that growing tension Maoists saw Deng Xiaoping's "theory of the productive forces" as fundamentally anti-Maoist and counterrevolutionary.

Deng Xiaoping and the "Theory of the Productive Forces"

Whatever Deng's pragmatic accommodation to the increasing "leftism" of Maoism throughout the 1960s and early 1970s, in the judgment of contemporary Sinologists, he nonetheless remained, throughout his career, a "staunch nationalist" who, like Sun Yat-sen, sought the regeneration of China through the "creation of a modern industrial base."[46] In fact, Deng's clear and persistent commitment to the rapid development of China's productive forces ultimately created major strains between himself and the chairman. Mao had become an "ultraleftist" social revolutionary while Deng had remained a developmental nationalist.

By the mid-1960s, Mao planned, launched, and directed what was to become known to the twentieth century as the Great Proletarian Cultural Revolution in China. It was a political movement predicated on the conviction that the real issue facing the Chinese people was the defense of the "socialist" and "proletarian" class character of the revolution. For Mao, "ferocious class struggle" rather than development of the productive forces was the "key link" in the realization of socialism.[47]

In fact, the Cultural Revolution, with its anarchic class struggles, succeeded only in severely damaging the Chinese economy. It impaired China's economic development, wasted its resources, and devastated its population. It neither produced a new "proletarian" consciousness among the masses of China nor generated the burst of creative energy that was supposed to carry the nation to a new level of revolutionary maturity.

Upon his advent to power, Deng Xiaoping was to reject all of that in its entirety. He was to reject its rationale, its economic strategies, and its political postures. In doing that, Deng was to renounce almost the entire legacy of Mao. That legacy was identified and deplored as "leftist"—and "leftism" was charged with obstructing the economic growth and industrial development of the nation. Maoists had systematically opposed any simple emphasis on the rapid development of the nation's productive forces.[48] The cost was the failure of the People's Republic of China to match the performance of the rapidly developing Asian economies of Taiwan, South Korea, or Japan.

In opposition to the Maoists, Deng was to insist that the responsibility of China's revolutionaries was to foster and sustain the growth of the productive forces of the People's Republic, in accordance with what he called "objective and natural laws."[49] In accordance with those "laws," Deng was to introduce a constellation of non-Maoist and fundamentally non-Marxist economic policies: the reintroduction of market modalities into what had been, for years, an essentially command economy; the restoration of qualified private property rights; the solicitation of joint venture investment from foreigners; and the creation of conditions that allowed an important sector of the domestic Chinese economy to be export oriented. True to apparently long-held convictions,[50] Deng restored free markets for the exchange of a substantial proportion of producer and consumer goods and allowed the employment of property for personal profit. He opened the Chinese economy to capital and technology transfers from the advanced industrial economies.[51]

The response to Deng's initiatives was the rapid expansion and technological improvement of the Chinese productive system. As a consequence, after 1980, the Chinese system was to become one of the fastest growing economies in the world.

Western commentators have found it curious that Deng Xiaoping—having securely established his historic eminence by liberating one of the largest economies in the world from the dysfunctional constraints imposed upon it by the Maoist variant of Marxism—gives no particular evidence of theoretical sophistication.[52] Deng has never said anything particularly original about economics or economic policy and seems to display few insights into the functioning of the economy.[53]

That judgment overlooks the fact that, as we have seen, Deng Xiaoping, early in his career as a revolutionary, found the developmental policies of Sun Yat-sen persuasive. He not only instructed the revolutionaries of the 1930s and 1940s in the doctrines of the *Sanmin zhuyi*,[54] but he also sought to implement its policies during the Communist party's long struggle to political dominance. The economic strategies introduced upon his own accession to power after the death of Mao are all but indistinguishable from those advocated by the non-Marxist and anti-Marxist followers of Sun Yat-sen.

Although Deng never overtly opposed Mao during the catastrophic years of the Great Leap Forward and the Cultural Revolution,[55] by the middle of the 1970s it had become evident to everyone that China had not only failed to keep pace with the economic development of Asia's "little tigers," but the gap between it and the industrialized democracies had grown steadily larger. By the end of the 1970s, major economic reform could no longer be resisted.

By the mid-1980s, the reformed economy that took shape under Deng's auspices began to look more and more like that recommended by Sun Yat-sen and the developmental nationalists of half a century before. Sun and developmental nationalists in general characteristically argued that the accelerated growth of the forces of production was the critical responsibility of revolutionaries. It was they who first articulated what was subsequently to be called Deng Xiaoping's "theory of the productive forces."

All of this is part of the long and complicated story of revolutionary thought in the twentieth century. Within that story can be traced the transformation of Marxism in the face of challenges totally unanticipated by Marx and Engels and bungled by Lenin. As suggested earlier, the emergence and dominance of developmental nationalism, and Fascism as a variant of that nationalism, is a critical part of the narrative.

At the turn of the century, revolutionaries in the less-developed periphery of world capitalism decided that there was little in the orthodox Marxism of the nineteenth century that had anything of importance to say to their times. Nonetheless, at the core of classical Marxism was a theme that was to emerge and reemerge in the revolutionary literature of the next half century. Amid all of the irrelevancies identified by the revolutionaries who found themselves in retrograde economic environments, there was an issue, raised by Marx and Engels, that seemed to have engaged the interest of almost everyone. In their most basic works, the founders of Marxism had argued that "the multitude of productive forces accessible to men determines the nature of society."[56] More than anything else, history for them proceeds as a function of the development of the material productive forces. Marx argued that "in the final analysis, the productive forces . . . are the basis of all . . . history."[57]

The argument was eminently clear. As early as the publication of his *Poverty of Philosophy* in 1847, Marx had written that "in acquiring new productive forces men change their mode of production; and in changing their mode of production, in changing the way of earning their living, they change all their social relations."[58]

Such a conviction confirms what revolutionary developmental nationalists had already recognized. Before Marx and Engels had developed their notions of socialist revolution, Friedrich List made his case for the critical significance of each nation's *Produktivkraefte* (productive forces) in shaping its life circumstances in the modern world. In fact, he called his account "the theory of the productive forces."[59] There was little that was specifically Marxist in the revolutionary emphasis on the productive forces of society.

Almost a century and a half before Deng Xiaoping introduced his reforms into the irrational economic system left to him by Mao Zedong, List had argued that what was required to bring a retrograde economy into modernity was the inspiration of revolutionary nationalism, the regulatory role of commodity and capital markets, the incentives provided by the possession of private property, the implied personal profit to be gained from individual enterprise, the utility of indicative planning by the state, the encouragement of capital and technology transfers from developed systems, the implementation of import substitution policies and protection for infant industries, the control of labor, with constraints on wages and consumption in order to allow for the rapid domestic accumulation of capital, and a policy of export sales of labor-intensive commodities in order to acquire foreign reserves—all under the administration of authoritarian rule. Only such a program offered the promise of the rapid development of the productive forces essential to the future of the community.[60]

With Friedrich List, all major revolutionaries at the turn of the twentieth century were prepared to recognize the critical role played by the forces of production in the search for "national salvation." Those in dynastic and postdynastic China, many of them familiar with the theoretical contentions of classical Marxism,[61] rejected its eschatology but took up its emphasis on the determinate role of the productive forces in the history of the modern world.

Until the "dialectical" innovations introduced by V. I. Lenin, almost every revolutionary in economically backward countries failed to see the relevance of Marxism as a guide to revolution.[62] What the best among them recognized was the critical importance of the rapid and intensive development of the productive forces to their purposes. Revolutionaries in primitive economic environments did not anticipate the suppression of private property, the abolition of commodity and capital markets, or the incorporation of "proletarian internationalism" and domestic class warfare as part of their program. Whatever their ultimate political vision, it was economic growth and industrialization, the accelerated development of the productive forces, that occupied much of their attention.

By the end of the First World War, for example, Sun Yat-sen was talking about China's inviting foreign capital and enlisting "foreign experts and organizers"[63] to manage joint ventures. Any constraints imposed on the transfer of capital and technology from the more advanced industrial states would seriously impair China's modernizing potential. Sun argued that given foreign capital, technology, and entrepreneurial skills, China's abundant resources and cheap labor would provide exports[64] that could be sold to supply the foreign exchange to service its international debt.[65]

At the heart of Sun Yat-sen's developmental ideology[66] was an anti-Marxist, nationalist, class-collaborationist, and productivistic "theory of the productive forces" that looks remarkably like that of Deng Xiaoping. That Marxists like M. N. Roy identified that developmental "theory" as "protofascist" is apparently a matter of little consequence to Deng Xiaoping and his followers.[67] That the "paramount leader" of a "Communist" China should pursue a policy that might be, in whatever sense, "fascist," seems to be a matter of relatively little concern to the present rulers in Beijing. Nevertheless, it is a matter of some interest to the present discussion.

Sun Yat-sen and "Protofascism"

The identification of Sun's developmental nationalism with "protofascism" recalls, once again, the similarities shared by many reactive nationalisms in the twentieth century. As has been suggested, a number of commentators have recognized some doctrinal similarities between the turn-of-the-century revolutionaries of China and those of Nationalist and Fascist Italy. That they all were nationalists facing the arrogant imperialism of the advanced industrial powers goes some distance in explaining their real or perceived similarities. Beyond that, however, it will be argued that there were shared themes that gave particular character to their commonality and that those themes have now reappeared in the "thought of Deng Xiaoping"[68] and his "theory of the productive forces."

It will be further argued that those themes common to non-Marxist Chinese developmental nationalism and Italian Fascism have resurfaced in post-Maoist China. Some of them are explicit, and some are implicit, both in Deng Xiaoping's assessment of Mao Zedong's role in the Chinese revolution and his "pragmatic" program for the accelerated "development of the productive forces."

Central to Sun Yat-sen's "principle of the people's livelihood" was a recognition of the critical role played by the material productive forces in the history of nations. In his rejection of Marxism, Sun insisted that almost all of the complex theoretical arguments advanced by its founders were entirely unrelated to the problems that Chinese revolutionaries had to address.

For Sun, class warfare, the abolition of private property, the suppression of enterprise profits, the abolition of "wage slavery," the notion that the rising organic composition of capital would necessarily bring an end to capitalism, the commitment to international proletarian revolution, and the insistence that working men had no fatherland were all of little, if any, interest to China's revolutionaries. What was of urgency was *production*. "Production," Sun insisted, "is, economically speaking, the principal agent in the modern world."[69]

The rest of Sunism followed from that central conviction. Further repetition of Sun's doctrines is hardly necessary to make the case. Sun's strategy for the rapid economic and industrial development of China included indicative planning by a "powerful" and tutelary state, insistence on harmony between classes so that all "patriots" could be mobilized to developmental purpose, rapid accumulation of capital for a capital-poor country, insistence on discipline in the pursuit of real growth and development, opening trade to the advanced industrial powers, soliciting foreign technology and skill, and advocating export-led growth.

The Nationalists and Fascists of economically backward Italy anticipated virtually the same strategy in tracking the same ends. By the second decade of the twentieth century, some of Italy's foremost Marxists acknowledged that Marxist doctrine was irrelevant to the revolutionaries of the peninsula. By the time of the March on Rome, which brought Fascism to power, the major theoreticians of the movement—most former Marxist radicals[70]—had made rapid economic growth and industrial development the critical responsibility of the revolution.

Mussolini himself was to give that revolutionary prescription authoritative expression. At the end of the Great War, he ventilated his own "theory of the productive forces." He charged Italians with the revolutionary obligation of overcoming the nation's economic backwardness. The revolution required that Italians "produce, produce with efficiency, with diligence, with patience, [and] with passion."

For Mussolini, organizing the first Fascists around the standards of developmental nationalism, it would be "producers [who would] represent the new Italy, as opposed to the old Italy of balladiers and tour-guides."[71] Prior to the war, he argued, Italy had been the "humble vassal" of foreign economic power. The people of Italy were defamed and despised as inferior, inept, and of little consequence.[72] To win a place in the modern world, he went on, required that Italians begin to accept the exacting responsibilities of modern "production." The conditions of the modern world compelled Italy to industrialize and modernize if it were to survive and prosper. "The essential thing," Mussolini urged his followers, "is to 'produce.' That is the beginning. In a nation burdened by a passive economy, it is necessary to exalt producers, those who work, those who construct, those who systematically increase wealth and general well-being."[73]

It would be necessary to mobilize "capitalists possessed of a sense of their historic function who are prepared to take risks" so that the "economy [of Italy] achieves its maximum intensity and extension." To that purpose, it would be necessary to mobilize proletarians "who comprehend the ineluctability of this . . . process and appreciate the mediate and immediate benefits it can deliver." Mussolini had decided that "to inhibit the development of the productive forces of Italy [would be] to condemn Italy" to perpetual inferiority.[74]

When Mussolini advocated making Italy "a nation of producers" and entitled his paper *Il popolo d'Italia*, "A Daily of Combatants and Producers," he communicated his commitment to the expansion and increasing technological sophistication of the forces of production of the peninsula.[75] Mussolini, the former leader of Italian Marxists, had made reactive nationalism and developmentalism the critical center of his revolutionary convictions.

The fact is that by 1915, the basic argument for reactive developmental nationalism had been formulated not only by Italy's Nationalists but by the most radical of Italy's heretical Marxists as well. They recognized not only that the productive base of the peninsula was painfully primitive and that "socialist" revolution was manifestly unrealistic[76] and could only devastate the nation,[77] but also that economic retardation meant not only poverty for the people of recently reunited Italy but national inferiority, foreign cultural domination, and collective humiliation.[78] These were the considerations that generated a reactive "proletarian nationalism" among revolutionary Marxists in Italy after the First World War.[79]

During the first quarter of the twentieth century, preoccupation with accelerated economic development and industrialization informed revolutionaries in both Asia and southern Europe. The salvific revolutionary doctrine had commitment to the rapid development of the nation's "productive forces" at its core.

The intrinsic logic of such a doctrinal position has now become familiar. Revolution in late-developing countries was no longer a question of undertaking a proletarian class revolution or participating in a worldwide socialist fraternity. It was a matter, Mussolini insisted, of making "proletarian Italy" a great nation—"respected, free, and secure."[80] To accomplish that, heretical Marxists would have to make of Italians "a new race of producers . . ."[81] committed to the rapid development of the material forces of production. Sun Yat-sen had said no less of China and the Chinese.

When, in 1993, Deng Xiaoping's "theory of the productive forces" was celebrated as the "newest fruit," produced by the union of Marxism with China's "concrete conditions" and elevated to the level of the creative thought of Karl Marx and V. I. Lenin,[82] no one had the temerity to allude to its similarities with the developmental nationalism of Sun Yat-sen or, for that matter, with the thought of Benito Mussolini. When Deng's "theory" was characterized as having "historic importance," pioneering "new territory within Marxism" so that it would be possible for China's revolution to build a modern and industrial "socialism with Chinese characteristics,"[83] no one reminded anyone that a similar "theory" was to be found as early as the mid-nineteenth century in the developmental nationalism of Friedrich List.

In retrospect, none of this is surprising. The classical Marxism of Karl Marx and Friedrich Engels was specifically designed for application in industrially mature economies, environments inhabited by politically sophisticated proletarian majorities, and characterized by monopoly production, investment saturation, falling wages, and an overall declining rate of profit.[84] List's *National System of Political Economy*, on the other hand, was written for those economically less developed nations that found themselves facing the arrogance of "imperialist" wealth and military power. Contrary to much of the folk wisdom of contemporary social science, it is the latter doctrine, rather than the former, that has really inspired revolution in the twentieth century.

"Proletarian" nations, facing developmental tasks, would have to anticipate, and contend with, the resistance of foreign "plutocracies."[85] In that challenging environment an adamantine resolve, an emphatic national unity, would have to sustain the revolutionary effort at economic growth and development.[86] It was that doctrine, implied by the "theory of productive forces," which Mussolini identified as the revolutionary socialism of poor nations[87] and Sun Yat-sen spoke of as the "true solution" to the political, economic, and social inequities and conflicts of the modern world.

Deng Xiaoping, Sun Yat-sen, and Fascism

Buried in the contemporary discussions taking place in Dengist China are issues long neglected by Marxist theoreticians. The discussions that have followed the death of Mao have brought them, once again, to the surface.

Fascist doctrine clearly gave expression to one form of what today in Communist China is called the "theory of productive forces." Revolutionary China has long been familiar with its own variants. One variant was that of Sun Yat-sen's Three Principles of the People. With the passing of Mao Zedong, Deng Xiaoping clearly made that variant the heart of "socialism with Chinese characteristics."

When Madame Mao, in the polemics that immediately followed the death of the "Great Helmsman," anticipated the rise of "fascism" with the advent of Deng Xiaoping,[88] the issues were reasonably clear. Maoists had insisted that Deng had "never been a Marxist." He was a "revisionist," and Zhou Enlai had warned that "revisionism" would inevitably produce a "fascist party" and a "fascist dictatorship."[89] Maoists identified Deng's "theory of the productive forces" as the critical concept that would transform China and "change the color" of its revolution.[90] More intuitively than substantively, Maoists recognized the fundamental changes in revolutionary priorities implicit in Deng's "revisionist theory of the productive forces."

All of this overwhelmed Marxist theoreticians in Maoist China because they have, in general, failed to understand much of the economic and political reality of China in the twentieth century. The failure of Maoism and its abandonment by the People's Republic immediately following Mao's death is stark testimony of that.

What is perhaps most interesting, for the purposes of the present discussion, is that however much the developmental reforms of Deng Xiaoping share features with those of Sun Yat-sen and Fascism, Deng's political postures have more in common with those of Mussolini's Fascism than anything else. Unlike Sun, Fascists specifically and consistently opposed liberal ideals and democratic institutions. In that clear sense, Fascists distinguished themselves from the followers of Sun Yat-sen.

However long the preliminary periods of military rule and political tutelage might have been that Sun anticipated for revolutionary China in the 1920s, China's non-Marxist revolutionaries always insisted that military rule and political tutelage would ultimately culminate in constitutional governance—in a system substantially like that of the Western industrial democracies. For Sun and his followers, the authoritarianism of the system they would initially impose on revolutionary China was always transitional.

For Fascists, their developmental programs required discipline, commitment, labor, and sacrifice from Italians. But more than that, Fascists refused to entertain the notion that their experiment would ultimately yield to some form of pluralistic and parliamentary democracy. Whatever they ultimately expected, Fascists resisted the re-creation of representative democracy as it is understood in the West. It is in that context that the "thought of Deng Xiaoping" is of interest.

It is clear that Deng has employed many of the central concepts of Sun's *Sanmin zhuyi* in his reforms, but it is just as clear that he has rejected its ultimate democratic aspirations. While there is ample talk of "democratization" in post-Maoist China, it is clear that it is the same kind of "democratization" spoken of by Fascists and Leninists.[91]

Deng has insisted that "we cannot do without dictatorship. We must not only reaffirm the need for it, but exercise it when necessary."[92] Whatever shape the political reforms might take, the "party must lead," Deng has insisted, and the reforms "must not imitate the West, and no liberalization should be allowed."[93] Deng committed himself to absolute domestic political stability, and the unrelieved submission of the Chinese people to the political dominance of the Communist party of China and its policies.[94]

For Deng—as it was for the first Fascists—the "soundness" of a political system is measured in terms of political stability, political unity, and unitary party rule. There is no real institutionalization of protection for individual political and civil rights—no defense of the freedom of association, expression, or choice.[95] There is a specific rejection of any system of political or governmental "checks and balances" or multiparty alternatives that would limit the discretion of the state or its agents. Governance, for Deng, involves proceeding "under unified central leadership"—the leadership of the party.[96]

For Deng, it is the "development of the productive forces"[97] that determines the merits of any political system and, in his judgment, it is political stability, party dominance, and ideological conformity that create the environment in which growth and technological development take place. The entire system seems to require the "ritualized charisma" of a "paramount leader" dominating a single-party state as its capstone.

To satisfy that requirement, Deng was suitably identified as a "giant," a "superman," and a "history-making great man," without whom China could only falter.[98] By the time of his death, the "thought of Deng Xiaoping" had become the "scientific compass that guides the . . . victorious progress of China." Deng, as an inerrant epistemarch, "found a way to build socialism with Chinese characteristics which Mao Zedong had sought, but was unable to find."[99]

In post-Maoist China, a clear effort has been made to routinize and institutionalize charismatic leadership, with the apparent intention of creating a durable vanguard party state. Together with the inculcation of patriotism, self-sacrifice, and obedience, the regime on the Chinese mainland has taken on those criterial features that have always been employed to identify fascist rule everywhere in the world.

Like Mussolini, Deng and his followers seem to imagine a disciplined developmental dictatorship being projected indefinitely into the future. Distinct from Sun Yat-sen, neither Fascists in their time nor followers of Deng Xiaoping in our own anticipated or anticipate a "bourgeois democratic" future for their respective countries.[100] In that sense, "Deng Xiaoping thought" ultimately seems to share more overt political features with Italian Fascism than it does with Sun Yat-sen's *Sanmin zhuyi*.[101]

That Marxist theory seems to have missed all this appears to be the consequence of Marxism's failure to understand very much about revolution in the twentieth century. Marxist theory—conceptually thin and embarrassingly ill-contrived—succeeded in convincing Marxists, and those academics influenced by Marxist theory, that Fascism was nothing more than "reaction," the "tool" of imperialism. Given the confusion, Sun Yat-sen became a "protofascist" and the Kuomintang of Nationalist China "fascist." By the end of the 1960s, both the Soviet Union and Maoism, to each other's Marxist theoreticians, had become fascist as well.

For a long time, scholarship in the West left many convinced that although the term "fascist" can legitimately be applied to almost any person, movement, or regime on the right,[102] it must never be employed when dealing with anything on the left. Prejudgment and distinctions based on pretheoretical categorization have left many without any perspective on the major political and economic developments of our century.

That developmental nationalism has assumed a variety of forms in our century hardly needs affirming. All the revolutionary developmental movements were, and are, different in different ways. All that notwithstanding, what is surprising is how closely they came, in many ways, to resemble each other in the course of time.

How many traits any developmental system must display to qualify as "fascist" is clearly a matter of judgment. For decades, the fact that Fascism acknowledged a citizen's juridical right to own equity and assets was enough to make it "bourgeois" and "right-wing." Now, we face the evident reality that post-Maoist China has allowed substantial citizen rights to private property, the accumulation of personal profit, class distinctions, and "bourgeois property relations." The distinctions between "right-wing" and "left-wing" no longer appear compelling.

Still more important, Soviet theoreticians and Maoists, in their time, dismissed the ownership of property as a distinction of any significance. Both in the Soviet Union and in Mao's People's Republic, Marxist theoreticians agreed that it is not the ownership of property that determines the character of a politicoeconomic system; it is a question of who controls it.

What is clear is that developmental systems change over time. Mussolini's Fascism between 1922 and 1925, initially an emergency regime of a constitutional system, could easily qualify as a traditional authoritarianism. After 1928, Fascism took on the major properties that now identify the class of "fascisms."

Although the system that Mao Zedong imposed on China shared many of the overt features of paradigmatic Fascism, there were still enough differences to make academics loath to consider it a member of the class. In the case of Maoist China, the dissolution of the original system led to the emergence of features it now shares with the reactive developmental nationalisms of the turn of the century.

The charismatic and antidemocratic dispositions of Deng Xiaoping's China, combined with the entire syndrome of traits with which we are now familiar, render it an approximation of classic Fascism. We shall see that post-Maoist China manifests still more of the features of paradigmatic Fascism. It may well qualify for membership in that special subspecies of the class of reactive, developmental nationalisms.

Notes

1. See Ross Terrill, *Madame Mao: The White-Bone Demon* (New York: Simon & Schuster, 1992), pp. 323, 359, 381, 403.

2. Neil Burton and Charles Bettelheim, *China Since Mao* (New York: Monthly Review Press, 1978), pp. 42, 73, 112.

3. Michel Chossudovsky, *Towards Capitalist Restoration? Chinese Socialism After Mao* (New York: St. Martin's, 1986), chap. 11. The works of Bob Avakian make the same claims. See Bob Avakian, *Phony Communism Is Dead . . . Long Live Real Communism!* (Chicago: RCP, 1992); and Avakian, *For a Harvest of Dragons* (Chicago: RCP, 1983).

4. See the discussion in Ruan Ming, *Deng Xiaoping: Chronicle of an Empire* (Boulder: Westview, 1994), pt. 1.

5. See the discussion in Chi Hsin, *The Case of the Gang of Four—With the First Translation of Teng Hsiao-ping's "Three Poisonous Weeds"* (Hong Kong: Cosmos, 1977), chap. 5.

6. Ruan, *Deng Xiaoping*, pp. 94f.

7. The full title of the resolution is *Resolution on Certain Questions in the History of Our Party Since the Founding of the People's Republic of China* (adapted by the Sixth Plenary Session of the eleventh Central Committee of the Communist Party of China on June 27, 1981).

8. See the discussion in Chi Hsin, *Teng Hsiao-ping—A Political Biography* (Hong Kong: Cosmos, 1978), pt. 2.

9. See the discussion in A. James Gregor, *The Fascist Persuasion in Radical Politics* (Princeton: Princeton University Press, 1974), chaps. 1–3.

10. See *Resolution*, pp. 30–34, 44f.

11. Ibid., p. 30.

12. Deng Xiaoping, "On the General Program of Work for the Whole Party and the Whole Nation," in Chi Hsin, *Gang of Four*, p. 221.

13. For a substantial treatment of the issues joined by this question, see Michael Sullivan, "The Ideology of the Chinese Communist Party Since the Third Plenum," in *Chinese Marxism in Flux 1978–84: Essays on Epistemology, Ideology and Political Economy*, ed. Bill Brugger (Armonk, N.Y.: M. E. Sharpe, 1985), pp. 67–97.

14. There is a convenient collection of articles giving expression to Maoist objections to Deng's "theory of the productive forces" in "Criticize Teng and Beat Back the Right Deviationist Wind," in *And Mao Makes Five: Mao Tsetung's Last Great Battle*, ed. Raymond Lotta (Chicago: Banner, 1978), pp. 257–397.

15. In 1993, Bo Yibo, in an interview, said that Deng had "found a way to build socialism with Chinese characteristics which Mao Zedong had sought but

was unable to find." As cited in *Shijie ribao* (World Journal), 9 November 1993, p. A2.

16. See the discussion in Hu Sheng, *Imperialism and Chinese Politics* (Beijing: Foreign Languages, 1955). The Chinese-language edition of Hu's book was first published in 1948. In the text, the publisher affirmed that the "struggle against imperialist aggression and for national independence" constituted the core of the Chinese revolution. The thrust of the revolution was to further "China's progress." The clear implication was that the revolution was committed to the nation's economic growth and industrial development (pp. 3–4).

17. See the collection of Marx's articles (and one article by Friedrich Engels) from the *New York Daily Tribune, 1853–1860* collected in Dona Torr, ed., *Marx on China* (London: Lawrence & Wishart, 1968)—and the discussion in A. James Gregor, *Marxism, China and Development* (New Brunswick, N.J.: Transaction, 1995), chap. 2.

18. See the discussion in Richard Evans, *Deng Xiaoping and the Making of Modern China* (London: Penguin, 1995), pp. 22–24.

19. See the discussion in Mary Backus Rankin, *Early Chinese Revolutionaries: Radical Intellectuals in Shanghai and Chekian, 1902–1911* (Cambridge: Harvard University Press, 1971).

20. David Shambaugh, "Introduction: Assessing Deng Xiaoping's Legacy," in *Deng Xiaoping: Portrait of a Chinese Statesman*, ed. David Shambaugh (New York: Clarendon, 1995), pp. 1f.

21. Ibid., pp. 3, 19.

22. Ibid., p. 76.

23. Ibid., pp. 44f.

24. Ibid., pp. 30–34.

25. Ibid., pp. 30f.

26. The criticism of Mao by Mainland Chinese economists is very extensive; it is conveniently summarized in Gregor, *Marxism*, chaps. 4–5.

27. In the *Resolution*, the "tragedy" of Mao Zedong is identified as his believing that his practice was "Marxist" when, in fact, it was not. See *Resolution*, pp. 41, 44–45. Mao, who was responsible for the Cultural Revolution, was guided by "erroneous theories." See ibid., pp. 41, 49. We are told that "the history of the 'cultural revolution' has proved that Comrade Mao Zedong's principal theses for initiating this revolution conformed neither to Marxism-Leninism nor to Chinese reality" (ibid., p. 33).

28. In 1980, Deng insisted that "modernization" was "at the core" of all of China's revolutionary tasks. Deng, "The Present Situation and the Tasks Before Us," in *Selected Works* (Beijing: Foreign Languages, 1984), 2:65. In the mid–1970s, I argued that the Chinese revolution was essentially nationalist and developmental in character and only Marxist as a consequence of circumstance. See Gregor, *Fascist Persuasion*, chap. 6.

29. In the *Resolution*, Mao was charged with having "an entirely erroneous appraisal of the prevailing class relations and political situation in the Party and state" (*Resolution*, p. 34).

30. Deng, "Mobilize New Recruits and Conduct Political Work Among Them," in *Selected Works*, 1:9, 11.

31. Deng, "The Party and the Anti-Japanese Democratic Government (1941)," in ibid., 1:17; Deng, "A General Account of the Struggle Against the Enemy over the Past Five Years," in ibid., 1:42; Deng, "The Establishment of Base Areas and the Mass Movement (1943)," in ibid., 1:76. Immediately before the Communist seizure of power, Deng was particularly emphatic about suppressing "left errors." See Deng, "The Situation Following Our Triumphant Advance to the Central Plains and Our Future Policies and Strategy (1948)," in ibid., 1:107; "Carry Out the Party Central Committee's Directive on the Work of Land Reform and of Party Consolidation (1948)," in ibid., 1:111, 113–115, 116, 118, 123; "Some Suggestions Concerning Our Entry into New Areas in the Future (1948)," in ibid., 1:131.

32. Deng, "Carry Out," 1:119.

33. Ibid., pp. 119–123.

34. Deng, "Establishment of Base Areas," pp. 75–76.

35. Deng, "The Party and the Anti-Japanese Democratic Government," p. 17.

36. See the entire discussion in Deng, "The Situation," p. 105–109.

37. Deng, "Economic Development," p. 83.

38. Deng, "In Celebration of the Fiftieth Birthday of Comrade Liu Bocheng (1942),"in *Selected Works*, 1:37.

39. See Uli Franz, *Deng Xiaoping* (New York: Harcourt, Brace, Jovanovich, 1988), pp. 235–247.

40. See Deng, "The Situation," "Carry Out," and "Some Suggestions," pp. 107, 111–114, 131.

41. Deng, "Report Delivered at a Conference on the Press in Southwest China," in *Selected Works*, 1:149; see the discussion in "The Situation," pp. 105–109.

42. "Report Delivered at a Conference on the Press in Southwest China," in *Selected Works*, 1:149.

43. See "Economic Development," p. 83; this essay was written in July 1943.

44. See Deng, "The Situation," p. 106.

45. Mao's entire discussion in "On Coalition Government," in *Selected Works* (Beijing: Foreign Languages, 1965), 3:255–320, is replete with Sunist themes. Mao insisted that the Communist Party was "carrying forward" Sun Yat-sen's "revolutionary Three People's Principles" (p. 261). The Communist Party intended to put those principles "into practice" (p. 263). Mao insisted that the views of the Chinese Communist Party were "completely in accord" with those of Sun (p. 280). That Deng expressed similar sentiments is not surprising. What is notable is that Deng apparently remained convinced of the efficacy of Sun's ideas long after Mao abandoned them.

46. Shambaugh, "Introduction: Assessing Deng Xiaoping's Legacy," in Shambaugh, *Deng Xiaoping*, p. 1.

47. See Chao Hua, "Has Absolute Music No Class Character?" *Renmin Ribao* (People's Daily), 14 January 1974, translated in *And Mao Makes Five*, p. 141f.; and "Never Forget the Class Struggle," in *Jiefangjun Bao* (Liberation Army Daily), 4 May 1966, translated in *The Great Socialist Cultural Revolution in China* (Beijing: Foreign Languages, 1966), 1:25.

48. Ibid., p. 76.

49. Ibid., p. 77.

50. Still in dispute is the question of whether Deng entertained any "long held" beliefs about economic theory. There are those who have held that he did not (see Shambaugh, "Deng Xiaoping: The Economist" in Shambaugh, *Deng Xiaoping*). Others have argued that in 1958–1961, his views on economic development underwent "fundamental change" (Evans, *Deng Xiaoping and the Making of Modern China*, p. 163), implying that he did have some views on economic development. What is clear is that by the time he assumed power, he held that "development is the only hard truth" (as cited in Shambaugh, *Deng Xiaoping*, p. 98). In general, whenever he dealt with economic matters, Deng tended to emphasize eclectic and antidoctrinaire approaches. Nonetheless, by the time he wrote "On the General Program of Work for the Whole Party and Whole Nation" in 1975, most of the elements of his subsequent reforms are discernible. The Maoists of the time recognized as much. See the exchange in *Teng Hsiao-ping and the "General Program"* (San Francisco: Red Sun, 1977).

51. These are the features of Deng's reforms that are typically identified as most important by commentators on the Chinese mainland. See Yao Ping, ed., *Xin shiqi Deng Xiaoping zhanlue sixiang yanjiu* (Studies in the strategic thought of Deng Xiaoping during the new era) (Xian: Shaanxi renmin chubanshe, 1989).

52. As a matter of fact the political leaders of Communist China have never demonstrated much theoretical sophistication. It would be hard to argue that Mao Zedong had anything like theoretical competence. See Maria Hsia Chang, "What Is Left of Mao Zedong Thought?" *Issues and Studies* 28, no. 1 (1992).

53. Barry Naughton, "Deng Xiaoping: The Economist," in Shambaugh, *Deng Xiaoping*, p. 83.

54. See Evans, *Deng Xiaoping and the Making of Modern China*, pp. 40–41.

55. It is generally accepted that Deng was never principled in his political pragmatism. It would have been very uncharacteristic of him to fail to follow Mao's directives. There is good evidence to indicate that he supported Mao's unrealistic and ultimately counterproductive Great Leap Forward. Deng admits to the responsibility of not opposing Mao's mistaken policies. Deng, "Replies to the American TV Correspondent Mike Wallace (1986)," in *Selected Works*, 3: 175.

56. Karl Marx and Friedrich Engels, *The German Ideology* (Moscow: Progress, 1964), p. 41.

57. Marx, letter to Annenkov, 28 December 1846, in Karl Marx and Friedrich Engels, *Selected Works* (Moscow: Foreign Languages, 1955), 2:442.

58. Karl Marx, *The Poverty of Philosophy* (Moscow: Foreign Languages, n.d.), p. 122.

59. See Hartfrid Voss's introduction to Friedrich List, *Kraefte und Maechte* (Munich: Wilhelm Langewiesche-Brandt, 1942), pp. 23, 44, 71–78.

60. See the discussion in A. James Gregor, *Marxism, China and Development: Reflections on Theory and Reality* (New Brunswick, N.J.: Transaction, 1995), pp. 134–142.

61. It is sometimes suggested that the theoreticians around Sun were unfamiliar with classical Marxism. That is, in substantial part, untrue. By 1919, some of the most substantial treatments of Marxism, as social and economic theory, are to be found in *Jianshe* (Reconstruction), a journal published by Sun's followers. See Gregor, *Marxism, China and Development*, pp. 194, 204 n. 62.

62. See the discussion in A. James Gregor, *A Survey of Marxism: Problems in Philosophy and the Theory of History* (New York: Random House, 1965), chap. 6.

63. Sun, *International Development*, p. 135.

64. See the discussion in Gregor, *Marxism, China and Development*, chap. 7.

65. See the discussion in ibid., pp. 306, 309–310, 323.

66. See the account in A. James Gregor, *Ideology and Development: Sun Yat-sen and the Economic History of Taiwan* (Berkeley: Institute of East Asian Studies, 1981).

67. As has been argued, it was of little consequence to the leaders of the Chinese Communist Party that some Marxists identified Sun Yat-sen as a "protofascist." For years, well into the 1940s, the Communists of China insisted that their revolution was devoted to Sun's Three Principles of the People. It was within that kind of doctrinal accommodation that Mao Zedong, before the accession of Communism to power, spoke of a "coalition government" that would not only ameliorate class tensions, and protect private property and private profits, but accelerate industrial development as well. See Mao's discussion in "A Comment on the Sessions of the Kuomintang Central Executive Committee and the People's Political Council" and "Coalition Government," in *Selected Works*, 3:147, 261, 280–284; and "The Present Situation and Our Tasks," in ibid., 4:167–169.

Only with his full accession to power did Mao Zedong decide to abandon all of those convictions, reject the advice of his closest collaborators, and follow his own strategies. That was to cost China much in blood and treasure. By the time of his death, Mao had driven the economy of China to the brink of disaster. See the discussion in Gregor, *Marxism, China, and Development*, chaps. 4–5; Peter Lichtenstein, *China at the Brink: The Political Economy of Reform and Retrenchment in the Post-Mao Era* (New York: Praeger, 1991), chap. 2; Henry K. H. Woo, *Effective Reform in China: An Agenda* (New York: Praeger 1991), chap. 2; and George C. Wang, ed., *Economic Reform in the PRC in Which China's Economists Make Known What Went Wrong, Why, and What Should Be Done About It* (Boulder: Westview, 1982).

68. The "thought of Deng Xiaoping" is now identified as "China's precious treasure." Reported in *World Journal*, 17 June 1992, p. A12.

69. Sun Yat-sen, *The Triple Demism of Sun Yat-sen* (1931; reprint, New York: AMS, 1974), p. 424. Reprint of the 1931 Yuchang edition.

70. See the discussion in A. James Gregor, *Phoenix: Fascism in our Time* (New Brunswick, N.J.: Transaction, 1999), chap. 2.

71. Mussolini, "Orientamenti e problemi," in *Opera omnia*, 11:283.

72. Mussolini, "Scoperte," in *Opera omnia*, 11:288.

73. Mussolini, "Orientamenti e problemi," p. 283.

74. Ibid., pp. 283ff.

75. When he announced the change on the masthead of *Il popolo d'Italia*, Mussolini said that to "defend producers signified the recognition that the bourgeoisie must complete its historic function." Mussolini, "Novità," in *Opera omnia*, 11:243. See A. James Gregor, *Young Mussolini and the Intellectual Origins of Fascism* (Berkeley: University of California Press, 1979), p. 219.

76. See A. O. Olivetti's discussion in "L'altra campana," *Pagine libere*, 15 November 1911.

77. Filippo Corridoni, *Sindacalismo e repubblica* (Rome: SAREP, 1945), pp. 19, 23, 25–26. Originally published in 1915.

78. Ibid., p. 4. See the discussion in Paolo Orano, *Lode al mio tempo, 1895–1925* (Bologna: Apollo, 1926) in which he defends *Latinità* from the disdain expressed by northern Europeans.

79. See the discussion in Roberto Michels, *L'imperialismo Italiano* (Rome: Libraria, 1914), p. viii. Michels, himself an early syndicalist, regularly referred to Italy's political, military, and economic subordination to the more advanced industrial powers (see, for example, pp. xii, 3). Michels spoke eloquently of the industrial retardation of the peninsula (pp. 56); he affirmed that "it is industry that allows people to live and prosper" in the modern world (p. 57). He spoke of the disdain with which Italians were treated (e.g., pp. 83–89).

80. Mussolini, "Ancora un discorso," in *Opera omnia*, 11:277.

81. Mussolini, "Il mio collaudo sullo 'SVA'," in *Opera omnia*, 11:171.

82. See *World Journal*, 23 August 1994, p. A10.

83. See the editorial comment in ibid, 22 August 1994, p. A2.

84. For a discussion of these issues, see Gregor, *Fascist Persuasion*, chaps. 1–3.

85. Mussolini, "Atto di nascita del fascismo," in *Opera omnia*, 12:323.

86. See, for example, Mussolini, "Il fascismo e i problemi della political estera Italiana," in *Opera omnia*, 16:158–159; and "Discorso di Verona," in ibid., p. 335.

87. See Mussolini's discussion at the end of his life in *Testamento politico di Mussolini* (Rome: Tosi, 1948).

88. Ross Terrill, *Madame Mao: The White-Boned Demon* (New York: Simon & Schuster, 1992), pp. 359, 381, 403.

89. See "Reversing Correct Verdicts Goes Against the Will of the People," *Peking Review* 11 (March 1976); and Zhou Enlai, *Report to the Tenth National Congress of the Communist Party of China* (Beijing: Foreign Languages, 1973), both reproduced in Lotta, *And Mao Makes Five*, pp. 85, 263.

90. See Cheng Yueh, "A General Program for Capitalist Restoration," *Hongqi* 4 (1976), cited in Lotta, *And Mao Makes Five*, pp. 281–286.

91. Fascists recognized their kinship with Stalinism in this regard. They pointed to the "radically antidemocratic" orientation of Josef Stalin as evidence of the transformation of Marxism-Leninism into a variant of Fascism. Felice Chilanti, "Stalin contro la democrazia," *Gerarchia* 19, no. 10 (1939): 692–693.

92. Deng Xiaoping, "Take a Clear-cut Stand Against Bourgeois Liberalization," in *Selected Works (1982–1992)* (Beijing: Foreign Languages, 1994), pp. 195f.

93. "On Reform of the Political Structure," in ibid., p. 179.

94. See Deng, "We Must Carry Out Socialist Construction in an Orderly Way Under the Leadership of the Party," in ibid., pp. 210–212.

95. Although all of these rights are stipulated in the Constitution of 1983, they are qualified by the "interests" and "protection" of the state. Deng's China has a long history of infraction of its own criminal procedure codes. See, for example, John F. Copper, Franz Michael, and Yuan-li Wu, *Human Rights in Post-Mao China* (Boulder: Westview, 1985); and Ta-ling Lee and John F. Copper, *The Bamboo Gulag: Human Rights in the People's Republic of China, 1991–1992* (Baltimore: University of Maryland School of Law, 1994).

96. Deng, "The Central Leadership Must Have Authority," in ibid., p. 272.

97. Deng, "How to Judge the Soundness of a Country's Political System," in ibid., p. 213.

98. See Sheila Tefft, "From 'Little Red Book' to 'Thought of Deng'–China's New Personality Cult," *Christian Science Monitor*, 22 October 1992, p. 1.

99. See the editorial in *World Journal*, 22 August 1994, p. A2.

100. See the discussion provided by Sun in *Triple Demism*, pt. 2.

101. In this context, Deng has been identified as an advocate of a "New Authoritarianism" that leaves no room for Western democracy. See Ruan, *Deng Xiaoping*, chap. 12.

102. See the amusing collection in Claudio Quarantotto, *Tutti fascisti!* (Rome: Il Borghese, 1976).

7

The New Nationalism of
Post-Maoist China

There has never really been any serious doubt that nationalism, as a state-building sentiment, served as a major informing factor in the revolutionary ideology of the Chinese Communist party. Together with an emphasis on martial spirit and voluntarism, Mao Zedong himself made a "vigorous nationalism" an unmistakable element in all his revolutionary invocations.[1] No less than Mao, Deng Xiaoping, throughout his life, was inspired by a reactive nationalism that typified the mentality of almost all Chinese revolutionaries after the antidynastic revolution of 1911–1912.

The urgent nationalism that inspired the sacrifice of countless Chinese in the years after Mao's accession to power was larded with obligatory, if opaque, Marxist notions, and it seems to have been only dimly perceived by many in the West. Mao, almost completely incapable of dealing with theoretical concepts with any sophistication, buried his evident nationalism in cognitively meaningless Marxist expressions.

Specialists have acknowledged that "from 1920 to 1926, during his initial Marxist period, Mao was not familiar with Marxist theory." In his formative years, "from 1927 to 1935, Mao seemed even less interested in Marxist theory than before." Between 1935 and 1949, he was almost entirely preoccupied with revolutionary activity and, as a consequence, "not much interested in [Marxist] theory."[2] In effect, Mao was never seriously interested in anything that might credibly be identified as "theory," Marxist or otherwise. As a consequence, we find in his prose and his discourses very little of theoretical interest, much less any account of nationalism, that is in any sense memorable.[3]

Because he had early chosen, for whatever reason, to identify himself as a "Marxist," Mao pretended to employ its "dialectic" in order to formulate, and justify, his policies. What he did, in fact, was press ill-defined and remarkably confused notions that he had borrowed from Soviet theoreticians and Western revolutionaries into service—to no one's cognitive advantage. He used them to give the color of theory to his entirely tactical revolutionary postures.[4] "Mao," we are told, "awaited no theory: he made a revolution, knocking together a rationale as he proceeded, borrowing on the cultural flotsam of the Chinese and Western intelligentsia." As a consequence, "Marx was turned on his head."

Thus, for the Marxist notion of the "self-emancipation of the majority, [Maoism] substituted a romantic conception of socialism, incapable of realization except through its contradiction, a bureaucratic nationalist State."[5] For all his putative Marxism, the nationalist state became the capstone of the Maoist system.

Mao's revolutionary goals clearly included the re-creation of the Chinese nation-state. Like the revolutionaries of the late nineteenth and early twentieth centuries, Mao sought China's redemption. He sought the resurrection of the state that had fallen before the imperialists of the nineteenth century. He sought to accomplish his goals inspired by a nationalism that was confused and confusing.

Without the benefit of theory, Mao Zedong made revolution. In the making, there was precious little Marxism. Gone was any serious notion of proletarian revolution. Gone was the expectation of anarcho-syndicalist rule and a consequent "withering away of the postrevolutionary state" that classical Marxism had identified with the "leap from necessity to freedom." Gone was the sophistication of Marxist theory. What remained was irrepressible, if poorly expressed, nationalist sentiment.

Throughout the revolutionary years, there was scant Marxism to be found in the workings of Mao. In fact, there was little Marxism in the thought of the founders of Chinese Marxism. What Marxism existed was composed of a mixture of romanticism, voluntarism, idealism, and nationalism.[6] It was the sort of thing one would expect in an environment of reactive nationalism.

The founders and the leading members of the party being overwhelmingly drawn from the "respectable classes" rather than the peasants and illiterate workers of retrograde China, reactive nationalism found expression in the revolutionary posturing of the party.

Throughout much of the time before 1949, for example, Mao took care to avoid "radicalism." He regularly counseled his followers that "this is not the time for a thorough agrarian revolution." It was his intention not to "accentuate the anticapitalist struggle" but to convince workers to "cooperate with the capitalists, so that maximum production [could] be attained."

Beyond the tactical preoccupations of making revolution, national economic growth and industrial sophistication seems to have been central to Mao's policies. To that purpose, as a case in point, he was prepared to "welcome foreign investments, if such are beneficial to China's economy ... [We] shall be able," he went on, "to absorb vast amounts of foreign investments."[7] The real task, Mao insisted, was to secure the cooperation of workers and capitalists in order "to do everything possible to reduce costs [and] increase output."[8] Mao was repeating the nationalistic and developmental programmatic injunctions of Sun Yat-sen.

All that was deflected by the struggle against the Japanese invader through the years from about 1935 until the end of the Second World War. The subsequent civil war, which occupied the Chinese Communist party until 1949, further delayed the singularly non-Marxist developmental program that had been both explicit and implicit in Maoism.

During all those years, from the early 1930s until 1949, however much the Chinese Communist party was involved in resistance to Japan and the Kuomintang, Mao continued to insist that the real "task of the Chinese working class is to struggle ... for China's industrialization and the modernization of her agriculture." In the last analysis, the purpose was not to make proletarian revolution but to render the nation strong and independent. That could be accomplished only through economic growth and industrialization. Given the character of its policies, what was eminently clear was that the program of the Chinese Communist party was primarily a struggle for nationalism and development—a "struggle for Dr. Sun's ... Three People's Principles."[9]

Until the military success of his revolution in 1949, Mao's sustaining ideology had very little, if anything, to do with Marxism, however Marxism was understood. His belief system was essentially that of Sun Yat-sen—two of whose fundamental "principles" were *reactive nationalism* and *rapid economic growth and industrialization*. Clearly, for Mao, an inarticulate and inchoate nationalism remained the inspiration for revolution. Whatever else it was, nationalism, for Mao, was "revolutionary." It was to be employed to "oppose imperialism," which was the enemy of China's future.[10] Only insofar as capitalism was identified with imperialism was it the enemy of the Chinese revolution. During the years of revolutionary struggle, Mao had consistently argued that domestic capitalism was not the enemy of the Chinese nation—unless Chinese capitalists chose to "collaborate" with the foreign enemy.

Moreover, since nationalism provided the inspiration for rapid economic growth and industrialization, capitalists who were "patriotic" served the nation well by assuring China its ultimate sovereignty and independence. That was the legacy Deng Xiaoping sought to subsequently defend against the growing Maoist "leftism" of the 1960s and 1970s.

As we have seen, Deng's identification as a "capitalist roader" by Madame Mao and the Maoists of the Chinese Communist party during the catastrophic years of the Great Proletarian Revolution turned on his

defense of Mao's pre-1949 policies. The Resolution of 1981, in which Mao
was identified with the "leftist errors" that had brought China to the brink
of disintegration by the mid-1970s, sought to reaffirm Sun's nationalist
Three Principles of the People as the ideology of revolutionary China.

Although that was the unmistakable reality, the political fact was that
to defend the continuity and legitimacy of rule by the Chinese Communist party, Deng concealed what was essentially Sun's Three Principles of
the People behind a pretense of "Marxism-Leninism Mao Zedong
thought." In fact, there is very little in the ideology of post-Maoist China
that might qualify as "Marxist-Leninist" and still less that could count,
independently, as the thought of Mao Zedong.

By the mid-1980s, what passed as "Marxism" was Deng Xiaoping's unqualified commitment to the "development of the productive forces"
rather than "class struggle" or "proletarian internationalism."[11] Deng
mobilized all the support he could against the "leftism" of the Maoist period. He was particularly emphatic about the rejection of the class struggle as a "key feature" of "socialism." Deng held that internal strife threatened the political and social stability essential to rapid economic growth.

By the mid-1980s, Deng proceeded to stipulatively define "socialism
. . . in terms," he admitted, that had "never [been] used by the founders
of Marxism-Leninism." It was defined, in what Deng acknowledged
were "heretical terms,"[12] as the alleviation of China's poverty and the
rectification of its economic backwardness. That tied the Communist
party of China to a program of accelerated development of the material
productive forces. That, Deng argued, required the massive influx of foreign investment, the introduction of foreign managerial expertise and
technology, and the opening of special economic zones and coastal cities
to the flow of foreign, essentially capitalist, exchanges.[13]

Deng made it clear that during the process China would not only tol-
erate differential income in terms of class and region but would welcome
material incentives to ensure enterprise and commitment. Although it
was clear to Deng that "socialism means common prosperity, not polar-
ization of income,"[14] he was prepared to grant that the "heretical socialism" he advocated would witness "some regions and some people" pros-
pering before others,[15] reconstituting sectional and class differences that
the "socialist revolution" of Mao Zedung had presumably abolished.

It is abundantly clear that the post-Maoist "heretical socialist ideas" of
Deng Xiaoping were largely derivative. They were to be found in the
non-Marxist programmatic legacies left to revolutionary China by Sun
Yat-sen.[16]

Sun's cardinal incentive, the restoration of China to its proper place in
the world, was nationalistic. Neither "proletarianism" nor "world revolution" supplied the normative energy for Sun's revolution. Redemptive

nationalism provided that. It is evident that no less can be said of the new nationalism that supplies both the belief system and its legitimation for Deng Xiaoping's post-Maoist China.

The New Nationalism of Deng Xiaoping

What seems clear, in retrospect, is that "Chinese Communism," without the collateral support of Soviet socialism, the theoretical integrity of classical Marxism, and its "dialectical development" at the hands of V. I. Lenin and Josef Stalin, was left "ideologically bereft" with the death of Mao Zedong.[17] Whatever his ideological confusion, Mao had sustained the system with his charismatic authority. With his passing, China's Communism enjoyed little coherence and still less legitimacy.

There is no doubt that Deng was aware of that circumstance. True to the developmental and reactive nationalism that had always been his inspiration, Deng had been instrumental in deflating "Maoism." The immediate consequence was Deng's recourse to a "visceral nationalism" as the grounds for justifying the Chinese Communist party's "holding on to power" in the absence of the "inerrant" thought of Mao Zedong.[18]

For Deng Xiaoping, only a socialism "that helps to constantly develop the productive forces"[19] could be a socialism that was meaningful for retrograde China —and only the Communist party could assure the political stability that would provide the environment in which the productive forces could develop.[20]

In September 1994, the Propaganda Department of the Chinese Communist party issued an instructional manual, "Fundamental Principles on Implementing a Patriotic Education,"[21] intended to instill in the citizens of the People's Republic a commitment to a defense of the motherland. It was followed by a volume, *Selected Works for Instruction in Patriotic Education,* that contained the expression of nationalist sentiments by Mao Zedong, Deng Xiaoping, and Jiang Zemin. It was intended to "fill the ideological vacuum" that typified the belief system of China's 800 million peasants after the close of the Maoist epoch.[22]

More than a generation ago, David Apter anticipated that "weakness in solidarity and identity" in socialist systems, under some set of circumstances, might very well "result in political leaders turning toward greater nationalism" in the effort to sustain legitimacy and ensure collective cooperation.[23] For Deng Xiaoping, the crisis that followed the death of Mao produced just such circumstances. He made ready recourse to the reactive and developmental nationalism that had always been at the center of his revolutionary belief system.

By the early 1990s, publications in the People's Republic were perfectly clear on the role nationalism was to play in the future of revolutionary

China. By that time, Premier Li Peng had issued national guidelines in order to enhance what was identified as the "patriotic education" of China's youth.[24] The nation's youth was to be inculcated with sentiments that would identify the Communist party with Chinese nationalism[25]— and all citizens were enjoined to strengthen their patriotism.[26]

In November 1995, when the *People's Daily* announced the publication of the book intended to teach China's 800 million peasants to love their country, Jiang Zemin reminded his audience of the humiliation China had suffered at the hands of foreigners.[27] In the course of a century after the First Opium War, Jiang continued, China had suffered a series of indignities that had humbled the nation that had not long before been the "center of the universe." Only a studied union of all citizens, infused with a "consciousness of national defense" (*guofang yishi*) and an abiding nationalism might assure the independence and integrity, as well as restore the dignity and the historic place, of that nation—the ancestral homeland of all Chinese.[28]

In all of this, "class consciousness" and the international revolution of the proletariat plays no role whatsoever. The continuing revolution has to do with China's place in the modern world—its sovereignty, its security, and the respect it is accorded by the international community. It has to do with the redemption of the nation and the identification of its citizens with that redemption.

As well as being reactive, redemptive, and developmental, the nationalism of post-Maoist China is identified with the political state. It is spoken of as "state nationalism" (*guojia minzu zhuyi*)[29]—a form of nationalism that is given expression by the state.[30] It is *ideocratic*, animated by a conviction of its own ideological inerrancy.[31] For Deng Xiaoping, post-Maoist China drew its necessary substance from its ideology and its "patriotism."[32]

What emerges from all of this is a standard form of reactive and developmental nationalism familiar to the twentieth century. It is the nationalism that found expression in the thought of, among others, Sun Yat-sen and the Nationalists of Italy at the turn of the century—a nationalism that became the sustaining core of Fascism and echoes on in the ideologies of less-developed countries throughout our time.

Patterns of Reactive and Developmental Nationalism

Reactive nationalism is apparently so intense a sentiment that it finds expression, where it appears, in a recurrent pattern. Its advocates speak of nationalism as arising out of a "natural" and/or "primordial" generic "group consciousness" that is common to all sentient creatures.[33] They see primitive evidences of group-building behaviors, similar to nationalism, in the exclusive territoriality and endogamous breeding practices of all sorts of animals.[34]

In commencing his discussion on "nationalism," for example, Sun Yatsen spoke of nationalism as a natural sentiment akin to the spontaneous reverence the Chinese show for family ties and ancestral lineage. Ingroup sentiment "naturally" draws persons to associations of restricted size, clans, extended families, and politically defined communities. Within such communities they are disposed to amity, mutual aid, and sacrifice in the service of their compatriots. They are enhanced by the success of their community, and they suffer in its failures.[35]

Sun understood all of that to be "primary" and recognized that persons, over evolutionary time, identified with different communities of different size and character, among which the nation-state was only one—if, in the nineteenth and twentieth centuries, the most important.

Thus it was important for Sun to explain the absence of "nationalist spirit" among the Chinese.[36] If persons, by nature, are disposed to identify with others on the basis of biological, linguistic, and religious affinities, together with "habits and customs,"[37] then Sun had to explain the failure of his conationals to unite, labor, and sacrifice in the defense of the motherland[38] when it was faced by the "political and economic oppression" of foreign imperialism.[39]

Sun argued that nationalism was a common expression of group affinity among the Chinese, just as it was for all peoples. Its loss or abatement, he argued, was a consequence of China's peculiar history. Sun maintained that the Chinese would be expected to share, with all other peoples of the world, national feeling as a common sentiment.[40] He explained the absence of that common sentiment at the beginning of the twentieth century in several ways. In the first instance, Sun argued that China, one of the world's greatest empires, had crafted for itself a rationale for imperial expansion that was to influence the national consciousness of the Chinese.

That rationale, provided by intellectuals in the service of China's successive dynasties, sought to vindicate each regime's right to rule, as well as its rationale for expansion. Each dynasty expected the intellectuals, as a political stratum, to provide for the legitimation of the regime and its foreign policies.

Once dynastic China proceeded to conquer the lands on its periphery, narrow nationalism no longer provided the rationale for the expanded system. Some form of "culturalism" was invoked in the effort to legitimate a system that sought to absorb and assimilate "barbarians." China's intelligentsia argued that it was "culture," rather than conquest, that the dynasties were bringing to the non-Chinese peoples of Northeast and

Southeast Asia. Chinese culture was considered universal, an objectively "true" (as distinct from a "barbarian") vision of the world.

"Culturalists" argued that it was neither race nor religion nor territory with which the Chinese were to identify, but Chinese culture—and that culture could be adopted by anyone of whatever provenance. Chinese culture, in effect, was understood to transcend nationality. As dynastic China expanded, it extended its culture; and it was Chinese culture, not the Chinese race or the territory of China, that was to be defended.

Sun argued that "culturalism" resulted in a form of cosmopolitanism that was intrinsically antinational. It weakened Chinese nationalism and the instinct of survival of the Chinese people. It exposed China to the aggression of foreigners because the Chinese were not expected to resist—as long as their "culture" survived.

The conquest of the nation by northern invaders in the sixteenth and seventeenth centuries was one of the results of the enfeeblement of Chinese resistance to foreign aggression. With their victory, the Manchus did precisely what conquerors have always sought to do: They systematically suppressed the common sentiment of nationhood among those they had defeated. Only among those Chinese who had somehow escaped their antinational indoctrination had the sentiment of nationalism survived.

Sun maintained that among the secret societies, the outcasts and the poor of post-Ming China, nationalism had survived. As marginal persons, they had escaped the ministrations of their "superiors." They remained true to their national heritage. Those were the elements among whom Sun made his first appeals.

For Sun, cosmopolitanism and the antinationalism of alien conquerors had succeeded in weakening China even before the first imperialist incursions of the early nineteenth century.[41] Nationalism, systematically opposed by the Manchu rulers of China and undermined by the culturalism of the intellectuals, had languished—and China was overrun by foreigners. "The result," Sun concluded, was "that every corner of China [had] become a colony of the Great Powers. . . . We are slaves not only to one country, but to all the countries."[42] The Chinese were a humiliated people.

Redemption, Sun insisted, could come only by rekindling the natural sentiment of nationalism among the Chinese people. As a consequence, *nationalism* became the first of Sun's three revolutionary principles. Like many reactive nationalisms, it would be a nationalism firmly rooted in biological continuity. For Sun, the Chinese were to identify themselves, from hoary antiquity to the modern age, with an unbroken bloodline. He was to consistently maintain that China was the historic product of "one sole race [that] developed into one single nation."[43]

Clearly, Sun was convinced that China, reduced to the station of "the poorest and the weakest nation of the world,"[44] could redeem itself only by having its population inextricably identify itself with a biological community, a "natio-race," from which members could not escape and with which their destinies were forever associated.

In order to ensure infrangible commitment and a disposition to sacrifice for the national community, reactive nationalists often attempt to identify members of the national community with permanent, inescapable affinities. In the context of such an imperative, "blood" and race immediately recommend themselves. One can hardly escape one's ancestral inheritance. If one's "destiny" is unalterably associated with one's biological community, self-interest would drive one to labor and sacrifice in its service. Biological continuity serves as an instrument in forging a united nation.

Thus, the reactive nationalists of Italy at the turn of the twentieth century made essentially the same arguments found in Sun's *Sanmin zhuyi*. Italy was the purported victim of the advanced industrial powers. It was said to be an economic and cultural colony of those nations that had preceded it on the course of economic growth and industrial sophistication.

Italians had been rendered passive, "cosmopolitan," by foreign conquest and by the philosophical universalism of the Roman Empire and the religious universalism of the Catholic Church. Italians had been conditioned by the "culturalism" of universal belief systems that rendered nationality of little account. Those influences had reduced resistance to foreign oppression to negligible measure. Because of those induced infirmities, Italy was to become the booty of German "barbarians," Arabs, and Bourbons alike and, ultimately, in modern times, to be exploited by the industrialized "demoplutocracies" of northern Europe and North America.

The rationale, surprisingly similar to that of Sun, motivated Italian reactive nationalists to attempt to restore, among their conationals, the sense of commitment necessary for the salvation of the nation. By the turn of the twentieth century, Italy's reactive nationalists began to speak of the sentiment of nationalism as a "primordial" impulse, natural to group life. They began to refer to the biological continuity of the "Italian race."

The history of the "race" was reconstructed, beginning with the emergence of Rome, through the time of the caesars to the reunification of the Italic peninsula in the nineteenth century.[45] All of that passed into Mussolini's Fascism, and nationalism became intrinsically associated with some form of biological continuity. There was increasing reference to the biologically related "family" of 40 million Italians who constituted a modern "race" of "blood-related" conationals. As early as 1921, Mussolini spoke of the Italian people as a biologically related family, united in race and "blood,"[46] dedicated to resistance against the impostures of foreign plutocracies.

What seems clear is that there is a relatively common disposition among reactive nationalists to attempt to elicit community commitment on the part of their conationals by tying that commitment to some permanent and unalterable association. Affinities of "blood" and "race" seem to recommend themselves.

In such contexts, neither "blood" nor "race" carry the malefic connotations with which they are now regularly associated. For most reactive nationalists—certainly for Chinese and Italian reactive nationalists—"blood" and "race" were dynamic concepts, having very little to do, for example, with the invidious anthropological racism of National Socialist Germany.[47]

For reactive nationalists, "race" is often defined as a historic "breeding circle," in which reproductive populations are isolated for extended periods, sustained by in-group attraction and out-group diffidence. Reactive nationalists tend to argue that such "breeding circles," over time, correspond, in significant measure, to historic nations. They conceive such political entities as historic "natio-races"—peoples who share, to some degree or another, anthropological features. "Natio-races" are considered incipient anthropological races in one or another dynamic stage of formation.[48]

It would seem that reactive nationalists seek to involve entire populations in a permanent affiliation with the historic nation. The permanence of the affiliation tends to ensure the commitment of persons to the survival of the nation, and its prevalence in the modern world. The identification of persons with a real or fancied biological community sustains the sacrificial commitment to the historic nation as it resists the impostures of foreigners.

The evidence of the twentieth century suggests that reactive nationalists, more often than one might expect, fall back on biology in the effort to ensure permanent commitment on the part of populations they seek to mobilize.[49] Biology offers the permanence unavailable in subjective political beliefs.

Thus, when Chiang Kai-shek offered his *China's Destiny* in 1943 as the rationale for Chinese nationalism, he insisted on the conviction that "the Chinese nation" was of "one stock." As a reactive nationalist, and the political heir of Sun Yat-sen, Chiang insisted that the Chinese "all belong to the same blood stream"[50]—all inescapably members of the same community of destiny.

When Chen Boda, spokesman for Chinese Communism at that time, sought to critically assess the views of Chiang, he identified the notion that the Chinese were all of "the same blood" as a "fascist" conviction.[51]

Nationality, for traditional Marxism, was a function of "bourgeois" interests, having little to do with biology. That the theoreticians of the Kuomintang sought to associate the Chinese nation with the continuities of biology and race was immediately identified with "fascism."[52]

The fact is that reactive nationalists, with Fascists as a subset of the class, often associate nationality with biological continuities. At their best, the theoreticians of reactive nationalism conceive the nation as a restricted breeding community out of which, over time, a new anthropologically distinct race emerges. Sun Yat-sen, for example, speaks of a new race that emerges from the assimilation of foreign elements.[53] Fascist theoreticians argued the same thesis.

For reactive nationalists, the nation is often a "race-cradle," protected and cultivated by the state.[54] In the final analysis, nationalism, biology, and statism become all of a piece. They become an indissoluble union of material interest, sensibility, and commitment. Developmentalism becomes one of its expressions. The development of the community's economic base becomes essential to the provision of the weapons systems necessary for national defense.

The informal logic of such systems is transparent. The features shared by Sun's Three Principles of the People and the exacerbated nationalism of Italian Fascism emerge from that very logic. If the post-Maoist nationalism of Deng Xiaoping and Jiang Zemin belong to the same order of reactive nationalism that finds expression in the thought of Sun Yat-sen and Fascism, one would expect similar features to characterize it as well.

Biology and China's Post-Maoist Reactive Nationalism

With the transformation of Chinese Communism into an unqualified form of reactive nationalism, one has every reason to expect some variant of "biologism" to make its appearance in the rationale provided to legitimate the system. In fact, whatever the judgment of some Western scholars,[55] an unmistakable form of biological nationalism has made its appearance in the post-Maoist People's Republic of China.[56]

By the early 1990s, the intellectuals of the People's Republic of China, receiving government sanction, had chosen to identify Chinese nationality with the continuities of "blood" and "race" rather than culture.[57] However much the official spokespersons of Beijing avoid reference to biology and race, it has become evident that the contemporary nationalism of Communist China has "strong racial overtones."[58]

Since the mid-1980s, for example, the cult of the Yellow Emperor, Huang Di, has been officially endorsed by the leadership of the Chinese Communist party.[59] All Chinese, it is currently maintained, "are proud ... descendants of the Yellow Emperor."[60] Communist China is appar-

ently constructing its own biological "myth of descent" that can serve as
the instrument of a modernizing, reactive nationalist state.[61]

In 1994, Hsieh Shih-chung reminded his readers that in the 1930s and
1940s Chiang Kai-shek had insisted that all Chinese—if they were to defend the nation against the imperialism of the advanced industrial countries—must identify themselves with descent from the Yellow Emperor.[62]
Chiang invoked the sentiment of biological descent to foster and sustain
the sense of community in the course of a particularly arduous political
and developmental program.

In the mid-1980s, Deng Xiaoping urged the Chinese of Taiwan to acknowledge their descent from the Yellow Emperor and, as a consequence, seek the reunification of all Chinese in the Chinese nation. The
principle is that "all ethnic Chinese are supposed to be biologically attached to the Chinese state through their descent from the Yellow Emperor and the Chinese state, in turn, takes cognizance of the bond among
ethnic Chinese created by that common descent."[63] In effect, like Chiang
Kai-shek, Deng Xiaoping would have the commonality of biological inheritance serve political purpose.

The argument pretends that the bonds of common descent create a
common adherence to the prevailing political regime. The biological continuity of the Chinese is imagined to provide the rationale for "patriotic"
commitment. When Sun Yat-sen and Chiang Kai-shek advanced their arguments,[64] Marxists, domestic and foreign, did not hesitate to identify
those arguments as "protofascist" or "fascist." No one has yet similarly
chosen to identify the political character of the arguments of Deng.

Contemporary anthropologists in Communist China now assiduously
search for a common biological origin for all Chinese. They argue, for instance, in favor of an approach to human evolution that rejects the notion
that all modern humans originated in Africa. They maintain, instead, that
the Chinese evolved within what are now the borders of modern
China—on the Qinghai-Tibetan plateau, or in Guizhou province.[65] The
official anthropologists of the Beijing government maintain that the modern Chinese are considered to have an autonomous origin—within the
borders of their own nation.

According to Beijing, "Chinese civilization" appeared within the territorial confines of contemporary China with the first humans—and has
persisted in that same geographical area with descendants of that same
people to this day.[66] All Chinese are thus considered united in culture,
blood, descent, and common territory.

Today, Chinese anthropologists argue that the "Chinese nation" already existed *in potentia* during the Pliocene and lower Pleistocene eras,
more that a million years ago.[67] That insight is instrumental in propagat-
ing "concepts of the long history, splendid cultural traditions, continuity

and integration of the country"[68] so essential to reactive and developmental nationalism.

In effect, archaeology in contemporary China serves as a tool for the enhancement of nationalist sentiment. Research is conducted with an eye to "the relationships between archaeological resources and their sociopolitical implication for China's current milieu."[69] All that is not unique in the annals of the century's reactive nationalist regimes. We have illustrated elements of such a development in the doctrines of Sun Yat-sen. Similarly, archaeology, genetics, and evolutionary studies in Fascist Italy displayed some of the very same features. Under Fascist rule, the biological sciences were consumed with a preoccupation to support the reactive nationalism of the system. During the Fascist period some of the most responsible Italian population geneticists and physical anthropologists sought to provide evidence of the biological continuity of the "Italian race"—the "morphological" and genetic continuity of a timeless Italian nation.[70]

For most reactive nationalists, "race," however it was construed, was a function of nationalism.[71] Anthropological race was considered the end product of long assimilation and protracted inbreeding. Varying degrees of phenotypic variability only served to indicate that a "new race" had not yet fully emerged. More important was the fact that shared history, shared culture, and shared reproductive interaction generated a sense of amity and mutual regard that sustained collective purpose and, in circumstances of threat, generated a willingness to sacrifice that contributed to the survival of the community.

This search for a biological foundation for the nation, what Western commentators call a "myth of descent," seems to typify reactive and developmental nationalism in the twentieth century—and it has come to characterize the reactive nationalism of post-Maoist China. The "left-wing" posturing of Mao Zedong, together with all the pretenses of "Marxism-Leninism," have all been swept away in the frank reactive nationalism and the biological anthropologisms of Deng Xiaoping and Jiang Zemin.

Post-Maoist China has clearly traversed the distance between "Marxism-Leninism" and the presumably "right-wing" developmental nationalism that have come to typify revolution in the twentieth century. The abandonment of "Marxism-Leninism Mao Zedong thought" has been all but absolute.

Classifying the New Nationalism of Post-Maoist China

By the end of the last decade of the twentieth century, political historians found themselves embroiled in great confusion. It had become impossible to categorize the system that had emerged out of the wreckage of what had been Maoist China. By that time, it was totally implausible to identify it as a "Marxist" regime. Other than its sometime vocabulary, there was nothing Marxist about it.

Its overt properties had become well-known. Post-Maoist China was an antiliberal, one-party, ideocratic state that arose in a relatively primitive economic environment. Ruled by self-selected leaders and cloaked in ritualized charisma, the system was fundamentally undemocratic. Its economy, composed of a reasonably discrete hierarchy of classes and influenced on the margins by personal profit and the market exchange of goods, was dominated by an elitist and interventionist state. State influence took on many forms, from the state control of national credit and finance to indicative central planning of the entire economy.

The ebb and flow of information was almost entirely controlled by the state, and dissenters were subject to a variety of administrative sanctions, ranging from "reeducation" to penal servitude. The nation's security forces served at the political behest of the single party. The single party itself was an elite organization, with its members committed to faith in the system and obedience to its leaders. The entire psychology of the single party, and the revolution it fostered and sustained, was redemptive, animated by a passion to redress the humiliations suffered by the nation for almost a century at the hands of the major industrialized nations.

To accomplish the nation's redemption, the revolutionary single party embarked on a program of accelerated economic growth and industrialization. Agrarian and industrial workers were mobilized to serve at relatively low wages in a state-managed program of capital accumulation that was to be employed in the systematic creation and expansion of an education, communications, and transportation infrastructure.

There were clearly residual traces of totalitarianism in the system, but the introduction of elements of a discretionary market and the qualified permission to own, and profit, from the ownership of property relaxed some of the rigidities that had earlier given the dictatorship its distinctive identity. Some political taxonomists choose to refer to the altered incarnation of the post-Maoist system as an "administered society" or something similar.

At such a level of abstraction, post-Maoist China might qualify as any one of a number of reactive and developmental nationalisms common to the twentieth century. The features it shares with the doctrines and the programmatic intentions of Sun Yat-sen's Kuomintang are obvious. More than that, however, are the differences that distinguish the doctrines and political goals of post-Maoist China from those of Sun Yat-sen or the Kuomintang.

The commitment on the part of the leadership of post-Maoist China to political dictatorship clearly distinguishes the regime of Jiang Zemin and his entourage from anything identified with Sun's *Sanmin zhuyi*. However long martial rule and political tutelage lasted in republican China or on Taiwan—to deny the Chinese people representative democratic rule—Sun's unqualified commitment to ultimate democratic rule distinguished his ideology from that of the Chinese Communist party.

Representative democracy, as an aspiration, was forever a component of the political culture left to China by Sun Yat-sen. Even when political controls were most onerous, the doctrines left by Sun to the people of republican China and Taiwan held out the promise of democracy. Sun Yat-sen's political ideal was a representative democracy very much like that of the United States and some of the more advanced states of Europe. Sun spoke of a strong government of separated executive, judicial, and legislative powers, supported by collateral powers of impeachment and examination. He spoke of universal suffrage and popular referenda. He advocated legislation by popular initiative and the recall of those political leaders found to be objectionable.[72]

Sun acknowledged that the tasks to be faced by a less-developed nation in an environment of Darwinian struggle would be demanding—and, on those occasions, he spoke of the need for an "all-powerful" government. It is clear, for example, that Sun favored an interventionist state that would control entire sectors of the developing national economy. Equally clear was the special role he anticipated for the revolutionary party. For Sun, the revolutionary party was charged with the responsibility of building the revolutionary, developmental state. It was on those occasions that Sun spoke, with evident admiration, of the new Soviet government of V. I. Lenin.[73]

All of this must be understood within the context of an anticipated reactive and developmental regime. As we have seen, Sun considered Lenin's government at the time of the New Economic Policy to be a developmental regime, like his own, having literally nothing to do with Marxism, class struggle, proletarian revolution, or internationalism.[74] As has been argued, Sun consistently held that Marxism was a system designed to resolve the problems of advanced industrial economies—not those of less-developed nations attempting to achieve a respected place in the universe of modern states.

Whatever Sun's conception of a reactive, developmental, and initially authoritarian regime, his ultimate commitment was to popular sovereignty. In the last analysis, he maintained that "self-government is the foundation rock of a country."[75] He insisted that whatever the political concessions to exigency, the government of a redeemed China must ultimately be democratic. In that sense, the regime Deng Xiaoping left to his political heirs differs fundamentally from the essentially democratic regime that has established itself, in Sun's name, on Taiwan.[76]

Among the "Four Cardinal Principles" left by Deng Xiaoping as the most essential "pillars" of the mainland regime are "the democratic dictatorship" and the single-party dominance of the Communist party.[77] Deng insisted that Communist China, however it reforms itself, must never allow the introduction of "bourgeois" political checks and balances to undermine "leadership by the party." He made very clear that "in reforming our political structure, we must not imitate the West, and no liberalization should be allowed."[78]

In that clear sense, the political system left by Deng Xiaoping to China was very different from anything anticipated by Sun Yat-sen or the Kuomintang. The system that Deng left to post-Maoist China is unmistakably more akin to paradigmatic Fascism than to anything advocated by Sun Yat-sen. However much post-Maoist China, the China of Sun Yat-sen, and Fascist Italy all resemble each other, their relationship to political democracy, as a goal or a reality, distinguishes that of Sun from the others.

The post-Maoist China of Deng Xiaoping more closely resembles paradigmatic Fascism than it does almost any other modern system, extant or received. What that implies is difficult to discern with complete confidence.

Post-Maoist China is clearly a member of a class of reactive and developmental regimes with which the twentieth century has become familiar. Mussolini's Fascism was a member of a subset of that class. The China of Deng Xiaoping and Jiang Zemin appears to be nothing less. It is a variant of contemporary fascism.

Should the China of Deng Xiaoping survive into the twenty-first century—and there is no assurance that it will[79]—the Western industrialized democracies will face a number of problems. First of all, Communist China can hardly be expected to respect "human rights" as they are understood in liberal democratic environments. Deng Xiaoping was very forthright in his judgments concerning human rights in general. "Our concept of human rights," he told the world, "is, in essence, different from that of the Western world, because we see the question from a different point of view."[80] Fascists had insisted on precisely the same difference more than fifty years before.

As long as the People's Republic of China continues to defend the "Four Cardinal Principles" of Deng Xiaoping, one can hardly expect the leadership in Beijing to allow nonparty dissidence to articulate opposition to the Chinese Communist party. Under the prevailing political circumstances, there will be little opportunity to aggregate nonparty sentiment in voluntary associations.

Thus the United States and the industrialized democracies will continue to be irritated. Nonetheless, business interests will foster continued "engagement" with a fascist China. The prospects of profit will tend to mitigate the sense of outrage produced among Americans and Europeans by the behaviors of the leadership in Beijing. Beyond that, however, there are other concerns that engage the interests of the advanced industrial nations.

Since the beginning of the twentieth century, reactive nationalists have tested both the patience and the strategic concerns of the advanced industrial nations. In their search for "living space" and restoration of "lost lands," revolutionary, reactive nationalist regimes have threatened what the industrialized democracies consider their vital interests. In an intelligible sense, the Second World War was a war of "redivision," a demand by "proletarian" nations for what they considered adequate "living space" and the restoration of "lost territories."[81]

If post-Maoist China has taken on the features of an exacerbated reactive nationalism, sharing some of the passion of fascism, one would expect the issues of "lost lands" and "living space" to aggressively and persistently occupy its leaders. That clearly seems to be the case. The recent history of post-Maoist China is a story of China's search for the territorial restoration of a China that once was.

Notes

1. See the discussion in Stuart R. Schram, ed., introduction to *The Political Thought of Mao Tse-tung*, rev. ed. (New York: Praeger, 1969), pp. 22–23; and Schram, *Mao Tse-tung* (Baltimore: Penguin, 1967), pp. 44, 54.

2. Donald M. Lowe, *The Function of "China" in Marx, Lenin, and Mao* (Berkeley: University of California Press, 1966), pp. 138–139.

3. See the discussion in Maria Hsia Chang, *The Labors of Sisyphus: The Economic Development of Communist China* (New Brunswick, N.J.: Transaction, 1998), chap. 2. Whatever can be said about Mao's anti-Japanese and anti-Kuomintang military strategy, that strategy was hardly the consequence of his knowledge of Marxist theory. There is nothing that might be identified as "Marxist" in Mao Zedong, *On Guerrilla Warfare* (New York: Praeger, 1961) or *Selected Military Writings* (Beijing: Foreign Languages, 1967).

4. See the discussion in Lowe, *Function of "China,"* chap. 5.

5. Nigel Harris, *The Mandate of Heaven: Marx and Mao in Modern China* (New York: Quartet, 1978), p. 297.

6. See the account in A. James Gregor, *The Fascist Persuasion in Radical Politics* (Princeton: Princeton University Press, 1974), chap. 6.

7. Mao, "On Coalition Government," a passage omitted in the standard editions. See Harris, *Mandate of Heaven*, p. 33 n. 49.

8. Ibid., pp. 25–26.

9. Mao, "On Coalition Government," in *Selected Works* (Beijing: Foreign Languages, 1965), 3:284, 304.

10. Mao, "Talks at the Beidaihe Conference"; Roderick MacFarquhar, Timothy Cheek, and Eugene Wu, eds., *The Secret Speeches of Chairman Mao from the Hundred Flowers to the Great Leap Forward* (Cambridge: Harvard University Press, 1989), p. 401.

11. In 1984 Deng defined "Marxism" as a fulsome commitment to the development of "the productive forces," i.e., the economic growth and rapid industrialization of the nation's system of material production. Deng Xiaoping, "Building a Socialism with a Specifically Chinese Character," in *Selected Works* (Beijing: Foreign Languages, 1994), 3:73. He identified making "class struggle" the "key link" in China's socialism as the "major error" of Maoist "leftism." Deng, "Speech at the National Conference of the Communist Party of China," in ibid., p. 144.

12. Deng, "Speech at the Third Plenary Session of the Central Advisory Commission of the Communist Party of China," in ibid., p. 97.

13. Ibid., pp. 74–75. See the discussion in Deng, "Our Magnificent Goal and Basic Policies," in ibid., pp. 85–87.

14. Deng, "Bourgeois Liberalization Means Taking the Capitalist Road," in ibid., p. 129; see Deng, "Reform Is the Only Way for China to Develop Its Productive Forces," in ibid., p. 142.

15. Deng, "There Is No Fundamental Contradiction Between Socialism and a Market Economy," in ibid., p. 152.

16. In this context, see Sun Yat-sen, *The International Development of China* (Taipei: China Cultural Service, 1953).

17. See Nayan Chanda and Kari Huus, "China: The New Nationalism," *Far Eastern Economic Review*, 9 November 1995, p. 20.

18. See the editorial "Stay Back, China," *Economist*, 16 March 1996, p. 15.

19. Deng, "No One Can Shake Socialist China," in *Selected Works*, 3:318.

20. See Deng, "Two Kinds of Comments About China's Reform," in ibid., pp. 138–139; "Reform Is the Only Way for China to Develop Its Productive Forces," in ibid., pp. 140–143.

21. As has been suggested, the pretended distinctions between "patriotism" and "nationalism" cannot survive scrutiny. As will be argued, the Communist Chinese notion of the distinction disappears with the doctrinal elaboration now taking place in the People's Republic of China. See, in particular, the discussion below on "Biology and China's Post-Maoist Reactive Nationalism."

22. See "China Prints Book to Educate Farmers," *San Francisco Chronicle*, 28 November 1995, p. A11.

23. See Maria Hsia Chang, "The Nationalist Ideology of the Chinese Military," *Journal of Strategic Studies* 21, no. 1 (1998): 46.

24. See Patrick E. Tyler, "China's Campus Model for the 90s: Earnest Patriot," *New York Times*, 23 April 1996, p. A4.

25. George Wehrfritz, "China: Springtime Perennial," *Newsweek*, 10 June 1996, p. 17.

26. See "An Open Letter to All Citizens," published by the *Qingdao Chinese Communist Party Municipal Committee's Propaganda Department*, 21 March 1996. In Chinese.

27. See "China Prints Book to Educate Farmers," *San Francisco Chronicle*, 28 November 1995, p. A11.

28. See Xiang Wenrong, "Consciousness of National Defense and Patriotism," *Guofang* (National defense) 9 (1996): 32. In Chinese.

29. For Fascists, nationalism was always defined in terms of the prevalence of the state. Nationalism was always seen as *political*, i.e., a function of the state. See A. James Gregor, "Fascism and the New Russian Nationalism," *Communism and Post-Communist Studies* 31 (1998): 1–15.

30. See the discussion in Li Xing, "On the Concept of State-Nationalism," *Minzu yanjiu* (Nationality studies) 4 (1995): 10–14. In Chinese.

31. See, for example, Deng, "The Party's Urgent Tasks on the Organizational and Ideological Fronts," in *Selected Works*, 3:47–58.

32. Deng, "The Party's Urgent Tasks on the Organizational and Ideological Fronts," in ibid., p. 50; and "Speech at the National Conference of the Communist Party of China," in ibid., p. 147.

33. These notions had their origin in the sociological work of the late nineteenth century. Prominent among the theorists of "group consciousness" one finds Ludwig Gumplowicz and Gabriel Tarde. By the turn of the century, that kind of sociological thought tailed off into the literature of the "group" or "crowd" mind. In the modern period, much of that kind of "theorizing" appears in the literature of "ethnocentrism." See the discussion as it relates specifically to nationalism in Eugen Lemberg, *Nationalismus*, 2 vols. (Reinbek bei Hamburg: Rowohlt, 1964); A. James Gregor, *The Ideology of Fascism: The Rationale of Totalitarianism* (New York: Free Press, 1969), chaps. 2, 6, provides some indication of the relationship between the sociological tradition of the nineteenth century and paradigmatic Fascism.

34. In this context, Fascist theorists made ready recourse to the general theory of human evolution and raciation to be found in the works of Sir Arthur Keith—where many of these claims are systematized. Keith is regularly referred to in the professional and apologetic literature of Fascist Italy. See, for example, the works of Mario F. Canella, particularly *Razze umane estinte e viventi* (Florence: Sansoni, 1942). For Keith, see Arthur Keith, *Nationality and Race from an Anthropologist's Point of View* (London: Royal Anthropological Institute, 1919). For a full statement of the position, see Arthur Keith, *A New Theory of Human Evolution* (New York: Philosophical Library, 1949).

35. Recently, Francis Fukuyama has touched on some of these themes in *The End of History and the Last Man* (New York: Free Press, 1992).

36. See Sun Yat-sen, *The Triple Demism of Sun Yat-sen* (1931; reprint, New York: ANS, 1974), p. 64. Reprint of the Wuchang edition of 1931.

37. The "Chinese, having the same blood, the same spoken and written language, the same religion, the same habits and customs, [form] a complete and independent race." Sun, *Triple Demism*, p. 70; see pp. 68–70.

38. See the discussion in ibid., pp. 118–122.

39. Ibid., pp. 92–115.

40. Ibid., pp. 126–127. This is not the place, nor is there space, to enter into the discussion of whether the Chinese, prior to the incursions of the imperialist powers, ever really were animated by a sense of nationalism comparable to that

of Europeans. It has long been held that "culturalism," rather than "national-ism," defined the political sentiments of the dynastic Chinese. Recently, James Townsend has provided an interesting analysis of such claims, concluding that the advocates of Chinese "culturalism" have overstated "both the dominance of culturalism and the weakness of pre-modern nationalism in imperial times." Elements of premodern nationalism are to be found in considerable abundance in imperial China before the advent of the first Chinese reactive nationalists. See James Townsend, "Chinese Nationalism," in *Chinese Nationalism*, ed. Jonathan Unger (Armonk, N.Y.: M. E. Sharpe, 1996), pp. 1–30; quotation from p. 24.

41. Ibid., p. 131.
42. Ibid., p. 97.
43. Ibid., p. 65.
44. Ibid., p. 71.
45. See the discussion in Gregor, *Ideology of Fascism*, chap. 2.
46. See the entire discussion in Benito Mussolini, "Discorso di Bologna," in *Opera omnia* (Florence: La Fenice, 1953–1964), 16:239–246.
47. See the discussion in Gregor, *Ideology of Fascism*, chap. 6.
48. Fascist theoreticians sought to explicate these concepts in fairly substantial works. Sun left only the outline of such concepts, but he clearly conceived "race" to be a historic product. He argued that "new races" develop out of preexisting races united in breeding populations under a variety of historic circumstances. Thus Sun maintained that "many different human races (in the strict sense) can unite and form all kinds of homogeneous races (in the broad sense). . . . The American race is more heterogeneous than any other race; it includes immigrants from all countries and from all continents. . . . [These] immigrants undergo a process of fusion; they are said to be 'welded in the melting pot,' and they form a new race." Sun, *Triple Demism*, pp. 70, 79.
49. In this context, see Moses Hess, *Rome and Jerusalem* (New York: Philosophi-cal Library, 1958), as a case in point. The same was true of Japanese nationalism before the end of the Second World War. See contemporary instances among the new Russian nationalists. See A. James Gregor, *Phoenix: Fascism in Our Time* (New Brunswick, N.J.: Transaction, 1999), chap. 7.
50. Chiang Kai-shek, *China's Destiny* (New York: Roy, 1947), pp. 29, 31.
51. Chen Boda's "Critique of *China's Destiny*" is available in mimeographed English translation at the Center of Chinese Studies, University of California, Berkeley.
52. Philip Jaffe, who wrote a commentary on *China's Destiny*, identified the no-tion of a biological foundation for the nation as a clearly "fascist" concept. See Philip Jaffe, "Commentary on *China's Destiny* and *Chinese Economic Theory*," in Chiang, *China's Destiny*, pp. 307–308.
53. Sun, for example, speaks of a new race that emerges from the assimilation of "foreign races" that learn Chinese. He states that "if foreign races learn our lan-guage, they will be more easily assimilated by us, and after a long while they will become one race with us" (Sun, *Triple Demism*, pp. 68–69).
54. See, in this context, the formal statement of Fascist "racial doctrine," pub-lished in "The Manifesto of Fascist Racism," in Gregor, *Ideology of Fascism*, pp.

383–386. One expression of the theoretical discussion is to be found in Mario F. Canella, *Lineamenti di antropobiologia* (Florence: Sansoni, 1943).

55. See, for example, the assessments of Lucien Pye, "How China's Nationalism was Shanghaied," in Unger, *Chinese Nationalism*, p. 110.

56. Much of the following discussion depends on the insights of Barry Sautman, who presented his views in a paper, "Racial Nationalism and China's External Behavior," before the American Political Science Association Annual Meeting, San Francisco, 30 August 1996.

57. Ismail Amat, "Multinationality, State and Patriotism," *Guangming Ribao* 2 (February 1995): 1–2 (see FBIS-CHI–95–045, pp. 35–37). In Chinese. Chinese intellectuals have had a long preoccupation with race and biology; see Frank Dikoetter, *The Discourse of Race in Modern China* (Stanford: Stanford University Press, 1992).

58. See the discussion in Chris Berry, "Race: Chinese Films and the Politics of Nationalism," *Cinema Journal* 31, no. 2 (1992): 45–58; and Ian Johnson, "Actor Captures China's Mood," *Baltimore Sun*, 8 October 1995, p. 2A.

59. See the account in *Xinhua*, 16 September 1995, in which members of the Communist Party's Standing Committee of the Politburo visited the tomb of Huang Di.

60. *Xinhua*, 15 April 1993.

61. See the discussion in Alaine Touraine, *Critique of Modernity* (London: Blackwell, 1995).

62. Hsieh Shih-chung, "A New Voice of Self-Interpretation: Han-Chinese Ideology on National Territory vs. Territorial Rights of Non-Han Aboriginal Peoples," in *The Territorial Rights of Nationals and Peoples*, ed. John Jacobson (Lewiston: Edwin Mellen, 1989), pp. 143–157.

63. Sautman, "Racial Nationalism," pp. 25–26.

64. See Sun, *Triple Demism*, p. 65; and Chiang, *China's Destiny*, p. 31.

65. See the report in the *South China Morning Post*, 6 April 1996; Jia Lanpo, *Early Man in China* (Beijing: Foreign Languages, 1980); and "A Few Questions of Paleoanthropological Research [in Chinese]," in *Anthropology and Its Applications*, ed. Chen Guoqiang and Lin Jiahuang (Shanghai: Xuelin Chubanshe, 1992).

66. See *Xinhua*, 10 April 1989.

67. See Jia Lanpo and Ho Chuan Kun, "Lumiere nouvelle sur l'archaeologie paleolithique chinoise," *L'Anthropologie* 94, no. 4 (1994): 851–860.

68. See Chen Chun, "Chinese Archaeology and the West," *Archaeological Review from Cambridge* 8 (1989): 1, as cited in Sautman, "Racial Nationalism."

69. John W. Olsen, "The Practice of Archaeology in China Today," *Antiquity* l, no. 6 (1987), as cited in Sautman, "Racial Nationalism," p. 32.

70. See, for example, Armando Lodolini, *La storia della razza italiana da Augusto a Mussolini* (Rome: Unione Editoriale d'Italia, 1939); Giovanni Marro, *Primato della razza italiana* (Milan: Principato, 1940).

71. In that reactive nationalism was distinguished from the biological racism of National Socialist Germany. For the National Socialists, nationalism was a function of race. The primacy was given to race rather than the nation. See the discussion in A. James Gregor, *Contemporary Radical Ideologies: Totalitarian Thought in the Twentieth Century* (New York: Random House, 1968), chap. 5.

Fascist theoreticians consistently distinguished their "racism" from that of National Socialism. Fascist "racism" was identified with the nation, and race was conceived as a dynamic product of national history.

72. See the discussion in Sun, "Five Power Constitution," in Sun, *Fundamentals of National Reconstruction* (Taipei: China Cultural Service, 1953), pp. 19–60.

73. Sun, *Triple Demism*, pp. 331, 346.

74. See Sun, "Statement on the Formation of National Government," in *Fundamentals*, pp. 162–163.

75. Sun, "Self-Government as the Basis of Reconstruction," in *Fundamentals*, p. 132.

76. See the discussion in John F. Copper, *The Taiwan Political Miracle: Essays on Political Development, Elections and Foreign Relations* (New York: East Asia Research Institute/University Press of America, 1997).

77. See Deng's comments in "The Party's Urgent Tasks on the Organizational and Ideological Fronts," in *Selected Works*, 3:52–53. For Deng, it was the "Party [that] exercises leadership over the government." Deng, "Help the People Understand the Importance of the Rule of Law," in ibid., p. 167.

78. Deng, "On Reform of the Political Structure," in *Selected Works*, 3:179.

79. See the discussion in Chang, *Labors of Sisyphus*.

80. Deng, "Bourgeois Liberalization Means Taking the Capitalist Road," in *Selected Works*, 3:130.

81. In this context, see the Fascist literature rationalizing the involvement of Italy in the Second World War. A. Messineo, *Spazio vitale e grande spazio* (Rome: Civiltà cattolica, 1942); Guido Puccio, *Lotta fra due mondi* (Rome: Edizioni italfiani, 1942). Similar arguments were given for National Socialist German and Japanese involvement.

8

Fascism, Post-Maoist China, and Irredentism

The argument that has been made in the preceding chapters attempts a classification of post-Maoist China that includes it in the class of reactive and developmental nationalisms and identifies it as an instantial case of "fascism." One of the reasons for the identification, among the several rehearsed, turns on Beijing's singularly insistent irredentism.

Fascist Italy's aggressive irredentism served to distinguish it from alternative reactive nationalisms. There is scant trace of such an aggressiveness, for example, in the foreign policy recommendations of Sun Yatsen. Although he was clearly aware of the territories China had "lost" to "oppressor" nations in the past, there is little, if any, suggestion of the use of force in seeking their restoration.[1]

Italian irredentism, at the very commencement of the twentieth century, had already assumed the aggressiveness that was to characterize Fascism. The architects of Italian reunification in the mid-nineteenth century spoke of the "lost lands" of the motherland[2] but without the intensity that was to typify the organized Nationalists of the first years of the new century—and that of Fascism during the interwar period.

Marxism and Marxism-Leninism had almost no theoretical grasp of nationalism, much less irredentism. Having failed in that regard, Marxism and its variants never really understood either Fascist or Chinese irredentism and hence failed to understand a good deal of the international politics of our time.

Nationalist and Fascist Irredentism

Irredentism is generally identified with the political sentiment attached to the restoration of lost lands, portions of national territory presumably languishing under "alien rule." More often than not, the inhabitants of those lands are considered members alienated from the motherland by the interposition of foreigners.

Irredentism was a constant among Italian nationalists from the time of the Risorgimento and, as a political sentiment, it persisted into the twentieth century. After public interest was fostered by a roster of publications, a formal organization of nationalists was undertaken in 1910.[3] The very first articles of organization of the Italian Nationalist Association (Associazione Nazionalista Italiana) announced that Italian nationalism was, and would remain, unequivocally irredentist.[4]

The threads that made up the fabric of organized Italian Nationalism can be traced back into the nineteenth century, at a time when irredentism already occupied the concerns of many. But the "new nationalism" of reactive response and developmental intent that began to find expression about the time of the organization of the Associazione Nationalista was certainly more than irredentism. Within the new constellation of factors, irredentism was to be singularly transformed.

The new nationalism probably first received fulsome expression in the work of Giuseppe Prezzolini and Giovanni Papini in 1903 and 1904.[5] That new nationalism, to distinguish it from the "literary" and "aesthetic" nationalism of the preceding century, not only sought the return of lost lands and alienated populations but also advocated the rapid economic and military development of the peninsula in order to secure those lands and that population—and defend the nation from the exactions of international "plutocracy." Economic growth and industrial development were understood to constitute the only means through which Italians might achieve dignity, security, independence, and place in the twentieth-century world of "Darwinian" international competition.

Some argued that Italy's defeat at Adowa, Ethiopia, in 1896, when 10,000 Italians and Askaris were humbled by the 100,000 riflemen of King Menelik, provoked the frenzied reactive nationalism that was to persist into the middle of the twentieth century.[6] Others were to argue that modern Italian nationalism appeared only in 1908 as a reaction to the annexation of Bosnia-Herzegovina by Austria-Hungary[7]—an event that exposed the entire eastern coast of the Italian peninsula, its cities and its major communications arteries, to the threat of offshore naval assault.

The Dalmatian coast, peopled in part by ethnic Italians but annexed by the Austrians, was characterized by protected waters, cluttered islets, and sheltered coves, rendering it ideal for naval staging areas, whereas the Italian coast on the Adriatic was featureless, lacking suitable naval anchorages between Venice and Brindisi, and afforded little natural defense from sea-based attacks. Control of the entire Adriatic littoral thus became not only an issue of irredentism but a vital strategic concern for the kingdom of Italy.

By 1910, the passion of the nationalist movement was further fueled by a deep sense of inferiority born of Italy's weaknesses with respect to the industrialized Great Powers. While Britain and France swept over Africa and Asia, Italy had not only failed in its efforts on the "Dark Continent" but found itself threatened at home by the ramshackle empire of the Hapsburgs.

The Great Powers, against which Italy measured itself, were feared and resented. They were feared because of their evident strength and resented because they had preempted space and resources throughout the Mediterranean and Africa.[8] Defeat in Africa and the exposure to Austrian naval threats in the Adriatic confirmed the sense of vulnerability and inferiority that impassioned the intellectuals who made up the leadership of Italian Nationalism. Once economic growth and industrial development became a programmatic concern for Italian Nationalism, the advanced industrial powers were conceived to be more than partly responsible for Italy's circumstances.

Italy's inability to obtain secure access to resources necessary for accelerated economic growth and industrial maturation—which might mitigate its vulnerability and assuage its sense of inferiority—was attributed to the "egoism" of those powers that had early achieved industrial maturity. According to the thesis, the industrialized powers had not only arrogated to themselves much of the earth's resources but had used their market and financial advantages to penetrate the peninsula and thwart its independent growth and maturation. That analysis generated a measure of resentment against the industrially advanced nations of the Continent and was to influence politics on the peninsula for decades.[9]

The Nationalist sense of outrage grew with the passage of time. Not only had Austria-Hungary seized military advantage on the Dalmatian coast, but the Austrian initiative was played out against the background of domination exercised by the Great Powers in the Mediterranean. Great Britain controlled access to, as well as egress from, the Mediterranean at Gibraltar and Suez. Within the waters of the Mediterranean, the French controlled Corsica and Tunis, bringing the French fleet both within immediate striking distance of the west coast of the Italian peninsula and positioning it, should there be conflict, to interdict Italy's strategic sea lines of communication.

By the end of the first decade of the new century, "Italy was just about the most thoroughly encircled nation on earth. No Great Power could ever allow itself to lose strategic defensibility in [such a] way—still less could a power wishing to establish itself as one of the Great."[10] All of this animated Italian Nationalism with a fierce passion. Irredentist sentiment was intense. By then it was associated with Italy's strategic vulnerability and the nation's disabling lack of raw materials. Each passion reinforced the other.

In their determined effort to "cancel the profound consequences of centuries of servitude,"[11] Italian Nationalists sought what is today termed "comprehensive security," an assurance that the nation commands sufficient human and material resources to resist and prevail against any plausible combination of potential enemies. Motivated by a search for that security, Italian Nationalists spoke not only of a credible armed forces capability, together with the ability to deploy those forces when and where necessary, but of the "problem of raw materials"—the fact that the Italian peninsula was malprovisioned with resources necessary to foster and sustain the economic growth and industrial development necessary for a modern military.[12] All of these imperatives implied "expansion"—commercial, intellectual, political, military, demographic, and territorial.[13] If Italy was to redeem itself after centuries of humiliation and abuse, it would be compelled to move with assertiveness against its "plutocratic" oppressors to satisfy the comprehensive requirements of its renewal.

These were the passions Italian Nationalism was to share with Fascism.[14] They were the passions that were to influence Italian external politics for almost half a century.

At least in part as a response to that abiding sentiment, monarchial Italy began to make some response to the evolving threat environment in which it was compelled to operate. The first effort made manifested itself in the Italo-Turkish War of 1911–1912. With the tacit approval of Great Britain, and provoked by the increasing expansion of a French presence in North Africa, the Italians undertook initiatives against the Ottoman Turks in order to secure for themselves some of the remainder of the North African littoral. The conflict of 1911–1912 was the first major effort to mitigate what were taken to be Italy's major strategic vulnerabilities. It proved to be little more than a preamble to Italy's second effort to redress what it saw as its geostrategic disadvantages.

In 1915, the kingdom of Italy chose to enter the First World War—against Germany and Austria-Hungary—as an ally of the Entente composed of Russia, France, and Great Britain. In the bargaining that was intended to secure Italy's entrance into the war, the ministers of Russia, France, and Great Britain—with the Treaty of London—were prepared to offer Italy, at the expense of Austria-Hungary, the province of Trentino, long considered ethnically Italian, together with the Tyrol as far as the Brenner Pass. Trieste, a port city on the Adriatic at least partly populated by ethnic Italians, and the Julian Alps as far as the port of Fiume were added as further incentives—to be supplemented by Istria and the Dalmatian coast as far south as the River Neretva, as well as the offshore islands as far south as Ragusa. Saseno and Valona in Albania were added to the territorial concessions, together with the northern Epirus hinterland. The clear impression was that Italy was being offered supremacy in the Adriatic and Ionian seas—as well as unspecified privileges in the Balkans and elsewhere.

In all of this, several things merit attention. In the first place, many of the Italian claims, and the Entente's response to those claims, could hardly be identified as involving irredentism —unless one made recourse to "historic" allusions to the Roman Empire, whose forces, in antiquity, occupied most of the Mediterranean littoral. Only if one were prepared to argue that all "the cultural elements of the [Dalmatian] population spreading inland from the sea coast and indeed all traces of true civilization . . . were Latin—Roman, Venetian, Italian," might one argue that the claims on the Yugoslavian coast and Albania were essentially "irredentist."[15]

In the second place, Italy tendered no claims on Malta and Corsica, which had been Italian territories until the eighteenth century—and it was Malta and Corsica that provided the armed forces of Great Britain and France with significant potential strategic advantage vis-à-vis the Italian peninsula. Claims on Malta and Corsica would clearly be "irredentist" by any definition.

The problem was obvious. The Entente powers could grant Italy's claims at the expense of Austria-Hungary or the lesser nations of the region, but neither Britain nor France was prepared to bargain away any of their territories in the Mediterranean to assure Rome's entry into the war. Italians could make no claims on Malta or Corsica nor raise any objections to Britain's control of Gibraltar and Suez—for Britain and France were Italy's allies in a war that was to prove to be one of the most difficult and devastating in history.

In that war, Italy sacrificed the lives of more than 650,000 of its finest young men. The Italian losses in men and materiel in their forty-one months of involvement in the First World War were as oppressive as British and French losses in fifty-one.[16] With limited capital availability and still fewer assets, the war cost Italy a full 25 percent of its total financial resources and almost 60 percent of its merchant fleet.

In the peace treaties that followed the war, the British empire was enlarged by 2.3 million square miles and 28 million subjects; French holdings grew by 2.7 million square miles and 19 million subjects. Italy's total territorial gain was about 24,000 square miles, and its population was augmented by about 1.6 million subjects. Britain extended its presence in the Mediterranean to include the Palestine Mandate, providing its armed forces still further strategic advantages in the East. The French assumed control over Syria and Lebanon, to enhance their own strategic position in the eastern Mediterranean.

In the course of the peace conference that was to conclude the First World War, British and French representatives proceeded to challenge the binding validity of the Treaty of London and the commitments entered into with the agreements of St. Jean de Maurienne. Italy was to be denied many of the concessions for which it had bartered so many of its sons.

Almost immediately, Italy was compelled to renegotiate the agreements that had brought it into the war. Italy was to surrender many of it claims in the Aegean and on the Dalmatian littoral. In territorial and strategic terms, Italy's reward for its losses in the war against the Central Powers was disappointing.[17] In some respects, the kingdom was less defensible after the Great War than it had been before.

That was how Italian Nationalism interpreted the results of the war. Italian Nationalism interpreted the victory in the Great War to have been "mutilated" by the greed of the advanced industrial powers. That was the "mutilated victory" of which Fascism was to speak.

Having officially organized themselves in 1919, the first Fascists gave expression to much of the frustration and despair felt by those who had fought in the war. Mussolini not only became the heir of Italian Nationalism but in effect became its spokesman.[18] On 28 December 1919, ten months after the founding of his movement, Mussolini insisted that the duty of Italy, as a "warrior nation," was to "liberate [itself] from the yoke of international plutocracy."[19] Two days later, as though to leave no doubt as to the measure of his conviction, he reaffirmed his determination to liberate Italy from "the oppression of Western 'plutocracy.'"[20] Only months after the organization of the Fascist movement, Mussolini identified the principal members of the "Western plutocratic coalition" that threatened Italy and rendered her servile and contemptible. France, England, and the United States, the "sated" nations, those who had industrialized first, were united in that purpose.[21]

Fascists argued that it was the "grand coalition of interest"—a "coalition of plutocratic-capitalistic" states—that sought to perpetuate not only the inferiority of Italy but of "all the other proletarian nations."[22] To effect their purpose, the advanced industrial nations sponsored international organizations, purportedly in defense of world peace, when in fact such organizations served the almost exclusive economic, political, and military interests of the "plutocracies." The inequality in the League of Nations, in terms of representation and responsibility, was prima facie evidence of that.[23]

In order to assure its place in the hierarchy of nations, Fascists insisted, England required that Italy, as a "proletarian nation," recognize and acknowledge its subordination.[24] For its part, France was prepared to ensure Italian subordination by entirely controlling the Mediterranean—thereby rendering Italian redemption from "centuries of servitude" impossible.[25]

About eight months before Fascism's accession to power, given that set of convictions, Mussolini was prepared to provide what counted as an outline of his intended foreign policy. He spoke of an Italy confined to the Mediterranean by the hegemonic presence of Great Britain. It was Great Britain that dominated the "sea that was once Roman" by holding the keys to the Suez Canal at one end of the Mediterranean and to Gibraltar at the other. Only a significant decline in the British presence might provide space and opportunity for Italian expansion and, in the final analysis, allow Italy to once again establish itself as a maritime nation, having unencumbered access to the Red Sea, the Indian Ocean, and the Atlantic Ocean. Italy would follow the example of Rome and the maritime republics of seafaring Italy and would create, once again, an imperial center of civilization on the Italic peninsula.[26]

Before he became head of state for Fascist Italy, Mussolini conceived of all this as an inspirational "myth," a "faith," supporting the possibility of a true rebirth of an "old new nation." He envisioned the rise of metropolitan centers on a Mediterranean that would be, once again, an "Italian lake."[27] Italians, Mussolini insisted, would no longer "shine the shoes" of "Anglo-Saxon tyrants" or "Anglo-American plutocrats." Italians would have earned the dignity and status for which they had sacrificed, fought, and died. They would receive respect through diplomacy and law if possible, but, should it be required, they would exact that respect through the use of arms.[28]

To complete the picture of a modern reactive and developmental nationalism, Mussolini emphasized that economic growth, and particularly industrial expansion, required predictable access to raw materials at costs that would foster and sustain extensive and intensive development.[29] Any effort at political independence would necessarily imply significant economic independence, the ability to feed a population and arm a nation without dependence on the sufferance of others.[30]

Italian industrial development required ready and secure access to coal, iron, and oil, together with most of the essential minerals. Bereft of the most basic raw materials required for modern industrial growth, Italy would be compelled to seek solutions if it entertained any hope of achieving not only the political independence but the "grandeur," the "greatness," to which it aspired.[31]

Once empowered to govern the nation, in one of his first speeches given as head of state, Mussolini announced that Fascism would "direct [Italy] toward its glorious future." Resurgent Italy would become a power ready to assume global tasks. The first steps in that process would include "making the Mediterranean an Italian lake."[32]

Thus, before its advent in October 1922, Fascism had already outlined the foreign policy it would pursue for the next two decades. Its irredentism was only part of a larger geostrategic program of Italian development and aggrandizement. It was a program intended to transform a nation, its people, and the world around them.

Fascist Geopolitics

Only decades after the termination of the Second World War did commentators fully acknowledge the geopolitical sweep of Fascist foreign policy.[33] Obscured as they were during the interwar years by traditional diplomatic niceties and pragmatic conversation, Fascist intentions, since then, have been interpreted and reinterpreted in any number of ways. Only recently has it become possible to trace the major features of that policy and appreciate it in its fullness.

Almost immediately upon assuming responsibility for the nation's foreign policy, Mussolini reasserted his intention to guide Italy into a "new era of development."[34] "Fascism," Mussolini proclaimed, "wishes to maximally develop its national production."[35] Italy would no longer remain industrially "retrograde."[36]

Fascists had consistently argued that without such development, Italy could neither be the equal of the other Great Powers nor enjoy true political independence.[37] To adequately develop the peninsula, however, the nation required resources that the peninsula did not offer.[38] To secure such resources at a time when Italy was capital poor and could deploy neither the power projection capabilities nor the requisite diplomatic weight to impose its will required a foreign policy that, throughout the interwar years, could only be "extremely circumspect."

The Fascists insisted that the new, emergent Italy, like the Rome of antiquity, once having chosen a goal, would persist, with whatever tactical prudence was required, until that goal was attained.[39] Prudence would be essential, Mussolini reminded his followers, for foreign policy must operate in an environment in which options are constrained by the realities dictated by concrete forces and events outside one's control.[40]

However prudent and circumspect over the years, Fascist Italy's policies toward Yugoslavia, Albania, Greece, Ethiopia, and Spain, in retrospect, become immediately comprehensible given the geostrategic context and Mussolini's chosen goals, and its posturing toward the "proletarian" Arab and Muslim world as their "protector" becomes equally transparent.[41]

With Great Britain and France dominating the Mediterranean with military power that exceeded anything available to Italy, Fascist policy pursued its goals as far and as rapidly as circumstances allowed. At the close of the Fascist period, Mussolini, no longer circumspect, admitted, in perfect candor, that Italy's struggle had been sustained by the decision that the nation could and would no longer remain "a prisoner in the Mediterranean."[42] Throughout the interwar years, Fascist policy had sought control of Italy's internal seas and free access to the oceans.

The Corfu incident, coming less than a year after Mussolini's accession and making an overwhelming display of Fascist force, was designed to demonstrate to Greece that Great Britain would not, or could not, respond to any and every demand for protection made anywhere and everywhere in the Mediterranean.[43] The protectorate over, and the ultimate annexation of, Albania was part of Fascist Italy's program for controlling the Adriatic and Ionian seas—its internal seas. Fascism sought to gradually diminish England's uncontested control of the entire Mediterranean.

The invasion of Ethiopia was undertaken not only to acquire resources and to provide colonial territory for the settlement of the peninsula's excess population but to establish an Italian presence outside the confines of the Mediterranean, beyond the Suez Canal, with access to the Indian Ocean.[44] For its part, involvement in the civil war in Spain held out the promise that Fascist Italy would have a military ally facing the Atlantic and positioned immediately across the straits from Gibraltar—gateway to the open ocean.[45]

Although Mussolini was compelled, by every pragmatic consideration, to be circumspect in his public statements after assuming the responsibilities of head of state, the documentary evidence records, for example, a continued interest in irredentist movements in Malta and in Corsica[46]—two of the major strategic positions held by Britain and France in the Mediterranean. Irredentism provided the public rationalization for Fascist Italy's pursuit of its geostrategic purposes.

Although Fascist claims on Malta and Corsica, arguably Italian,[47] were made in the language of irredentism, it is clear that Fascist interests were emphatically geostrategic. Malta, occupied by Britain in 1798, provided London a naval staging area that protected its critical sea passages from Gibraltar to the Suez through the choke points of the central Mediterranean. Those sea lines of communication were essential to the maintenance and defense of the British empire in India, South and Southeast Asia, and the Far East.

At the same time, British naval facilities and combat elements in Malta, so close to metropolitan Italy, threatened Italian freedom of movement throughout the region and diminished the credibility of peninsular defense. Irredentist claims on Malta were clearly linked to strategic interests.

Similarly, claims on Corsica, occupied by the French in 1769, satisfied the demands of irredentism but also served geostrategic purposes. The island is only eighty kilometers from the Italian coast, and both Italian Nationalists and Fascists conceived its occupation by France as part of a comprehensive plan by "plutocratic powers" to control developments on the peninsula as well as the flow of maritime traffic through the surrounding sea. Occupying both Corsica and Tunisia in North Africa, the French fleet could exercise potential control over all movements in the central Mediterranean and the Tyrrhenian Sea.

The rest of Fascist Italy's claims were often bruited in the language of irredentism and appealed to the ancient Roman presence in Africa as far to the southeast as Aux—modern Ethiopia—and the Balkans. But they were clearly geostrategic in intent.[48] Many of the claims, recurrent in the literature of Italian Nationalism, have little immediate ethnic, linguistic, or historic justification. They were clearly geostrategic, serving the needs of an emergent nation convinced of its oppression by those more industrially advanced[49] and desirous of establishing itself as an equal among them.

The conviction was that the "plutocratic nations, having arrogated to themselves the bulk of the world's raw materials . . . imposed on poor nations onerous conditions for the acquisition of all those components necessary for the life and well-being of a people."[50] This monopoly over resources by the advanced industrial powers was seen as particularly disabling for those nations coming late to industrialization. The pace and extent of the process of industrialization "is undermined by the insufficiency of raw materials . . . and the dependence on foreign sources of supply which predictably increases the costs of production and confines enterprise to a low rate of return." More than that, "a dependency on foreign sources of raw materials, allows foreigners an inordinate measure of control over the life of the nation."[51]

Developing nations so circumstanced are driven to resolve their disabilities by obtaining immediate access to, or extending their control over, sources of raw materials and/or bargaining from a position of strength.[52] By the interwar years, the argument had become familiar: Sated and privileged nations, possessors of the bulk of the world's resources, are disposed to resist any change in the relationship between themselves and their real or potential dependencies.

Often, the argument continued, the only recourse open to "proletarian nations" is war.[53] Nations denied by nature or circumstance the very necessities of a dignified modern existence find it necessary to carve for themselves a "living space" *(spazio vitale)* that would afford them the material prerequisites for economic growth and intensive industrial development—all necessary for continued cultural evolution and to assure a secure place in the international community.[54]

For Italy, its immediate "living space" was the Mediterranean—with Africa as its resource base. That "vital space" would satisfy the nation's urgent need for raw materials—and provide territory on which to settle its excess population. That space would be knitted together by secure internal sea lines of communication throughout the Mediterranean.[55]

More than that, Fascists conceived their "Greater Italy" endowed with the same maritime potential that made ancient Rome and the city-states of the peninsula powers of international significance.[56] Italy could not perform the functions of a world power without, once again, becoming a major commercial and military maritime power.[57] As a consequence, "the foreign policy of Mussolini always followed the classic geopolitical directive: seek an outlet to the ocean, to 'open' waters, by controlling the requisite strategic accesses."[58] Only then would Italy become the "third Rome" of which the first Italian nationalists of the nineteenth century had spoken.

In the years immediately preceding the advent of the Second World War, Mussolini spoke with evident passion of the "sacrosanct right" of "poor people to refuse to suffer forever the [prevailing] inequalities in the distribution of the resources of the earth."[59] Without confident access to the raw materials necessary for robust industrial extensive and intensive growth, less-developed nations are reduced to the dependents of the industrially advanced "demoplutocracies."

For Fascist strategists, the resolution of all these problems, as well as the fulfillment of all their aspirations, would have to await a major change in the European balance of power. Italy, alone, contending with the major powers, could not change power relations on the European continent.

The requisite change in the European balance of power evidently came with the advent of Adolf Hitler's National Socialist Germany. An economic and military union of Italy, Germany, and Japan gave the appearance of possible success in the anticipated contest with the advanced industrial democracies.

On the fateful day in June 1940, when Italy declared war on Great Britain and France as an ally of National Socialist Germany, Mussolini made Fascist Italy's intentions, prefigured twenty years before, eminently clear. "Proletarian and Fascist Italy," he told the multitude in the Piazza Venezia, "seeks to breach the suffocating territorial and military barriers that confine the nation to the Mediterranean. A people composed of forty-five million souls cannot be free," Mussolini insisted, "if it does not have free access to the open ocean."

"This gigantic battle," he continued, "is a phase in the logical development of our revolution; it is a struggle of poor people . . . against those determined to monopolize all the riches of the earth."[60] It was a restatement of convictions long held and goals long sought.

"Italy's war," Italians were told in the Fascist literature of the time, "is a struggle for liberty and vital living space. . . . [It is a war] for national political unity, for security within its borders, for freedom of life and movement in the Mediterranean, the Tyrrhenian and the Adriatic seas and access to the oceans. . . . for the direct possession or control of sources of necessary natural resources for the development of heavy industries and for the peaceful and productive organization of a union of

Mediterranean peoples."[61] Fascist Italy would serve as the "defender" of the "proletarian" nations of the Mediterranean against the impostures of the "plutocracies."[62]

Fascist Italy's objectives were those of an exacerbated reactive and developmental nationalism. As such, its decisions were all too often governed by vindictiveness and a ready hostility generated by a deep sense of humiliation and longsuffering.[63]

By whatever criteria such decisions are measured, Fascist Italy's decision to enter the Second World War was just short of criminally reckless.[64] Italy's wars in Ethiopia and Spain had consumed much of its military resources, had destroyed substantial numbers of its combat units, and had exhausted some of its most effective troops. By any standard, Fascist Italy required at least a decade to refurbish its armed forces before it could reasonably be expected to face armed conflict with opponents as formidable as the advanced industrial democracies or the Soviet Union.[65] Nonetheless, its armed forces were committed to conflict with an enemy that had not only immediate advantages in the combat zones but vast industrial potential and powerful allies. The decision to enter the conflict was driven, in part, by the very psychology of reactive nationalism. It was to cost Italy hundreds of thousands of lives and devastate the peninsula. Both the "empire" and Fascism were extinguished in that war. In its last days, Mussolini himself was to fall at the hands of anti-Fascist partisans.

Reactive nationalist movements, and the regimes they inform, display traits that make them dangerous to others and probably to themselves. For that reason, the identification of contemporary China as a reactive and developmental nationalism is important for our purposes. That post-Maoist China may qualify for entry into the subclass of reactive nationalisms classified as "fascist" is troubling.

The Irredentism of Post-Maoist China

As China's long revolution took on more and more of the reactive nationalist and developmental traits of modern revolution, irredentism became a common theme that linked all of its revolutionaries. By the end of the first twenty-five years of the twentieth century, Sun Yat-sen gave what was to become standard expression to the almost universal lament concerning China's "lost territories."[66]

He listed as lost all the territories China had "leased" to the more advanced industrial powers, among others, territories at the southern end of the Liaotung Peninsula and the "New Territories" adjacent to Hong Kong. He spoke of all the territories in the Russian Far East, lost through "unequal treaties" to the "imperialist" government of the czars. He also alluded to as lost all the lands of the tributary states—Korea, Siam, Borneo, Java, Ceylon, Nepal, and Bhutan—that had shown their deference to China by paying it tribute before China's humiliation at the hands of the imperialists.

The exactions imposed on China by Europeans hardly requires rehearsal here. It is all very familiar to the least-informed undergraduate. That Chinese intellectuals suffered a profound sense of personal and collective grievance is as easily understood as the reactive nationalist sentiments that inspired the revolutionary politics of both Sun's Kuomintang and the Chinese Communist party.[67]

A constituent of that nationalism was an abiding commitment to the restoration of "lost lands," which has continued to this day and has most recently involved China, Japan, the United States, and Taiwan in tense exchanges. Beijing's claims to the tiny islands in the East China Sea, which the Chinese identify as "Diaoyutai" and the Japanese as "Sengaku," as well as Beijing's claims on Taiwan and associated territories, have generated a degree of tension that has alarmed observers.

In July 1996, Tokyo formally extended its national exclusive economic zone to include the Sengaku Islands, and the United States, in domestic law, has committed itself to the defense of Taiwan should force be employed to resolve Beijing's claims.[68] These circumstances create an atmosphere of potential conflict with post-Maoist China.

Although the authorities in Beijing have shown considerable prudence in dealing with the conflicting claims that sustain current tensions,[69] it is equally clear that the leadership of the Chinese Communist party considers the restoration of such contested territories to the motherland to be a matters of grave significance. There is little doubt that the irredentism of post-Maoist China might well be a source of increasing political and strategic difficulties between the People's Republic of China (PRC) and the industrialized democracies in the twenty-first century.[70] For the purposes of the present discussion, focusing on a specific area of disputed territorial claims is particularly instructive.

Post-Maoist China's Claims in the East and South China Seas

Ever since the founding of the People's Republic of China, the authorities in Beijing have insisted that the islands, cays, banks, sandbars, and lagoons in the East and South China Seas are part of sovereign Chinese territory, having been "discovered" during the Han Dynasty in the reign of Emperor Wudi (140–186 B.C.). The precise extent of the "discovery" and the associated claims have never been formally tendered, so Beijing's claims are not specific.[71] What Beijing has done, instead, is to impress on all the littoral, insular, and archipelagic nations of the region that con-

struction will not be permitted on any of the territories nor will exploration or exploitation of seabed resources be undertaken in the East or
South China Seas without the active participation of China.

The Chinese People's Liberation Army Navy (PLAN)—the Chinese
Communist navy—has engaged in armed conflict with Vietnam over
Hanoi's attempt to extract oil from the contested regions in the Gulf of
Tonkin and the South China Sea. In 1988, the Chinese armed forces
seized islets in the Spratlys (Nansha), in the course of which three Viet-
namese vessels were sunk and about eighty Vietnamese nationals killed.
That was followed by further seizures of contested maritime territory in
the Spratlys in 1992.

In that same year, Beijing consented to a nonbinding code of conduct
concerning contested claims in the South China Sea, based on the Association of South East Asian Nations (ASEAN) Manila Declaration, which
repudiated unilateral action or the use of force in resolving maritime territorial disputes. At the same time, the National People's Congress, at the
explicit urging of Premier Li Peng, passed the Territorial Waters Act de-
claring that China's "sovereign territory" included all the territorial and
maritime space of the East and South China Seas, as well as the airspace
above them. Article 14 of the act specifically reserves the right to control
traffic through and above China's "sovereign regions."[72]

Thus Beijing has sent conflicting signals to the international community, concerned as it is with the free flow of maritime traffic through some
of the world's most heavily utilized sea lines of communication.[73] The
United States is fully aware of the implications of the Territorial Waters
Act and has insisted that Beijing agree to fulfill all its obligations under
international law concerning the rights of innocent passage of foreign
vessels or aircraft through the South China Sea.[74]

The fact is that Beijing's behaviors are often at variance with its formal
international declarations. For example, after its formal agreements with
ASEAN concerning contested territorial claims, Beijing acted unilaterally
in dealing with the Republic of the Philippines. In 1994, the Philippines
contracted with a U.S. company, Alcorn, for a seismic survey in the waters west of the Palawan, well within Manila's own 200-mile exclusive
economic zone recognized by the U.N. Convention on the Law of the Sea
(UNCLOS).[75] Beijing responded, early in 1995, by marking islands in the
region as Chinese sovereign territory and erecting structures on Mischief
Reef, 130 miles west of Philippine national territory.[76]

The United States became involved in the sequence of events when
Philippine spokespersons made recourse to clauses in the U.S.-Philippine
Mutual Defense Treaty that called for bilateral consultation in the event
of attack upon the Filipino armed forces. It was on that occasion that the
then U.S. secretary of state, Warren Christopher, reminded the Chinese
foreign minister that the United States did have treaty obligations with

the Philippines and urged "in the strongest possible terms that . . . [the territorial disputes in the South China Sea] should not be settled by force."[77] Military confrontation was avoided on that occasion seemingly by the intervention of the United States and the reaction of the ASEAN community. Nevertheless, Beijing has proceeded to act with proprietary deliberation to dredge the access to Mischief Reef in order to accommodate larger Chinese vessels.[78]

At almost the same time, Jakarta discovered that the PRC has an outstanding claim on a section of the continental shelf off the Indonesian coast, within Indonesia's own 200-mile exclusive economic zone, in which natural gas reserves estimated at over 55 trillion cubic feet have been identified. Jakarta's attempt to resolve the disagreement bilaterally with Beijing has not been successful.[79] Conflict has been avoided, but Beijing has insisted that exploitation of resources in the region can continue only if pursued jointly.[80]

In March 1996, the armed forces of post-Maoist China conducted joint air and naval exercises north and south of the Republic of China on Taiwan, launching missiles whose impact areas were in close proximity to Taiwan's two largest ports. Washington considered it "prudent" and "precautionary" to deploy two carrier battle groups to the waters off Taiwan, bringing overwhelming firepower into the tensions created by Beijing's provocative live fire exercises.[81]

In effect, while Beijing has generally proceeded with diplomatic "circumspection" and prudent deliberation, it has not avoided provocative behavior. It has proceeded to behave as though the waters off its coast constitute part of its sovereign national perimeter, and it suffers violations only because its armed forces are not yet capable of fully securing its defense.[82]

For the United States, unobstructed passage through the East and South China Seas is of critical importance. The economies of its major security partners in East Asia are abjectly dependent on the inflow of fuel oil, lubricants, and natural gas from the Middle East and Indonesia. Any obstruction to that flow would negatively impact the life circumstances and the defense capabilities of all the nations of Northeast Asia, primarily Japan and the Republic of Korea.[83] Obstruction of free passage through the region, for whatever reason, would be a matter of grave concern to the security and economic interests of the United States.

"Vital Living Space" and the Geostrategy of Post-Maoist China

In the context described above Beijing has declared the East and South China Seas part of its "vital living space" *(shengcun kongjian)*—necessary if the Chinese people are to survive and prosper in the twenty-first century.[84] That post-Maoist China is already a net importer of both food grains and oil prompts its concern for the protection of offshore oil reserves and fish harvests in the East and South China Seas. With 22 percent of the world's population confined to about 7 percent of the world's land surface, feeding its growing population has always been a critical preoccupation of the government in Beijing.[85]

Given China's current rate of real industrial growth, the availability of energy reserves will become increasingly important in the next several decades. If Beijing insists on a real measure of "self-sufficiency" in order to maintain its political independence, it is evident that China must jealously guard any real or fancied offshore resource reserves. Depending on how Beijing deals with its growing shortages, domestic political pressures may precipitate military action in the contested waters of East and Southeast Asia, with Beijing acting to secure not only the resources for China's continued accelerated economic growth and industrial development but also for its political independence.[86]

These are the kinds of concern that have given rise to, and sustain, the conviction throughout East Asia "that naval power is essential for self-reliance."[87] China has given every evidence of being prepared to aggressively defend its claims in the East and South China Seas, and its neighbors have correspondingly devoted more and more attention to maritime defenses.

For the People's Republic of China, an active defense offshore is now a major part of Beijing's comprehensive national security strategy. In the perception of the leadership of Communist China, an "offshore active defense" of the mainland is dictated not only by immediate self-interest and prevailing military doctrine but by a long-term geopolitical strategy as well. Such considerations go some distance in explaining Chinese behavior in the East and South China Seas region. Only such concerns could explain the series of provocations that have troubled all the nations in those waters, which China chooses to call a "Chinese lake."

Whatever Beijing's declarative policies, however ardently the post-Maoist China involves itself in confidence-building measures, and however frequently its spokespersons participate in regional conferences,[88] there remains its commitment to an "offshore active defense"—the full implications of which remain obscure.[89]

As early as 1985, it became clear that the strategic and defense thinking of post-Maoist China had significantly changed. The conviction arose, for a variety of reasons that need not detain us, that armed conflict between the major military powers, involving early, large-scale engagements and nuclear exchange, was very unlikely.[90] Rather, the political and military leaders of post-Maoist China anticipated that armed conflict for the foreseeable future would involve conventional weapons, would be of short duration, and would probably be a response to immediate territorial and/or maritime disputes.

Post-Maoist China's new strategic doctrine has changed the responsibilities of the PLAN from the support of land operations to the conduct of war at sea.[91] Those responsible for naval planning now anticipate a different set of potential missions, some involving relatively brief conflicts in local environments in which the major military powers would not have the lead time required to mount credible countermeasure responses.[92] Those missions were constituents of a general strategy (originally termed "People's War under Modern Conditions") designed to provide post-Maoist China "comprehensive national security" in a post–Cold War world conceived by Beijing as "a dangerous neo-Darwinian jungle."[93]

The PLAN, under the new dispensation, has prepared a war-fighting doctrine calculated to complement Beijing's notions of comprehensive national security. The PLAN is charged with the responsibility of providing mainland China the strategic depth necessary to survive in the event, however improbable, that a major military power would attempt to contain or defeat the PRC.[94] More important, for present purposes, is the fact that to meet its new responsibilities the leadership of the PLAN put together a policy of "offshore active defense" that has major geostrategic implications.

Admiral Liu Huaqing, former commander of Chinese naval operations in the Spratly Islands and subsequently vice chairman of the Central Military Commission, was the architect of the PLAN's blue-water ambitions and its new interpretation of "defensive" offshore operations. Those operations involve precisely those military activities in East Asia that are threatening regional security and international trading interests.

Liu's conception of an "offshore active defense" is part of a larger strategic concept that is certainly more than a concern with irredentist claims. It involves an in-depth maritime defense of the Chinese mainland in the unlikely event of any conflict involving a major military power. Such a defense would require effective military control over the chain of islands that Liu identifies as the "first island chain,"[95] commencing with those in the Yellow and East China Seas in the north, through those in the South China Sea, to the territorial waters as far south as the Greater Sunda Islands.

Control over those maritime territories would deny any enemy secure access to base facilities, launch sites, and staging areas in proximity to the mainland. It would render any enemy operations within the boundaries of the first island chain extremely hazardous.

The preconditions for any effective control over the waters bordered by Liu's first island chain involve the resolution of post-Maoist China's irredentist claims. To prepare to control the waters of the East and South China Seas in any contingency recommends to Beijing a deliberate effort to press its territorial and maritime claims. That entails dealing with the claims of the Republic of Korean, Japan, the Republic of China on Taiwan, Indonesia, the Socialist Republic of Vietnam, Malaysia, Thailand, Brunei, Singapore, and the Republic of the Philippines. It is in this context that China's promulgation of its February 1992 domestic Territorial Waters Act takes on particular significance. Article 2 of that legislation identifies Taiwan, the Pescadores, the Diaoyu Islands (Sengaku Shoto), the Pratas, the Paracel Islands, the Macclesfield Bank, and the Spratly Archipelago as components of the sovereign and inalienable territory of the PRC.

Not only do such affirmations lay the foundation for Chinese claims to preclusive economic exclusion zones in the region, but they include a suggestion that Beijing might restrict passage along the sea routes under unspecified conditions, as well as authorize the use of military force to prevent other claimants from occupying the contested maritime territories.[96]

The ability to deploy the requisite combat capabilities would free China from the confines of the first island chain. With control of the waters and some of the strategic islands of the first island chain, China would have free access to the open Pacific Ocean. Like the China of the dynastic past, post-Maoist China would once again become a maritime power of worldwide significance.[97]

In 1993, the government presses of post-Maoist China published *Can China Win the Next War?* in which analysts, most probably naval officers, discussed in considerable technical detail the planning strategies necessary to assure victory in the armed struggles attendant to seizing and maintaining control over the waters within the boundaries of the first island chain.[98] The physical acquisition and defense of those territories would be the responsibility of the naval forces of the PLA.

Recently, Zhang Liangzhong, commander of the PLAN, affirmed that "to defend China truly and effectively from raids and attacks from the sea, we must strengthen the defense in depth at sea and possess naval forces that have the capability to intercept and wipe out the enemy."[99] That would require major air and surface capabilities enhancement. What seems evident is that the leadership of post-Maoist China is increasingly prepared to provide suitable budgets for just such enhancements.[100]

Faced with major procurement requirements, the Chinese navy has sought, in the immediate past, an increasing share of China's defense budget, which has escalated at double-digit rates since the late 1980s. Estimates of the PRC's annual defense-related outlays range widely, from as little as an official $7.48 billion to $140 billion, the most responsible estimate being about $48.5 billion.[101]

The inability to estimate the military budget of the PRC turns not only on all the difficulties inherent in trying to fix the purchasing power parity of a nonconvertible currency with any precision, but on the fact that so much of China's military expenditures are buried in opacity. Analysts will probably never be able to provide a precise figure for Beijing's spending on national security.[102] What seems reasonably clear is that post-Maoist China is spending proportionately more in expanding the capabilities of its naval forces than almost any other modern nation.

Post-Maoist China's geostrategic plans thus involve the construction of a major blue-water navy, including suitable aircraft carriers together with the support and attack machines that make such carriers effective defensive and offensive weapons. Such weapons platforms and delivery systems would allow China to control the waters within the first island chain and commence its strategic and tactical planning for controlling the waters up to the "second island chain" in mid-Pacific—a "chain" that includes the U.S. island Guam.[103]

Consequently, some fear not only a potential "threat to Western interest in the free movement of shipping" in the East and South China Seas region that could generate the "strong possibility" of "limited war" between one or another ASEAN nations but a major conflict with the United States as well.[104]

Beijing's determined effort to establish its territorial and maritime claims in the South China Sea has implications for the international community as well as the economies and the security of nations in the region. Certainly, in their effort to secure military control over the first and second island chains and secure access to the open oceans, the Chinese authorities would have to anticipate the resistance of nations in the region, and the threat of retaliation by the major international trading nations. Such considerations would serve as major disincentives.[105]

It is difficult, however, to have absolute confidence in the deterrent efficacy of such disincentives. Before the Tiananmen massacre in 1989, most analysts were convinced that the authorities in Beijing would not consider employing violence against their own unarmed civilian population in their effort to suppress political dissent because it would alienate foreign investors and bring down trading sanctions that would threaten China's ambitious programs of economic modernization. The leaders of the Chinese Communist party were well aware that the predictable international response would threaten continued economic modernization, reduce the nation's access to foreign markets, and outrage those prepared to provide the investment capital China so desperately needed. But none of that dissuaded the leadership in Beijing from its purpose. Before the eyes of the world, the leaders in Beijing massacred innocents in Tiananmen Square.

It is not certain that fear of foreign reaction would do much to deter Beijing if it were determined to exercise "benign" and "legitimate" control over 15 percent of all the world's ship traffic passing through the East and South China Seas in the pursuit of its irredentist intentions and the security of controlling the waters to the far reaches of the second island chain. It is evident that whatever Beijing chooses to do in the waters between the Chinese littoral and the first or second island chain will depend more on its military capabilities than almost anything else. The measure of the capabilities required would depend on China's identification of its potential opponent in the region.

The United States has expressed its determination to assure freedom of navigation in the South China Sea.[106] The question is whether Beijing, under one or another set of circumstances, might decide that some political or security imperatives override any of the risks implicit in aggressive action in the region. Then the test could well be military and would be measured in capabilities.

It is clear that the People's Republic of China will remain an assertive and increasingly arms-capable actor in East Asia, particularly in the South China Sea. That, together with the general conviction that post-Maoist China is "a growing regional military power—and a major non-*status quo* power—with extensive irredentist claims,"[107] suggests that there is a real possibility of armed confrontation in the East and South China Seas.

Those who dismiss such possibilities as unlikely tend to base their judgments on the fact that major conflict in East Asia would not serve China's "rational" interests. What may seem "rational" to "sated" Western powers may not appear "rational" to a reactive nationalist regime. Only within a given context can behaviors be considered "reasonable." The authorities in Beijing measure the rationality of their activities within the framework of an emerging "patriotism" that defines the survival of China in terms of a strong state, an equally strong military, and an emphatic nationalism.[108] The Chinese Communist party's Program for Education in Patriotism, animated by the conviction that nationalism will serve as the "spiritual foundation for a strong and prosperous country and a rising nation," shares some of the features of the aggressive nationalism with which the twentieth century is all too familiar.

The Chinese people are taught that the industrial democracies are "decadent" and are the source of "spiritual pollution," as well as the active agents of an arrogant "imperialism" against which only "patriotism" offers defense.[109] There is regular reiteration of the humiliations that China has suffered for a century and a half at the hands of those same "imperialists"—the United States foremost among them.

China's new nationalism, with its attendant irredentism and its geostrategic plans, is a serious matter. In a recent poll, about 90 percent of Chinese youth identify the United States as an "imperialist" power attempting to "dominate" China.[110] The mainland Chinese authors of the best-selling *China Can Say No–Political and Emotional Choices in the Post Cold War Era* did not conceal their admiration of Vladimir Zhirinovsky,[111] the radical Russian nationalist who has called upon his countrymen to embark on an adventure in irredentism that would bring them to the shores of Alaska in the quixotic effort to restore "lost" lands.

More recently, mainland Chinese authors have published a collection of enormously popular essays entitled *The Demonization of China*, in which the United States is charged with a determined policy of vilification—the ultimate purpose of which is the total subjugation of China. The United States is typified as inherently racist, anti-Chinese, inhumane, and aggressively militaristic, as well as a threat to the survival of China.

How much China's new nationalism influences its present behavior is difficult to determine with any confidence. Even less is it possible to predict its influence in the immediate future. Although exacerbated nationalism has provoked military adventure and violence everywhere in the world after the Second World War, it is impossible to anticipate how much it will shape events in East and Southeast Asia.

The experience of the twentieth century, however, cannot leave us sanguine. Reactive nationalism has everywhere inspired political communities to embark on harrowing misadventures in unequal combat if sufficiently inspired by irredentist incentives. This is not limited to Fascism's commitment to conflict in the Second World War without the military inventory or the resources necessary to make that involvement "rational." The Iraqi invasion of Kuwait and the Argentine invasion of the Falklands were similarly "irrational" in the judgment of commentators in the "imperialist" nations.

Yet the abeyant irredentist claims of post-Maoist China far exceed those we have considered here. In various places and different times, Chinese authors have spoken of the Russian Far East and Sakhalin Island as "lost territories." They have spoken of the western half of the Sea of Japan and the Korean peninsula as somehow "lost" territories. There has been talk of the Ryukyus, and Vietnam, Laos, Thailand, Cambodia, Burma, Malaysia, and all the tributary states as having been "lost." "Lost" also have been Andaman Island, Nepal, Bhutan, Kirghizstan, the eastern half of Kazakhstan, as well as the Russia Altay and Sayan mountains and Mongolia.[112]

In an imaginable future, the rise of dissidence at home, the accumulation of unmanageable social problems, economic dislocations, and political factionalism might recommend nationalist and irredentist adventures to China's leaders. Even when China pretended to be animated by "proletarian internationalism," it came perilously close to war with the overwhelming military power of the former Soviet Union over territorial disputes in the Russian Far East.[113] Under Deng Xiaoping, China was similarly prepared to embark on an apparently unequal "punitive war" with Vietnam for much the same reasons.

The leaders of post-Maoist China, like the leaders of Fascist Italy, see their nation as the paladin of those poor, less-developed nations that suffer at the hands of the "imperialist" powers. In one of the more recent publications of China's controlled press, the authors stated with doctrinaire certainty: "We can predict with full confidence and pride that the twenty-first century will be the time of the Third World. The Third World will play an important role on the world stage in the coming century. As the Third World's largest developing nation," they continued, that time would be "China's day of ascendance."[114] China, long humbled by the advanced industrial powers, would assume its rightful place as a "proletarian central kingdom" in a world in which the greed, selfishness, and hegemonic aspirations of rich nations no longer have a place.

Notes

1. Sun Yat-sen, *The Triple Demism of Sun Yat-sen* (1931; reprint, New York: AMS, 1974), pp. 92–95. Reprint of the Wuchang edition of 1931.

2. See Giuseppe Mazzini, "To the Italians," in *The Duties of Man and Other Essays* (New York: E. P. Dutton, 1907), pp. 244–245.

3. See the discussion in Paola Maria Arcari, *Le elaborazioni della dottrina politica nazionale fra l'unità e l'intervento (1870–1914)*, vol. 3 (Florence: Marzocco, 1934–1939), pt. 2.

4. See the Model Statute of the first group of the Association that met in Turin to prepare for the formal organization of the national body in 1910. "1909," in Arcari, *Le elaborazioni*, 3:57.

5. See the account made available in Giovani Papini and Giuseppe Prezzolini (1914; reprint, Rome: Volpe, 1967), where they trace the origins of the "new" nationalism to articles in *Leonardo* and *Il Regno* in 1903 and 1904.

6. Arcari, *Le elaborazioni*, 1:5. Mussolini, who was thirteen at the time of the Italian defeat at Adowa, is reported to have been obsessed by the event throughout his life. See James Dugan and Laurence Lafore, *Days of Emperor and Clown: The Italo-Ethiopian War, 1935–1936* (New York: Doubleday, 1973), p. 60.

7. Gualtiero Castellini, *Fasi e dottrine del nazionalismo italiano* (Milan: Quinteri, 1915), p. 2.

8. See the discussion in Scipio Sighele, *Pagine nazionaliste* (Milan: Treves, 1910), particularly "Risveglio italico," where Sighele argues that the "Latin nations" suffer from a deep sense of inadequacy, the result of their inferiority vis-à-vis the "Germanic" peoples of the North. He advocated the rapid economic development of the motherland, so that Italians might satisfy their "will to be strong and respected in the world."

9. See the discussion in A. James Gregor, *Phoenix: Fascism in Our Time* (New Brunswick, N.J.: Transaction, 1999), chap. 2.

10. Glen Barclay, *The Rise and Fall of the New Roman Empire* (New York: St. Martin's, 1973), p. 40.

11. See "Order of the Day," 1919 Congress of Rome, in Arcari, *Le elaborazioni*, 3:40.

12. Ibid., p. 51.

13. See ibid., p. 38, and Model Statute, in ibid., p. 57.

14. It is not the case that Fascism simply inherited its external policies from organized Italian Nationalism. There was a parallel ideological development among Marxist Revolutionary Syndicalists (with whom Mussolini had an intimate intellectual association). Fascist nationalism was more complicated than is suggested here. See the account in A. James Gregor, *Young Mussolini and the Intellectual Origins of Fascism* (Berkeley: University of California, 1979).

15. See Luigi Villari, *Italian Foreign Policy Under Mussolini* (New York: Devin-Adair, 1956), p. 18.

16. See the account in Barclay, *Rise and Fall*, pp. 116–117; Virginio Gayda, *Perchè l'Italia e in guerra* (Rome: Capriotti, n.d.), pp. 25–26.

17. Barclay, *Rise and Fall*, p. 126; Gayda, *Perchè l'Italia*, p. 26.

18. In 1923, the Italian Nationalists officially merged with Fascism. The ideological relationship between the Nationalists and Fascists was always acknowledged. See the discussion in Carlo Terracciano, "Direttrici geopolitiche coloniali dell'Italia nell'era fascista," in *Geopolitica fascista: Antologia di scritti*, ed. Carlo Terracciano, Giorgio Reletto, and Ernesto Massi (Milan: Barbarossa, 1993), pp. 8–10.

19. Benito Mussolini, "Il nostro dovere e quello di liberaci del giogo della plutocrazia internationale," in *Opera omnia* (Florence: La fenice, 1954–1963), 14:223. Hereafter cited as *OO*.

20. See Mussolini's comments in "I diritti della vittoria," *OO*, 14:50–55.

21. Mussolini, "Gesto di rivolta," *OO*, 14:5.

22. Ibid.

23. See the "Programma e statuti del Partito nazionale fascista," *OO*, 17:336.

24. Mussolini, "Noi e l'estero," *OO*, 18:274–275.

25. Mussolini, "Italia e oriente: Libertà alla Siria," *OO*, 18:244–246.

26. Mussolini, "Italia e Mediterraneo: L'Egitto indipendente?" *OO*, 18:76–78.

27. Mussolini, "Il discorso di Napoli," *OO*, 18:457–459.

28. See the discussions in Mussolini, "Il programma di Mussolini," *OO*, 18:466; "Il bavaglio," *OO*, 14:13; "Fatto decisivo!" *OO*, 14:19; "Decidersi o perire!" *OO*, 14:28–29; "La stolta vociferazione," *OO*, 14:32–33.

29. See Mussolini, "Il discorso," *OO*, 14:30–31.

30. Mussolini, "Per rinascere e progredire: Politica orientale," *OO*, 14:225.

31. In his first speech to the Chamber of Deputies after acceding to power in 1922, Mussolini spoke specifically of Italy's dearth of natural resources. See Mussolini, "Il primo discorso presidenziale alla Camera dei deputati," *OO*, 19:19.

32. Mussolini, "Dal malinconico tramonto liberale all'aurora fascista della nuova Italia," *OO*, 18:439.

33. Robert Mallett, *The Italian Navy and Fascist Expansionism, 1935–1940* (London: Frank Cass, 1998); Terracciano, *Geopolitica fascista*, pp. 5–20.

34. Mussolini, "L'Italia e le grandi potenze," *OO*, 19:3.

35. Mussolini, "Le elezioni e la riforma elettorale," *OO*, 19:10.

36. Mussolini, "Ai metallurgici Lombardi," *OO*, 19:57.

37. Mussolini, "Agli industriali italiani," *OO*, 29:224.

38. Mussolini, "Il primo discorso presidenziale all Camera dei deputati," *OO*, 19:19.

39. Mussolini, "La nuova politica estera," *OO*, 19:130; and "La nuova politica estera," *OO*, 19:148.

40. Giorgio Rumi, *Alle origini della politica estera fascista* (Bari: Laterza, 1968), p. 235.

41. See, for example, Giovanni Selvi, "L'Islam e l'impero dell'Africa Italiana," *Gerarchia* 18, no. 5 (1938): 323–328.

42. Mussolini, "Alle gerarchie trentine," *OO*, 29:394.

43. Fascist commentators recognized that the Corfu incident was designed to demonstrate to Great Britain that Fascist Italy was prepared to challenge its dominance in the Mediterranean. See Guido Puccio, *Lotta fra due mondi* (Rome: Edizioni italiane, 1942), p. 187.

44. See the discussion in Leopoldo Checchi, "Italia sul mare," *Gerarchia* 17, no. 9 (1937): 619–625; and in Emilio Canevari, "Il Medeterraneo frontiera italiana: Noi e l'Inghilterra," *Critica fascista* 14, no. 19 (1936): 299–301.

45. See the discussion in G. Fioravanzo, "Il problema del Mediterraneo," *Gerarchia* 19, no. 2 (1939): 77–84; see p. 83; Marco Maffei, "La Spagna e l'equilibrio Mediterraneo," *Gerarchia* 19, no. 8 (1939): 530–543.

46. See Guido Pucci, *Il conflitto Anglo-Maltese* (Milan: Treves, 1933); see Rumi, *Alle origini*, pp. 235–238.

47. See the accounts in Guido Puccio, *Malta italianissima* (Rome: Maltesi, 1940); and Giovanni Selvi, "Corsica, terra italiana," *Gerarchia* 19, no. 1 (1939): 3–8.

48. As Italy entered the Second World War, Fernando Gori, in his *Roma nel continente nero* (Rome: Tupini, 1940), reiterated all the same arguments, ranging from the occupation by the Roman Empire to then contemporary geostrategic issues.

49. See the editorial "L'Italia e la nuova situazione europea," *Critica fascista*, 15 April 1938, pp. 178–179.

50. Leopoldo Checchi, "La politica navale," *Gerarchia* 18, no. 3 (1938): 219–222.

51. Gayda, *Perchè l'Italia*, p. 47.

52. See the discussion in Vito Beltrani, *Il problema delle materie prime* (Rome: Tupini, 1940), chaps. 5–7.

53. See the discussion in ibid., chap. 4.

54. See the discussion in Lauro Mainardi, *Nazionalità e spazi vitali* (Rome: Cremonese, 1941).

55. Domenico Soprano, *Spazio vitale* (Milan: Corbaccio, 1942), pp. 12–13.

56. See the comments of Giuseppe Bottai, "Sul piano imperiale," *Critica fascista*, 1 September 1936, pp. 321–323

57. See the discussion in Leopoldo E. Checchi, "La politica navale," *Gerarchia* 13, no. 2 (1935): 193.

58. Terracciano, *Geopolitica fascista*, p. 15.

59. Mussolini, "Il capestro di demos," *OO*, 29:28.

60. Mussolini, "'Popolo italiano! Corri alle armi,'" *OO*, 29:404.

61. Gayda, *Perchè l'Italia*, p. 95.

62. In 1940, in the effort to document the continuity of Fascist geopolitical thought on the occasion of Italy's intervention in the Second World War, *Gerarchia* republished articles written by Dino Grandi at the time of Italy's intervention in the First World War. In those articles Grandi wrote that "modern wars, the wars of tomorrow will inevitably involve poor nations against those that are rich, between those nations that labor and produce and those nations that already possess capital and riches. . . . It will be a war between those who would do more against those who have more. It will be class struggle between nations." Dino Grandi, "Interventismo 1915 e interventismo 1940," *Gerarchia* 19, no. 11 (1940): 571. See the last interview with Mussolini in which he restated his case, *Testamento politico di Mussolini* (Rome: Pedanesi, n.d.), pp. 26–35. See the discussion in Domenico Soprano, *Spazio vitale* (Milan: Corbaccio, 1942), pp. 125–151.

63. In his final interview before his death, Mussolini spoke of Italy's oppression and humiliation in terms of "eighteen centuries of invasions and misery . . . and servitude" (*Testamento*, p. 33).

64. For the complicated process of deciding to intervene, see Renzo De Felice, *Mussolini il duce: Lo stato totalitario, 1936–1940* (Turin: Einaudi, 1981), chaps. 6–7.

65. See Emilio Faldella, *L'Italia e la seconda guerra mondiale* (Rocca San Casciano: Cappelli, 1967), chap. 2; see the three-part article by Luigi Emilio Longo, "Il fallimento militare italiano 1940–1943 e le sue origini," *Storia verità* 1, nos. 4–6 (1992).

66. Sun, *Triple Demism*, pp. 92–95.

67. See the recent discussion in Liu Xiaozhu, "Beware the Rise of Extreme Nationalism on the Mainland," *Shijie ribao* (World Journal), 3 April 1994, p. A6. In Chinese.

68. See the discussion in Edwin K. Snyder, A. James Gregor, and Maria Hsia Chang, *The Taiwan Relations Act and the Defense of the Republic of China* (Berkeley: Institute of International Studies, 1980).

69. This has led some commentators to see post-Maoist China as amenable to diplomatic treatment. See Yong Deng, "Managing China's Hegemonic Ascension: Engagement from Southeast Asia," *Journal of Strategic Studies* 21, no. 1 (1998): 21–43. Similar arguments were made during the interwar years concerning Fascist Italy.

70. See Maria Hsia Chang, "Chinese Irredentist Nationalism: The Magician's Last Trick," *Comparative Strategy* 17, no. 2 (1998): 83–100.

71. See William J. Dobson and M. Taylor Fravel, "Red Herring Hegemon: China in the South China Sea," *Current History* 96, no. 611 (1997): 259–260.

72. "The People's Republic of China's Territorial Waters and Adjacent Territories Act," *1995 Zhonggong nianbao* (1995 China yearbook) (Taipei: Zhonggong yanjiu zazhishe, 1995), sec. 6, pp. 36–37.

73. See John H. Noer, "Southeast Asian Chokepoints: Keeping Sea Lines of Communication Open," *Strategic Forum* 98 (December 1996): 1; John H. Noer with David Gregory, *Maritime Economic Interests and the Sea Lines of Communication Through the South China Sea* (Washington, D.C.: Center for Naval Analyses, 1996), pp. 4–5.

74. See Eric A. McVadon, "China: An Opponent or an Opportunity?" *Naval War College Review* 49, no. 4, sequence 356 (1996): 78.

75. To which Beijing became a signatory in 1996. See Jusuf Wanandi, "ASEAN's China Strategy: Towards Deeper Engagement," *Survival* 33, no. 3 (1996): 123.

76. See Rodney Tasker, "A Line in the Sand," *Far Eastern Economic Review* [hereafter *FEER*], 6 April 1995, pp. 14–16.

77. See *Indochina Digest*, 21 April 1995, p. 1.

78. In mid-May 1997, the PRC complained that Philippine naval vessels had "driven away" Chinese ships from the contested Scarborough Shoal. "Philippines: Showing the Flag," *FEER*, 29 May 1997, p. 13.

79. There have been reports that negotiations continue. Although Beijing has agreed that Netuna island is Indonesian, the dispute about the offshore shelf apparently remains unresolved. In the interim, Jakarta has proceeded to purchase 12 Su–30MK multirole fighters from Russia to provide enhanced defense of the giant Natuna gasfield in the South China Sea. See John McBeth, "Turn and Burn," *FEER*, 21 August 1997, pp. 20–21; Charles Bickers, "Bear Market," *FEER*, 4 September 1997, p. 25.

80. John McBeth, "Oil Rich Diet," *FEER*, 27 April 1995, p. 28. Beijing has consistently maintained that the PRC must be consulted in any activity in the South China Sea region. That insistence is now increasingly backed by military capabilities.

81. See A. James Gregor, "China, the United States, and Security Policy in East Asia," *Parameters* 26, no. 2 (1996): 92–101.

82. The deficiencies of the Chinese PLA are well-known and will take considerable time to remedy. See the discussion in A. James Gregor, "Qualified Engagement: U.S. China Policy and Security Concerns," *Naval War College Review* 52, 2 sequence 366 (Spring 1999): 69–89.

83. See Marwyn S. Samuels, *Contest for the South China Sea* (New York: Methuen, 1982), chap. l; A. James Gregor, *The Philippine Bases: U.S. Security at Risk* (Washington, D.C.: Ethics and Public Policy Center, 1987); Steven Butler et al., "Refocusing in Asia," *U.S. News and World Report*, 22 April 1996, p. 49.

84. Nayan Chanda and Karl Huus, "China: The New Nationalism," *FEER*, 9 November 1995, p. 20. See the discussion in Samuel S. Kim, *China's Quest for Security in the Post-Cold War World* (Carlisle Barracks: U.S. Army War College, 1996), pp. 16–17.

85. For a careful analysis of China's agricultural problems, see Vaclav Smil, "Who Will Feed China?" *China Quarterly* 143 (September 1995): 801–813.

86. See the discussion in A. James Gregor, *In the Shadow of Giants: The Security of Southeast Asia and the Major Powers* (Stanford: Hoover Institution, 1989), chap. 5; and Henry J. Kenny, "The South China Sea: A Dangerous Ground," *Naval War College Review* 49, no. 3, sequence 355 (1996): 96–108.

87. Ibid., p. 118.

88. Stanley Roth, assistant secretary of state for East Asian and Pacific Affairs, provides a catalog of Beijing's declaratory commitments concerning the peaceful resolution of conflict in Southeast Asia in "The China Policy Act of 1997," *Topics*, October 1997, pp. 40–46.

89. China's bilateral military arrangements with Burma have become a matter of concern. If reports are correct, the PLA has now acquired signal intelligence sites on the Bay of Bengal coast of Burma that allows Chinese forces to monitor

ship passage through the Strait of Malacca. See Yossef Bodanky, "The PRC Surge
for the Strait of Malacca and Spratlys Confronts India and the U.S.," *Defense and
Foreign Affairs Strategic Policy*, 30 September 1995, pp. 6–13.

90. See Nan Li, "The PLA's Evolving Warfighting Doctrine, Strategy and Tac-
tics, 1985–95: A Chinese Perspective," *China Quarterly* 146 (June 1996): 443–463;
Paul H. B. Godwin, "People's War Revised: Military Doctrine, Strategy, and Op-
erations," in *China's Military Reforms: International and Domestic Implications*, ed.
Charles D. Lovejoy and Bruce W. Watson (Boulder: Westview, 1986), pp. 2–4;
Wang Chengbing, *Deng Ziaoping's Modern Military Theory and Practice* (Nanchang:
Jiangxi People's Publishers, 1991), pp. 272–319. In Chinese.

91. In 1950, the commander of Chinese naval forces insisted that the PLAN
"should be a light-type navy, capable of inshore defense. Its key mission is to accompany the ground forces in war actions." As cited in You Ji and You Xu, "In
Search of Blue Water Power: The PLA Navy's Maritime Strategy in the 1990s," *Pacific Review*, Summer 1991, p. 139.

92. See the discussion in Alexander Chieh-cheng Huang, "The Chinese Navy's
Offshore Active Defense Strategy: Conceptualization and Implications," *Naval
War College Review* 47, no. 3, sequence 347 (Summer 1994): 7–32, particularly p. 17.

93. Kim, *China's Quest for Security*, p. 6. Song Yimin describes the realpolitik of
the PRC's current strategic worldview in the following fashion: "In their eyes
world politics continues to involve a zero-sum game, and a hierarchy of power
inevitably exists within which the more powerful nations dominate the weak."
As cited in Wang Jisi, "Pragmatic Nationalism: China Seeks a New Role in World
Affairs," *Oxford International Review*, Winter 1994, p. 29. See Thomas J. Chris-
tensen, "Chinese Realpolitik," *Foreign Affairs* 75, no. 5 (September-October 1996):
37–52.

94. The notion that the defense of Mainland China required strategic depth
was a consequence of the recognition that the bulk of the economic assets of the
PRC were located on the littoral. Unlike the war with Japan, in which China
could trade space for time, any future conflict with a major military power would
put the nation in jeopardy if it could not adequately defend its coastal economic
base.

95. See the discussion in Ai Hongren, *Zhonggong Haijun Toushi: Maixiang
Yuanyang De Tiaozhan* (An inside look into the Chinese Communist navy: Ad-
vancing toward the blue-water challenge) (Hong Kong: October 1988). Translated
by the U.S. Information Service, Joint Publication Research Service, China (JPRS-
CAR–90–052), 16 July 1990, pp. 14–15. Zhang Lianzhong et al., eds., *Haijun Shi* (A
history of the PLA Navy) (Beijing: PLA, 1989), p. 247.

96. See Eric Hyer, "The South China Sea Disputes: Implications of China's Earlier Territorial Settlements," *Pacific Affairs*, Spring 1995, p. 41.

97. See the discussion in Bruce Swanson, *Eighth Voyage of the Dragon: A History
of China's Quest for Seapower* (Annapolis: Naval Institute Press, 1982); Irwin Mil-
lard Heine, *China's Rise to Commercial Maritime Power* (New York: Greenwood,
1989); David G. Muller Jr., *China As a Maritime Power* (Boulder: Westview, 1983).

98. See the discussion in Ulysses O. Zalamea, "Eagles and Dragons at Sea: The
Inevitable Strategic Collision Between the United States and China," *Naval War
College Review* 49, no. 4, sequence 356 (Autumn 1996): 64.

99. As cited in Ai, *Inside Look*, p. 25.

100. Paul H. B. Godwin, "Uncertainty, Insecurity, and China's Military Power," *Current History* 96, no. 611 (1997): 253–254.

101. David Shambaugh provides the figure of approximately $48.5 billion in "The United States and China: Cooperation or Engagement," *Current History*, September 1997, p. 243. That would provide the People's Liberation Army, annually, with the world's third- or fourth-largest military budget. The range of estimates provided in the text are to be found in David Shambaugh, "Growing Strong: China's Challenge to Asian Security," *Survival* 36 (Summer 1994): 54. See, in this context, Richard A. Bitzinger and Chong-pin Lin, *Off the Books: Analysing and Understanding Chinese Defense Spending* (Washington, D.C.: Defense Budget Project, 1994); and Richard A. Bitzinger, "China Defense Budget," *International Defense Review*, February 1995, p. 37; Harry Harding, "A Chinese Colossus?" *Journal of Strategic Studies* 18 (September 1995): 122 n. 5; Ricard D. Fisher Jr. and John T. Dori, eds., *U.S. and Asia Statistical Handbook (1995)* (Washington, D.C.: Heritage Foundation, 1995), p. 37.

102. See the discussion in Shaoguang Wang, "Estimating China's Defence Expenditure: Some Evidence from Chinese Sources," *China Quarterly* 147 (September 1996): 889–911; Arthur S. Ding, "China's Defence Finance: Content, Process and Administration," *China Quarterly*, 146 (June 1996): 428–442.

103. See the discussion in Ai, *An Inside Look*; Huang, "Chinese Navy," pp. 7–32.

104. Michael Pugh, "Is Mahan Still Alive? State Naval Power in the International System," *Journal of Conflict Studies* 16, no. 2 (1996): 119; see "Beijing Arming for Wars with West," *Washington Times*, 6 July 1997, p. 1; and Richard Bernstein and Ross H. Munro, *The Coming Conflict with China* (New York: Knopf, 1997).

105. See the account in Kenny, *Analysis*, pp. 19–20.

106. See the account in Department of State, *United States Policy on the Spratlys and the South China Sea* (Washington, D.C.: Government Printing Office, 1995).

107. Kim, *China's Quest*, p. 32.

108. See Jonathan Unger, ed., *Chinese Nationalism* (Armonk, N.Y.: M. E. Sharpe, 1996). For interesting insights into these issues, see Barry Sautman, "Racial Nationalism and China's External Behavior" (paper prepared for the American Political Science Association meeting, San Francisco, 30 August 1996).

109. See Tang Yongsheng, "Nationalism and the International Order" (paper presented at the Academic Conference on Nationalism at the Turn of the Century, Shenzhen, PRC, 17 November 1995).

110. The apparently accidental bombing of the Chinese embassy in Belgrade during NATO's Kosovo operations provoked widespread nationalist outrage among the Chinese.

111. See Zhang Xiaobo and Song Qiang, "China Can Say No to America," *New Perspectives Quarterly* 13, no. 4 (1996): 55–56.

112. See "The Dragon Awakes," *Browning Newsletter* 20, no. 2 (1996): 4; Maria Hsia Chang, "Chinese Irredentist Nationalism: The Magician's Last Trick," *Comparative Strategy* 17, no. 2 (1998): 83–100.

113. See Harrison E. Salisbury, *War Between Russia and China* (New York: Norton, 1969).

114. Zhang Zangzang, Song Qiang, and Ziao Bian, *Xiang zoutian, ma zouri: 2030 zhongguo di boyi tu* (Two paths: 2030 China's strategy) (Hohhot: Inner Mongolia People's Publisher, 1997), p. 22.

9
Conclusions

China has not yet concluded its long revolution. Its revolution is part of a continuing process that has seen the influence of the advanced industrial democracies radiate outward from northwestern Europe and North America into eastern and southern Europe to Africa and Latin America—and the Middle and Far East. Along the periphery and through time that penetration provoked a reactive response in the form of a series of revolutionary nationalist movements.

The reactive nationalist regimes that emerged as a response to the real or fancied impostures of foreign penetration gave shape and substance to the history of the twentieth century. Less-developed regions of the globe, long somnolent in the backwaters of history, were prodded into activity by the overbearing presence of foreigners armed with the most advanced technology. Peoples long content to live passively in relative isolation were shaken into a frenzy of activity to resist being culturally, politically, and militarily subordinated by powerful outsiders.

Great Britain's rise to virtual global hegemony in the nineteenth century, succeeded by the United States in the twentieth, served to galvanize peoples on their perimeters. In central, eastern, and southern Europe reactive nationalist movements made their appearance. In East Asia, developmental nationalist impulses coalesced around revolutionary intellectuals.

Throughout the less-developed regions of the world, these impulses gave rise to regimes that assumed a variety of forms. There were "restorative" authoritarianisms and "young Turk" modernizers. Some accomplished their purposes to a substantial degree. Some sputtered out and lapsed back into an accommodative lethargy. All had their difficulties with the "demoplutocracies" that had hegemonic influence over international developments.

Much, although certainly not all, of the violence that has come to distinguish our century turned on the efforts of reactive nationalists to secure for their communities what they considered a proper place in the sun. The resistance of the advanced industrial powers fueled the reaction that motivated the revolutionaries, almost always committed to the restoration of what was considered the dignity, independence, and security of their respective peoples. A commitment to an imposing military, with all its uniforms and aggressive posturing, became traits common to virtually all "redemptive," "palingenetic" nationalisms.

It goes without saying that the history of these movements, and the regimes they spawned, was and is different in many ways. Some were clearly uncertain about their ultimate purpose. Some infused their calls for sacrifice and dedication with talk of "proletarian" revolutions, the withering away of the state, and the consecration to class warfare. Some spoke of race wars and others of a revolutionary devotion to the restoration of treasured religious and cultural norms. All saw in the advanced industrial democracies their mortal enemies.

Although these responses are characteristically forthcoming in less-developed economic and industrial environments, there have been instances in which relatively advanced nations have succumbed to the siren call of securing that place in the sun denied them by circumstance. At the beginning of the twentieth century, Wilhelmine Germany was on the cusp of becoming one of the "powers." War and the reparations imposed on a defeated nation reduced a proud Germany to abject inferiority. The hundreds of thousands of young men who had poured their lives into the armed struggle of the First World War returned home to a humiliated and desolate Germany. Like denizens of less-developed nations, the Germans of the interwar years found themselves denied station and status in a world dominated by the advanced industrial democracies. The subsequent drive to achieve Germany's "proper" place in the international community caused Germany, and the nations around it, unspeakable devastation.

National Socialist Germany featured all the overt traits of reactive and developmental nationalism. Its seeming nationalism was aggressive and revanchist, its economic system specifically geared for conflict with the "plutocracies." While not "less-developed," its circumstances simulated those of peripheral peoples.

National Socialist Germany was not to be the last of these anomalies. After the First World War Russia was initially confused by a Marxism that was neither functional nor credible, and it quickly assumed the political posture of a nationalist developmental dictatorship that was neither humane nor internationalist and antimilitarist. Because of the uncertainty and confusion that accompanied the Bolshevik revolution, the new dictatorship was created under the pretended auspices of an internationalist and postdevelopmental Marxism. In the course of time, the jerry-built system disintegrated under the pressure of circumstances.[1] Out of the ruins of a "Marxism-Leninism" dialectically transformed into an uncertain developmental dictatorship, a "nuclear-powered Third World community" emerged that abandoned all pretense and took on the now familiar attributes of the paradigmatic Fascism of Mussolini.[2] The consequence has been the emergence of an antidemocratic, nationalistic, developmental, irredentist, militaristic, and redemptive political movement that identifies itself as "communist" but features all the properties of reactive nationalism.

It seems reasonably clear that the protracted humiliations suffered by political communities because of military defeat or catastrophic economic collapse—particularly in an environment of acute challenge—may be sufficient to precipitate the sequence of events that matures into the responses herein identified as fascist. Under some set of just such ill-defined circumstances, a reactive and developmental regime may transform itself into an identifiable variety of fascism.

In the case of contemporary China, its progressive transformation commenced with the incursions of the industrialized Western powers into the empire at the beginning of the nineteenth century. The response was initially reactive and ultimately developmental. By the end of the twentieth century, the process has given rise to an unmistakable form of fascism.

The political leadership of China continues to smart under what it perceives as the real and fancied, past and present humiliations endured at the hands of the advanced nations. That leadership remains convinced that only a politically unified, heavily armed nation can resist the depredations of the established "demoplutocracies" and their allies. Only so provisioned can an ill-used and exploited people restore their integrity and collective pride. Given such a view of the world, no sacrifice can be too great, no risk too hazardous, in the effort to restore the motherland and its people to that proper place denied it by the dominant powers.

Given China's unhappy history, all of this could only have been anticipated. Its long revolution had nothing to do with the advent of a "classless society" or the resolution of the problem of poverty. China's revolution was the consequence of its search for equity and place in the modern world. China has been only one of the reactive, developmental nationalisms that have been, and continue to be, observed in a variety of configurations in almost every environment in which communities suffer what they consider a subordinate station in the international community. In some places, because of a singular history and demographic and resource limitations, the reactive nationalism that manifests itself displays features peculiar to itself. Whatever the differences, however, at the core of the political and revolutionary response, a reaction to foreign "imperialism" and "hegemonic plutocracies" supplies the energy.

Marxism and Reactive Nationalism

None of the tortured history of the twentieth century is explicable in terms of classical Marxism. Neither classical Marxism nor any of its variants has helped us understand national resentment and the irrepressible desire of peoples on the margins of industrial capitalism to restore their respective nations to the status they once enjoyed in a real or fancied history.

During the first quarter of the twentieth century, some of the best Fascist theoreticians, denying the relevance of orthodox Marxism to revolution in our time, anticipated that modern revolutions would be characterized by conflict—not between classes but between those nations, "poor and proletarian," that found themselves "humiliated and discredited" by foreign "plutocracies."[3] They argued that the wars of the twentieth century would be conducted by poor nations against those nations that have arrogated to themselves all the world's material benefits. The wars of the twentieth century would be "class wars involving nations" and would take on the form of a revolutionary effort at "national palingenesis" in an environment dominated by advanced industrial powers.[4] Fascist theoreticians came to believe that the struggle of "proletarian" nations against the hegemonic "plutocracies" would shape revolutions in our time, help to explain their essential character, and account for their major properties.

In this kind of conceptual framework the revolutionary history of China makes increasing sense. The revolutionary ideology of Sun Yat-sen was reactive and developmental. It sought the restoration of China's ancient glories. After a century and a half, the Chinese mainland remains caught up in political, social, and economic tensions of an arresting magnitude—still seeking its redemptive place in the sun.[5] Pursuing that purpose, the authorities in Beijing have placed their nation in an intersection of accelerated domestic economic development, unbalanced international trade, unresolved irredentist claims, and contested security concerns, ensuring that the twenty-first century will continue to be a time of difficulty for China. The leadership in Beijing, the "third generation" after the advent of Maoism, will continue to pursue the "equity" that would restore to the Chinese their collective and individual dignity. The post-Maoist, nationalist leadership in Beijing continues to consider the advanced industrial powers, particularly the United States, the nation's mortal enemy—a conviction that assures tensions in the future.[6]

Neither the central concepts of classical Marxism nor the "creative" developments of Leninism, Stalinism, or Maoism accounts for any of this. Some of the early efforts of Marxists and Marxist-Leninists to grapple with revolution in less-developed environments had a transient relevance, but it quickly dissipated. For a brief period, Stalin acknowledged that Marxism had no place in "bourgeois nationalist" China and recognized that "anti-imperialism" mobilized *all* classes in the struggle for national rebirth. But that thought quickly dissolved in a welter of enjoinments to "class analysis," "class struggle," and "proletarian internationalism."

The conceptual preoccupations of Marxism made it all but totally impossible to understand what was transpiring in the China of the Kuomintang and the Chinese Communist party. Ruminations about "class struggle" and the working out of the "contradictions of capitalism" did very little to assist in tracing China's long, reactive, and redemptive revolution through its various stages and phases. Marxism has been even less helpful in trying to account for China's history after Mao Zedong's accession to power in 1949.

China's tragic years between 1956 and 1976 are inexplicable in standard Marxist or Marxist-Leninist terms. Most Western commentators have abandoned the notion of making Marxist sense of any phase of China's long revolution. In the effort to explain the appearance of nationalism, charismatic leaders, single-party dominance, mass mobilization, and the imposition of an ethic of sacrifice and obedience, contemporary analysts have completely abandoned Marxism and have fallen back to an eclectic fare of political, historic, social, and economic factors in the effort to account for the complex sequences of events involving revolution on the mainland of China.

Rarely does anyone now search through the works of Marx, Engels, Lenin, Stalin, or Mao to account for the political features of China's modern revolutionary history. One is counseled to abandon Marxist theory and rummage through the notions made available by non-Marxist Western scholarship. A number of alternative explanations suggest themselves. Not the least interesting is that offered by Fascist theoreticians.

Fascist Theory

Prior to the Second World War, Fascist theorists offered a schematic account of reactive and developmental nationalisms in an effort to explain many of the features that have now become familiar in the movements and regimes identified as members of the class. The best of the Fascist theoreticians argued that reactive nationalist and developmental regimes—because of the singular sense of vulnerability that afflicts their active populations—offer the occasion for the rise of many of the properties identified with generic fascism. As a case in point, Fascist theoreticians argued that the emotively charged environments of mass-mobilizing dictatorships[7] explained something significant about the rise of "charismatic" leaders.[8]

Because such regimes arise in circumstances of threat and protracted humiliation, they are typified by a degree of emotional susceptibility that tends to promote an investment of faith in a leader who is inerrant and gifted. The leadership and his entourage appeal to the sense of inadequacy and alienation common to members of their status-deprived communities. The leadership proceeds to cloak itself in the aura of infallibility. Such leadership tends to be personalistic in essence, idiosyncratic in expression, and capable of exercising singular influence on each system, rendering each, in one or more senses, unique.

Today, few deny that Josef Stalin left his indelible mark on the Soviet Union, just as Adolf Hitler made National Socialist Germany something of an extension of himself. Thus the volatility of reactive, developmental, and nationalist China amplified, and gave public expression to, all the confusion and hostility that made up the personal psychology of Mao Zedong.

In the past, scholars have identified some of the properties that characterize the environment of redemptive, reactive, and developmental dictatorships. They have spoken of communities "alienated" by dislocation, by rapid population growth, by the disintegration of institutions, and by the effects of modern war.[9] These are the circumstances associated with reactive, developmental nationalisms. They are the conditions that breed compliant masses, ferocious revolutionaries, and the commitment to struggle so familiar to the revolutions and revolutionaries of the twentieth century. They are the conditions that host the appearance of charismatic leaders.

Marxism, or Marxism-Leninism, did not prepare us for any such analysis. Marx's "ineluctabilities" of history did not allow for the impact of personalities. "Charismatic leadership" had no place in standard Marxist and Marxist-Leninist theory. Nonetheless, the issue of charismatic leadership ultimately forced itself upon Marxists and Marxist-Leninists. In each Marxist system, charismatic leadership made its appearance as "a cult of personality." No "Marxist" explanation has ever been forthcoming to account for its appearance. After the passing of Stalin, however much charisma was ritualized in the office of party leadership, the "cult of personality" simply became something to be deplored[10]—an inexplicable, if recurrent, feature of the history of Marxist-Leninist states.

Similar "cults" have appeared in Communist China, the North Korea of Kim Il Sung, Castro's Cuba, and Marxist-Leninist Albania. More than that, they have appeared in National Socialist Germany and Fascist Italy. Whereas the major theoreticians of Fascism have attempted an explanation, it has not been a serious concern of Marxists.

However confused the Marxist treatment of "charismatic leadership," ritualized charisma remained essential to the Soviet system and seems to remain equally essential to the current post-Maoist Chinese Communist system. Given the logic of political control, neither seemed (nor seems) capable of effectively operating without the presence of a "paramount leader" who becomes, however qualified, the ultimate repository of power in the system.

Epistemocracies seem to legitimate their single-party rule through the availability of inerrant leaders, who serve as capstones of unitary party systems. They provide guidance and direction for arrangements that allow neither dissident opinion nor political factions.

None of this makes any sense in terms of general Marxist, and Marxist-Leninist, theory. It makes sense in the context of some notion of emotively charged and demanding revolutionary single-party reactive and developmental nationalism.

Reactive and developmental nationalisms, in general, conceive themselves as dependent on the episodic and frequently stylized mobilization of "masses" in the service of identifying individuals and groups of individuals with the nation's rebirth and vindication. The leaders of reactive and developmental regimes imagine that national redemption and renaissance require the invocation of masses—identified with a "political genius" who intuits and embodies their sentiments and their aspirations.

Although the notion of a charismatic leader was only half-articulated in the work of Sun Yat-sen and Kuomintang theoreticians, they at least pretended to some theoretical grasp of the phenomenon. The theoreticians of the Blue Shirt Society in republican China argued that a humiliated China could only be redeemed through the identification of all citizens with the revolutionary party and its "strong" leadership. The party and its charismatic leadership could fuse all segments, strata, classes, and regions of the nation into one cohesive unity committed to one unalterable purpose—the nation's salvation.[11] Charisma was the emotional charge attendant upon the identification of masses with its leaders. The leader was the emotional mooring for an insurgent people seeking self-realization in a harrowing environment of threat, dislocation, and intense international competition.

Recently, Francis Fukuyama spoke of "Hegel's non-materialist account of History, based on the [human] 'struggle for recognition.'" He went on to speak of the disposition to be "recognized" as intrinsic to human beings as group animals. He spoke of the desire on the part of those group animals to be acknowledged as beings with "worth and dignity."[12]

The notion that entire peoples who have suffered real or fancied humiliation at the hands of others might identify with a redemptive revolutionary leadership that promises glory and "recognition" suggests an explanation of charismatic political systems.[13] In such circumstances, it is conceivable that the leader may become the "living and active incarnation" of the people as nation, and the nation as state.[14]

Within such a system, the talk is of communities mobilizing the virtues of loyalty, hard work, perseverance, and patriotism in order to wrest from others the recognition of their worthiness. Individuals, identifying with a larger "community of destiny," seek self-fulfillment in the fulfillment of that community. The account follows that of Fascist theoreticians.

Like many Western social scientists, Fascist theoreticians chose to speak in such fashion, employing similar conceptual materials. As has been suggested, Fascist theoreticians early argued that the twentieth century would be host to conflicts between the less-developed, "poor" nations seeking recognition in a world of intense competition and those that were "plutocratic." In such contests, the mass psychology of "proletarian" nations would shape not only the properties of the revolution and the regime revolution produces but the character of the revolutionaries themselves.

There is the pretense of explanation and the rudiments of a taxonomy in all of that—the first elements of theory construction. Fascist theoreticians were among the first to offer such notions as explanation—and among the first to make a serious effort at political taxonomy. However incomplete as explanation and taxonomy, the effort recommends itself.

Elements of a Taxonomy

Taxonomies often grow correlative to imagined explanations, but the actual purpose of a taxonomy is descriptive and pretheoretical—a convenient means of classifying knowledge to serve didactic, mnemonic, and heuristic purposes. In itself, a taxonomy is a classification of materials that result from extended observation and familiarization with forms of life; it becomes a synoptic characterization of a large and otherwise unmanageable amount of empirical data. Taxonomic efforts attempt to provide a summary account of observations within a given universe of discourse.

Thus political scientists speak of "pluralistic" systems. Although no single extant system may satisfy all the entrance criteria into the general category, the category captures, at an unspecified level of abstraction, at least some of the essentials of what is considered a generalizable phenomenon. Class properties are distributed over a collection of phenomena, summarizing them and providing a mnemonic convenience, a guide to exposition, as well as suggestions for possible research.

Everyone grants that political "pluralism" in contemporary Italy is different from the "pluralism" of the United States, and yet the term captures something of the essentials of both. But in regard to the empirical differences, each "pluralism" is unique. Similarly, there are essentials of "fascism" that distinguish the class from its alternatives. Within the class, all "fascisms" are different to one or another degree. It is clear that not all members of the class must be identical any more than all human beings must be identical to satisfy the entrance criteria for membership in the species.

Fascist theoreticians were prepared to attempt to reduce the complex political world of their time to a preliminary taxonomy by identifying classes of revolutionary movements and revolutionary regimes. The suggested taxonomies varied, but the best of the efforts produced interesting results.

Acknowledging the complexity of any proposed classificatory system,[15] Fascist theoreticians nonetheless undertook some interesting preliminary attempts.[16] For the purposes of the present discussion, it is reasonably certain that for Fascists, "fascism" as a class was a subspecific variant of the genus "reactive and developmental nationalism."[17]

In 1933, Mussolini acknowledged to visitors from East Asia that Fascism shared their political aspirations and many of their resentments. The Asian nations, like Fascist Italy, were "proletarian," suffering exploitation at the hands of the industrially advanced powers. Mussolini told his visitors that the "plutocracies" insisted on dealing with the Asian nations, as they had with Italy, as though they were nothing other than market outlets for surplus goods and territorial preserves for raw materials.

"We Fascists," Mussolini reflected, "recognize ourselves in the complaints of Asians, in their resentments and their reactions. The differences are in the particulars; the essentials are the same."[18] In effect, Mussolini was prepared to argue that the reactive and developmental nationalism of revolutionary China and redemptive Japan shared generic taxonomic features with Fascist Italy.

For Fascist theoreticians, "reactive and developmental nationalism" constituted a *family* or a *genus* of political systems featured in the modern world. Constituent candidate members of the general class ranged over all the reactive and developmental nationalisms from the German revolution of 1848[19] through the political systems of Mustafa Kemal Ataturk, José Martí, and Sun Yat-sen to the revolutionary movements, Marxist and non-Marxist alike, that typify the twentieth century.[20] Among the historic collection of democratic and nondemocratic reactive and developmental movements and regimes, Italian Nationalists and Fascists were a special subset, sharing clear affinities with the contemporaneous antidemocratic Russian and National Socialist revolutionaries.

Fascist theoreticians recognized that among the entire roster of contemporary reactive and developmental nationalisms only some qualified as "fascist." "Fascism," for Fascist theoreticians, was a form of reactive and developmental nationalism that found unique and defining expression in the commitment to "totalitarian" control of an emerging revolutionary society.[21]

Totalitarianism, for those theoreticians, constituted the effort to create an exemplary unity of all citizens, all aggregates, and all interests within the compass of the revolutionary party and the state that it constructs.[22] The agency of that unity is the "unitary party," a political party animated by a mass-mobilizing ideology that undertakes revolution and over time transforms the juridical rationale and structure of the preexisting state, attempting to absorb within itself all individuals and aggregates of individuals until "everything is within the state, nothing is opposed to the state, and nothing is outside the state."[23]

Fascist theoreticians recognized that although there were totalitarian tendencies among political parties that emerged in reactive and developmental nationalist environments,[24] they refused to classify them as "fascist" unless they possessed certain requisite defining properties. To be identified as "totalitarian," for example, required institutional expression rather than ideological velleities.

Thus, for Fascists, the grand council of Fascism became the political institution in which the Partito nazionale fascista "fused" with the state. The grand council was the creature of the leader as head of the party and became the tool of the leader as the head of state.[25] Below the grand council an entire infrastructure of institutions gave body to their political control. The revolutionary party had become the Fascist state.

Through a complex of state institutions—economic, social, communications, medical, and pedagogical—the party assiduously sought to influence the life of every citizen.[26] However complicated, overlapping, and conflicted the relations between all the institutions, the system was transparently more than that of an "authoritarian dictatorship."[27] The intention of authoritarian states is not to transform their subjects.[28]

However authoritarian systems are conceived, they are emphatically different from Fascist totalitarianism. Nor can a system be denied identification as totalitarian simply because its enterprise is unsuccessful. The identification turns on the clear intentions of its practitioners and the institutions constructed to achieve their essentially utopian ends, not on their success.

Because Fascism identified itself as totalitarian, potentially every aspect of Italian life fell under the purview of the party. The economy was directly and indirectly controlled by agencies of the interventionist state. The Fascist state was charged with daily involvement in all aspects of the nation's activities. It discharged "a predominant function in the life of the nation—not only to intervene in the nation's economy, for example, when there were dislocations in the normal course of things . . . , but in the daily life of every activity."[29] By the mid-1930s, the Fascist economy was the most regulated in all of Europe—save that of the Soviet Union.

Fascist theoreticians insisted that a "fascism" must be totalitarian in intention and practice, for they considered the descriptive concept "totalitarian" an intrinsic part of the *definition* of Fascism.[30] Since the concept implied, for Fascists, the involvement of "masses" in the revolution, the reconstruction of the state, and the remaking of human beings, "mass mobilization" became one of Fascism's defining attributes.

Any reactive and developmental nationalism that failed to mobilize masses—a factor "decisive" to fascist identification[31]—would not be "fascist." Masses provided the populist and plebiscitary base of the system. Although elements of formal election might subsist at some level somewhere in a revolutionary system,[32] they would be supplementary at best. For Fascist theoreticians, a fascist leader must necessarily "emerge from the people and from a great popular party. . . . from the most profound and immediate popular sources."[33] A fascist leader is never elected in the sense that political leaders are elected in pluralist political environments. Fascist leaders are "acclaimed." As an immediate, logical consequence of that, fascist movements and fascist regimes are intrinsically antiliberal and antidemocratic. Fascist movements are populist, dealing with masses rather than voters.

In other cases, Fascist theoreticians refused to identify a revolutionary movement or regime, however antiliberal and populist, as fascist because neither the movement nor the subsequent regime was defended by its own political army. The truly revolutionary party, determined to transform the state and society, Fascist theoreticians maintained, "appears as a true and virtual state in formation . . . by manifesting all the properties of a state, particularly by deploying its own armed forces."[34]

During the insurrectionary phase, the political army defeats the opponents of the revolution. After the revolutionary seizure of power, the revolutionary armed forces, under the direct orders of the leader,[35] become agencies of public control and political education. With the establishment of the new political system, the members of the party army and/or the armed forces are expected to serve as models for the general citizenry.[36] They become part of the vast machinery of public education that creates totalitarian consensus.[37]

As a consensus, plebiscitary regime, fascist systems organize education to serve the purposes of the revolution. Information and public instruction are ultimately controlled by the leader, who seeks to realize "a political, economic, social reconstruction. . . . in the service of national resurrection."

On the initiative of the leader, "the party mobilizes all the vital moral and ideal forces of the nation in order to create in the population a new soul and spirit."[38] A fascist system attempts to create "new human beings" for the "new society."

"In order to fully understand Fascism," it was said, "it is necessary to recognize it as the most ambitious educative effort in the history of the world since the propagation of Christianity."[39] The employment of education as an instrument of the regime reveals the epistemarchic character of the system.

Fascist systems are ideocratic. Their legitimacy is a function of the credibility of their ideological persuasiveness. Education serves to convey the "truths" of the system and assure the popular consensus, real or factitious, on which the entire political structure ultimately rests.[40]

Because political education is intended to instill in the masses a conviction in the legitimating normative and empirical "truths" of the system, the "pedagogical state," because of its apologetic role, necessarily takes on an "ecclesiastical" character.[41] All of the trappings of religion become evident—the liturgies, rituals, symbols, sacred history, saints and martyrs, transcendent glories, authoritative decalogue, and seemingly superhuman qualities of the charismatic leader.[42]

What emerges from the Fascists' assessment of their system is a primitive taxonomy. It provides a list of criterial attributes that attempt to distinguish "fascist" from nonfascist systems as subspecific variants of "reactive and developmental nationalism." However incomplete and uncertain their taxonomies, the best of the Fascist theoreticians nonetheless recognized the classificatory similarities between Fascism, Stalinism, and Hitler's National Socialism.[43] They were the "totalitarian" regimes recognized by Western scholars before, and more emphatically after, the Second World War.

In terms of their defining attributes, qualitatively identified, all such systems shared unmistakable properties. They were all animated by formal doctrines of national renovation, and their revolutionaries aggregated in exclusivistic and unitary parties, led by charismatic or pseudocharismatic leaders. They all committed themselves to the predominance of an interventionist state, in the service of creating a new order and new human beings to people it. They were all characterized by features of "masculine protest"—the prevalence of uniforms and the accoutrements of battle.

These revolutions and the state system they created were members of a class of systems of which paradigmatic Fascism was a member. The distinctions among them, turning on doctrinal differences and the particular history of each, justify ascribing different names to each, but that should not disguise some of their fundamental similarities.

Because the concepts of a primitive descriptive taxonomy are all characterized in qualitative, rather than quantitative, terms, there will always be doubt about the inclusion and exclusion of particular cases in the genus "reactive and developmental nationalism" as well as the species "totalitarianism" and the subspecies "fascism." These categories are all synoptic renderings of complex descriptions, subject to review and refinement with subsequent empirical assessment.

Fascism was neither Stalinism nor Hitler's National Socialism. Each totalitarianism had distinguishing characteristics. Stalinism insisted on its fictive "Marxism" with its ineffectual "proletarian internationalism" and its homicidal class warfare. Hitler's biological racism, for its part, rendered National Socialism distinctive. Marxism, or Marxism-Leninism, could tell us nothing about all of that. Fascist theoreticians, on the other hand, provided a preliminary and pretheoretical ordering of phenomena in the effort to obtain purchase on the universe of discourse.

Sergio Panunzio, among the best of the Fascist theoreticians, sought to distinguish modern reactive and developmental revolutionary movements and regimes on the basis of the criteria isolated by Fascist thinkers. Thus for Panunzio, Spanish Falangism displayed the major attributes of generic fascism during its insurrectionary phase. For all that, it remained uncertain whether its accommodation with the traditionalism of Francisco Franco would leave Spain "fascist" or traditionalist.[44]

Concerning China's Kuomintang, Panunzio was more certain. Although Chiang Kai-shek's Kuomintang was revolutionary and sought to inform the state, its totalitarianism was compromised by its commitment to an ultimate constitutional, democratic, and pluralistic order.[45] Sun Yat-sen never surrendered his conviction that a modern China would ultimately assume a democratic and pluralistic character—a conviction that distinguished the revolutionary ideology of the Kuomintang from generic fascism.[46]

Similarly, although Japanese nationalism was infused with reactive and developmental impulses and Japan was a military ally of Fascist Italy, Fascist theoreticians never considered imperial Japan a member of the class of generic "fascisms."[47] Japan was clearly animated by a reactive and developmental nationalism, but it shared few, if any, of the mass-mobilizing and single-party features of paradigmatic Fascism.

For Fascist theoreticians, the class of generic fascisms was exiguous. Neither Stalin's Soviet Union nor Hitler's National Socialism fully qualified. In both cases, doctrinal differences excluded them from the class. Fascist theoreticians argued that while both shared the form of generic fascism, both lacked its doctrinal substance. The Soviet Union was, in theory, opposed to the totalitarian state. Marxism sought the state's ultimate dissolution—its "withering away." More than that, the Soviet Union imposed a command economy on the developmental system put together by the Bolsheviks after the compulsory "socialization" of the economy following Stalin's accession to total control.[48]

Fascism, as its ideologues conceived of it, accorded the state the right to indicative, but not mandatory, planning. For Fascists, in general, the market served regulatory purposes, providing the essentials of a rational price structure for the allocation of resources and the distribution of goods. Stalinism was not a fascism, no matter how many of the properties of fascism it shared, because the Stalinist regime insisted on a command, rather than a market, economy.

Stalinism was not a fascism, for Fascist theoreticians, because Stalinism insisted on the centrality of class warfare, the transience of the state, and the nonmarket character of the economy. It failed to officially acknowledge the primacy of the nation. Like Hitler's National Socialist insistence on the primacy of biological race, the Marxist preoccupation with class made it a quasi-fascism, at best. There were, in effect, throughout the interwar years, few real members of the class of "fascisms." Most candidates failed to fully qualify.

Only after the Second World War did surviving Fascist theoreticians offer some alternatives. In the early 1960s, Ugo Spirito, one of Fascism's most celebrated theoreticians, delivered himself of judgments concerning Communist China. He recognized China as a member of the class of systems that were reactive and developmental, but more than that he identified it as a system that demanded sacrifice and discipline from an entire nation in order to restore the grandeur of the historic community.

Spirito dismissed Marxism, in any of its variants, as relevant to what was transpiring in China. Whatever the pretenses of Maoism, it was clear to Spirito that Marxism had nothing to do with what was happening in revolutionary China.[49] By that time, the Marxist-Leninists of the Soviet Union had identified Maoist China as a variant of European fascism and by the end of the 1970s, China's own dissidents saw, in Maoism, an emergent fascism.

By the end of the 1980s, Deng Xiaoping's reforms had transformed Maoism into a form of generic fascism sharing the criterial attributes of the original. By that time, the "dictatorship of the proletariat" had been transformed into the dictatorship of the most patriotic, and the command economy had given way to the fairly extensive market alternatives that sustained international trade and the transfer of foreign capital. Class warfare had been abandoned and the integral unity of all citizens in the support of national regeneration had become a political priority.

As a consequence, by the early 1980s, it seemed that "Communist" China might best be cognitively identified as "fascist." Not only had a host of traditional Marxist-Leninists so identified it, but it seems reasonably clear that Fascist theoreticians would have little serious objection to the classification.

What seems eminently clear is that Marxist theory had, and has, precious little to tell us about all that and still less to offer as an explanation for the revolutions and regimes that have peopled the twentieth century. Fascist theoreticians, for their part, provided a preliminary taxonomy and the outlines of a first attempt at explanation in the effort to understand the revolutions of our time. That effort remains suggestive and is perhaps more helpful than any alternative in trying to understand the history of China's long revolution and post-Maoist China's place in that history.

Post-Maoist China As Fascist

Little remains of the Marxism of Communist China. Contemporary China is a reactive and developmental regime that not only seeks parity with its "imperialist" and "plutocratic" counterparts but aspires to a place in the sun as the "central kingdom." It seeks not only its adequate "living space" but its role as hegemon in East Asia. Contemporary China gives every appearance of being the kind of antiliberal, collectivistic, party-dominant, elitist, militaristic, plebiscitary, reactive nationalist and developmental fascist system with which the twentieth century has become familiar.[50]

Even before the transformations that resulted from the revolutionary reformism of Deng Xiaoping, the Marxist-Leninists of the Soviet Union identified the emergence of a "great-power tradition" in China that threatened the security of all of East Asia and the future of the entire Pacific rim.[51] Communist China has emerged as a contender for place and status in East Asia and, as such, reveals itself as a potential threat to the peace and security of our time.

There is little doubt that revolutionary China, under the aegis of Sun Yat-sen, Chiang Kai-shek, or Mao Zedong, satisfied the requirements for entry into the class of reactive and developmental nationalisms.[52] More than that, it is now generally recognized that Marxism, as a revolutionary theory, played little, if any, role in the ideology that governed the emerging system. Everyone now agrees that there was scant Marxism in the regime that ruled mainland China from 1949 through 1976.[53]

Maoism was identified by many as "totalitarian" because of Mao's utopian attempt to transform the nation through mass-mobilization campaigns involving agencies of the party and the state.[54] Whatever the judgment, it is clear that Maoist China was a singular place. As we have seen, both foreign and domestic critics, over time, perceived unmistakable elements of fascism in the complex components that made up the ideology and practice of the system.[55]

Maoist China was reactive nationalist and developmental in character and intention. It was totalitarian in aspiration. It conducted mass mobilization to achieve its purposes, and its leadership characterized themselves as epistemarchs, possessed of inerrant knowledge of the world. Ideologically driven, the Communist party was an antiliberal and antidemocratic, hegemonic, and elitist organization that characteristically chose its unitary party leadership by acclamation.

The Communist party early created its own armed forces, and its leadership was always, and has remained, charismatic. In ideocratic systems, the leader is always endowed with practically supernatural powers. Where the charisma is routinized, those powers are not as immediately evident. Nonetheless, the leadership of the unitary party must always be possessed of the truth. That has been central to the convictions of the Bolsheviks, the National Socialists, and the Fascists.

In Communist China between 1949 and 1976, every word uttered by the "chairman," the "never setting red sun," was transcendently true. He was the magic talisman that promised triumph in all endeavors. His words could overcome material deficiencies, illness, and death.[56] Today, China's leadership celebrates the impeccable "theories" of Deng Xiaoping, flawlessly conveyed to the a billion citizens of China by Jiang Zemin (and whoever succeeds him).

In its own time, Maoism distinguished itself from paradigmatic Fascism by insisting on a command economy for China's expanding material base. Whatever its foreign or domestic critics might say, Maoism fostered a nonmarket economy or at least an economy that had suppressed almost all critical market exchanges. Fascists had always insisted on the role of the market, as well as the incentives provided by private property and profit, in the programmatic economy of their evolving system.[57]

Moreover, as we have seen, Maoism was inextricably committed to class struggle, a commitment fundamentally alien to paradigmatic Fascism. For Fascism, class struggle betrayed the nation, undermining its integrity and exposing it to threats emanating from the more powerful "plutocratic" states.

With the passing of Maoism and the advent of the revolution that followed the incumbency of Deng Xiaoping, those distinctions changed dramatically. Post-Maoist China displays almost all of the defining traits of fascism as characterized by the best Fascist theoreticians in the interwar years.

To classify a political system as *fascist* is to say that it shares generic descriptive properties with *reactive and developmental nationalisms*, with a *totalitarian* species of that genus, and a discrete subspecies of that species. As such the naming involved in the classification is part of an essentially descriptive enterprise.[58] That a political regime is characterized as "fascist" means that it displays properties that satisfy some list of entry criteria into the class.

The concern that is generated by such preliminary naming arises from the history of the entire class of such systems. In the past, such systems have been singularly hostile and aggressive. Convinced of the impeccable justice of their cause, they have been prepared to employ massive violence against those they conceive as obstructing their search for some kind of cosmic justice. All too often their search for justice cuts across the critical interests of others—often the interests of very powerful opponents. The Axis powers destroyed themselves in just such a confrontation. The Soviet Union exhausted itself in its attempt to compete with the industrialized democracies in an all-consuming arms race.

Given the circumstances in which they find themselves, and the individual and collective psychology that is a function of those circumstances, such systems pretend to see occult conspiracies everywhere. They conceive arabesque plots being marshaled against them by international bankers, capitalists, imperialists, plutocrats, the bourgeoisie, Jews, Masons, and "racial inferiors." The plots are calculated to destroy their community, enslave its members, and undermine their utopian goals. In response to the perceived threat, such systems have incarcerated and expelled hundreds of thousands of their own citizens in their efforts to abort such plots and contain the contagion of "spiritual pollution" or impairments to "racial consciousness." In the most psychopathic instances, and to the same ends, such systems have murdered millions.

We also know, by virtue of recurrent observation, that reactive nationalist systems, particularly when they are totalitarian in disposition, tend to be irrepressibly irredentist. Fascist systems as a subset will tend to conceive of irredentism as part of a larger program of securing both a "living" and a "civilizing" space in which a "great culture" can be restored and ancient glories rekindled.

It is in such a context that we consider post-Maoist China. Unlike the China of Jiang Zemin, the remnants of post-Nationalist China on Taiwan have transformed themselves into a fully democratic polity.[59] Inspired throughout its history by the democratic, nontotalitarian, reactive and developmental nationalism of Sun Yat-sen, the Kuomintang has led the Republic of China on Taiwan through the transitions from military rule and political tutelage to constitutional democracy.

Very little of that has been observed on the mainland of China. Whatever tentative and marginal political moves the leadership in Beijing has undertaken in terms of "popular representation,"[60] very little has changed in the one-party system that, for all intents and purposes, still dominates China. Major political reforms that would be required to move the system away from its party-dominant and antidemocratic form of governance do not seem to be in the predictable future.

Many Americans have invested considerable confidence in the fact that the People's Republic of China has remained open to Western trade, finance, and technology transfers since the 1980s. That is expected to mollify Beijing's positions on a variety of sensitive subjects. Unhappily, we cannot know with any predictable assurance what influence China's spectacular "opening to the West" might have on the regime of Jiang Jemin and those who will follow him. Fascist Italy had been similarly open to the West, trading and borrowing extensively from the "plutocracies." In the mid-1930s, the system retreated to a self-imposed autarky in an effort to insulate itself from the "corrupt" influence of, and the political constraints imposed by, the industrialized democracies. At least in part as a result, Italy lapsed into that fateful alliance with National Socialist Germany and Japan that precipitated the Second World War.

At the turn of the twenty-first century, most observers appear confident that post-Maoist China will persist in seeking foreign technology and capital investment—that China will continue to earn foreign exchange by selling its labor-intensive commodities to the advanced industrial economies—and that it will remain open to the "imperialist powers." It is argued that with foreign wares and foreign capital, foreign ideas—"bourgeois spiritual pollution"—will penetrate as well—to make of Communist China a "responsible member of the international community."[61]

It is the hope of the industrialized powers that a policy of "deep engagement" with China will lead to its increasing political liberalization. Unfortunately, Western social science has very little empirical evidence that might give us confidence in that outcome. Social science has had very little success anticipating complex political developments in the twentieth century—and there is little to suggest that its practitioners will be any better in the foreseeable future.

Few, if any, Western scholars anticipated the catastrophic collapse of the Soviet Union and the "Marxist" governments of Eastern Europe and the Balkans. Few predicted the unraveling of Communist Yugoslavia and the concomitant emergence of homicidal ethnic nationalisms. Few foresaw the appearance of a form of fascism arising out of the ruins of the Soviet Union.

At the turn of the century, there is little that inspires confidence in the predictions of peace, continued economic growth and development, and political stability in East Asia. Any serious dislocations in the expansion and increasing sophistication of the Chinese economy could throw the mainland regime into turmoil and precipitate an incalculable political response. Given all this, as long as the People's Republic of China remains central to the concerns of the region and the regime that controls it, continues to feature all the properties of a revolutionary, antidemocratic, irredentist, and belligerent reactive developmental nationalism, there remains the continuous threat of domestic violence within China and the prospect of international conflict throughout East Asia.

At the turn of the century, there are those who, given at least these kinds of consideration, see China as an "emerging hegemon" in the western Pacific that the United States is destined to confront.[62] China is seen as an economic and military peer/competitor in the twenty-first century—a competitor in a confrontation that might constitute a "clash of civilizations."

The People's Republic of China is a reactive and revanchist nationalist system, moved by profound sentiments of historic injustice. Like the systems of interwar Europe, post-Maoist China searches for its proper place in the sun. Unlike the reactive nationalism of the period before the Second World War, Communist China has a population of over a billion people and a resource base of vast potential. It is crafting for itself a military possessed of nuclear capabilities, sea-denial potential, manpower resources, and range that could easily mean that the twenty-first century will be a time of unmitigated troubles. Should all that be the case, Fascism will have cast its shadow over our own and our children's time.

Notes

1. See the discussion in Mikhail Agursky, *The Third Rome: National Bolshevism in the USSR* (Boulder: Westview, 1987); and Agursky, *Contemporary Russian Nationalism—History Revised* (Jerusalem: Hebrew University, 1982).

2. See the discussion in A. James Gregor, *Phoenix: Fascism in Our Time* (New Brunswick, N.J.: Transaction, 1999), chap. 7; Gregor, *The Faces of Janus: Marxism and Fascism in the Twentieth Century* (New Haven: Yale University Press, 2000), chaps. 5–8; Gregor, "Fascism and the New Russian Nationalism," *Communist and Post-Communist Studies* 31, no. 1 (1998): 1–15.

3. Dino Grandi, "Le origini e la missione del fascismo," in *Il fascismo e i partiti politici*, ed. R. Mondolfo (Bologna: Cappelli, 1922), pp. 52–53, 62.

4. Ibid., p. 52.

5. See Maria Hsia Chang, *The Labors of Sisyphus: The Economic Development of Communist China* (New Brunswick, N.J.: Transaction, 1998).

6. In 1985, the Communist government of China republished, without emendation, Hu Sheng's *Imperialism and Chinese Politics*, 7th ed. (Beijing: Foreign Languages, 1985). The book was originally published in 1955. Irrespective of the changes that have taken place both in terms of the system on the mainland and its relations with the "imperialist" powers, the government in Beijing gives every indication that it considers its relationship with the United States as fundamentally adversarial. In this context, see the very popular national best-seller by Song Qiang, Zhang Zangzang, Qiao Bian, Yiang Zhengyu, and Gu Qinsgsheng, *Zhongguo keyi shuobu* (China can say no) (Beijing: Zhonghua gongshang lianhe, 1996d); and Qiang et al., *Zhongguo haishi neng shuobu* (China can still say no) (Beijing: Zhonguo wenlian, 1996), which characterizes the United States as a committed enemy of China.

7. "Mass mobilization" is never clearly defined. The term seems to apply to government-sponsored festivals, ritualized performances, street theater, mass rallies, organized mobilization for specific public projects, party-dominated athletic events, and so forth. These activities all seem to serve one purpose: the maintenance of a sense of collective identity among the active members of the population.

8. See, for example, the discussion in Roberto Michels, *First Lectures in Political Sociology* (New York: Harper & Row, 1949), chap. 6.

9. See the discussion in A. James Gregor, *The Interpretations of Fascism* (New Brunswick, N. J.: Transaction, 1997), chaps. 4, 6.

10. For the Marxist-Leninists of the Gorbachev era, the "cult of personality" was explained in terms of Stalin's "mental illness" and thus recourse was made, once again, to the personal properties of the dictator. See Anatoly Butenko, Gavriil Popov, Boris Bolotin, and Dmitry Volkogonov, *The Stalin Phenomenon* (Moscow: Novosti, 1988), particularly pp. 48–52.

11. See the account in Maria Hsia Chang, *The Chinese Blue Shirt Society: Fascism and Developmental Nationalism* (Berkeley: Center for Chinese Studies, 1985).

12. Francis Fukuyama, *The End of History and the Last Man* (New York: Free Press, 1992), p. xvi.

13. The theory of "charismatic government of the national society has found . . . in Fascism its first complete realization." The party handbook, *Il partito nazionale fascista* (Rome: Libreria dello stato, 1936), pp. 49–51.

14. See the discussion of Michels, *First Lectures*, p. 126.

15. See, for example, Sergio Panunzio, *Teoria generale dello stato fascista* (Padua: CEDAM, 1939), pt. 5, particularly pp. 458–463, 471–473, 492–520. The difficulty with most of the Fascist writings turns on the evident confusion between "taxonomizing" and attempting an explanation.

16. See, for example, Antonio Canepa, *Sistema di dottrina del fascismo*, vol. 3 (Rome: Formiggini, 1937), pt. 5, chap. 1.

17. Throughout the present exposition, the point has been made that national humiliation was a constant theme in the earliest Fascist literature. So too was the theme of accelerated economic growth and production. In the early 1920s, for example, Sergio Panunzio wrote, "[The nation] is poor in natural resources, we have little opportunity to either save or accumulate capital. . . . We must break

out of the circle in which we find ourselves caged, making it impossible to demonstrate our talents and our labor and productive power." Sergio Panunzio, *Che cos'è il fascismo* (Milan: Alpes, 1924), p. 29; see pp. 14–15 for the statements concerning Italy's humiliations.

18. See Mussolini, "Oriente e occidente," in *Opera omnia* (Florence: La fenice, 1953–1964), 26:127–128.

19. It was during that period that Friedrich List wrote his *National System of Political Economy* (New York: Longmans, Green, 1916) (a translation of the writings of 1844), which was to influence both Italian Nationalist and Fascist developmental thought. See, in this context, Roman Szporluk, *Communism and Nationalism: Karl Marx versus Friedrich List* (New York: Oxford, 1988).

20. See the discussion in W. W. Rostow, *The Process of Economic Growth* (New York: Norton, 1962), pp. 315–318.

21. See the account in Salvatore Carbonaro, *Il partito nazionale fascista e la sua struttura giuridica* (Florence: Carlo Cya, 1939), paras. 17–19, pp. 96–118.

22. See the discussion in Sergio Panunzio, *Il fondamento giuridico del fascismo* (Rome: Bonacci, 1987), pp. 176–186.

23. See Umberto Renda, *Lo statuto del partito nazionale fascista* (Turin: Paravia, 1938), pp. 11–13; Carbonaro, *Il partito nazionale*, para. 21, pp. 124–131.

24. Thus Carbonaro speaks of the "distinct tendencies toward totalitarianism" in various environments. Not all emerge as "fascisms." See Carbonaro, *Il partito nazionale*, p. 114 n. 91.

25. See the comments in Panunzio, *Teoria generale*, p. 552 n. 1; and Panunzio, "Teoria generale della dittatura," *Gerarchia* 14, no. 5 (1936): 303–316.

26. See the discussion in Alfredo Rocco, "La trasformazione dello stato," in *Lo stato Mussoliniano* (Rome: La Rassegna Italiana, 1930), pp. 9–22.

27. Fascism, as a historic reality, may have failed to "totalitarianize" Italy. That is not the point. "Totalitarian" systems are those that aspire to total control and create institutions requisite to that intention. Thus, to find "personalism" and "authoritarianism" in Fascist Italy is not to deny its "totalitarian" character. See Alberto Aquarone, "The Totalitarian State and Personal Dictatorship," in *Totalitarianism Reconsidered*, ed. Ernest A. Menze (Port Washington, N.Y.: Kennikat, 1981), pp. 81–93. Compare the discussion with Leonard Schapiro, *Totalitarianism* (New York: Praeger, 1972); and Steven Paul Soper, *Totalitarianism: A Conceptual Approach* (New York: University Press of America, 1985).

28. See G. Bruni, "Sul concetto di stato totalitario," *Lo Stato* 10, no. 5 (1936): 99–118.

29. Arturo Assante, *Il nuovo regime economico sociale* (Naples: Alberto Morano, 1936), p. 243.

30. See Carlo Costamagna, *Dottrina del fascismo* (Turin: UTET, 1940), pp. 153–161.

31. Carbonaro, *Il partito nazionale*, p. 114 n. 91.

32. See Francesco Paloni, *Sistema rappresentativo del fascismo* (Naples: Rispoli, 1937); Gino Sottochiesa, *Il nuovo regime rappresentativo dello stato fascista* (Turin: Paravia, 1939); Vincenzo Zangara, *La rappresentanza istituzionale* (Bologna: Zanichelli, 1939).

33. "The Head of State [Capo dello Stato] no longer comes from parliament, but from the nation in its organic unity." Vincenzo Corsini, *Il Capo del Governo nello stato fascista* (Bologna: Zanichelli, 1935), p. 49; Panunzio, *Teoria generale*, p. 580.

34. Panunzio, *Teoria generale*, p. 462. In the Statutes of the Fascist Party in 1921, the Fascist combat squads were considered intrinsic to the party. They were the "voluntary militia in the service of the national state." G. A. Chiurco, *Storia della rivoluzione fascista* (Florence: Vallecchi, 1929), 3:647. In some revolutionary regimes (as in most "Marxist-Leninist" regimes), the party army becomes the armed forces of the state. In others, the party army remains essentially an adjunct to the armed forces.

35. Giovanni Corso, *Lo stato fascista* (Rome: Libreria del littorio, 1929), p. 225.

36. See the account in Antonio Canepa, *L'organizzazione del P. N. F.* (Palermo: Ciuni, 1939), pp. 224–230.

37. See Balbino Giuliano, *Elementi di cultura fascista* (Bologna: Zanichelli, 1929), pp. 104–106.

38. Corsini, *Il Capo del Governo*, pp. 289–90.

39. Luigi Romanini, *I principi del fascismo nel campo dell'educazione* (Turin: Paravia, 1939), p. 17.

40. The fascist state is thus an "educative state . . . possessed of 'pedagogical' rights." Panunzio, *Teoria generale*, p. 59. Roberto Michels, as a Fascist ideologue, recognized that should the epistemarchs be shown to be in error, the legitimacy of the system is compromised. See Roberto Michels, *First Lectures in Political Sociology* (New York: Harper, 1949), pp. 123–132.

41. See the discussion in Sergio Panunzio, *Il sentimento dello stato* (Rome: Libreria del littorio, 1929), chaps. 1–2, *Teoria generale*, pp. 19, 59; and Panunzio, *Il fondamento giuridico*, p. 187.

42. Fascists were supplied, for example, with handbooks containing the selected thoughts of Mussolini in order to guide them in their day-to-day behavior. See Ezio Maria Gray, ed., *Il pensiero di Benito Mussolini* (Milan: Alpes, 1927); and Asvero Gravelli, ed., *Vademecum dello stile fascista* (Rome: Nuova Europa, n.d.), which contains the commands issued in the "immortal name" of the Duce (see p. 12) so that all may be faithful to his "Idea" (p. 13).

43. Panunzio, *Teoria generale*, pp. 10, 461–463.

44. See Sergio Panunzio, *Spagna nazionalsindacalista* (Milan: Bietti, 1942). As late as 1939, Panunzio was uncertain whether Spain, tendentially "totalitarian, popular and authoritarian" would mature into a Spanish fascism. See Panunzio, *Teoria generale*, p. 499.

45. See Sergio Panunzio, *Rivoluzione e costituzione* (Milan: Treves, 1933), pt. 2, chap. 15; and Panunzio, *Teoria generale*, pp. 579–580.

46. See the discussion in Chang, *Chinese Blue Shirt Society*, chap. 5, particularly pp. 121–123.

47. See the discussion in Pompeo Aloisi, *La situazione geopolitica del Giappone* (Rome: Societa amici del Giappone, 1942); Carlo Avarna di Gualtieri, *La politica giapponese del "nuovo ordine"* (Milan: Principato, 1940), chap. 7.

48. See Panunzio, *Teoria generale*, pp. 40, 42–43.

49. See the discussion in Ugo Spirito, "Il comunismo cinese," in *Il comunismo* (Florence: Sansoni, 1965), pp. 225–267.

50. The question remains whether contemporary China is "mass-mobilizing." There are no universally satisfying responses to such questions. Clearly, Beijing can mobilize masses—as witnessed by the mass demonstrations organized by the state during the protests against NATO bombings of the Chinese embassy in Belgrade in 1999.

51. See S. L. Tikhvinsky, introduction to *China and Her Neighbours from Ancient Times to the Middle Ages* (Moscow: Progress, 1981), pp. 16–17.

52. It is interesting to note that one of the foremost of the Fascist theoreticians who survived the war identified Maoist China as a reactive and developmental regime. See Spirito, "Il comunismo cinese," in *Il comunismo*, particularly pp. 226, 228, 230, 258, 265.

53. See Chang, *Labors of Sisyphus*, chap. 2; A. James Gregor, *China, Marxism and Development* (New Brunswick, N.J.: Transaction, 1996), chaps. 2, 4.

54. See, for example, Richard L. Walker, *China Under Communism: The First Five Years* (New Haven: Yale University, 1955); and George Paloczi-Horvath, *Mao Tse-tung: Emperor of the Blue Ants* (New York: Doubleday, 1963).

55. See the discussion in A. James Gregor, *The Fascist Persuasion in Radical Politics* (Princeton: Princeton University Press, 1974), chap. 6; and the comments in Paul Johnson, *Modern Times: The World from the Twenties to the Nineties* (New York: Harper Perennial, 1991), chap. 16.

56. See George Urban, ed., *The "Miracles" of Chairman Mao* (Los Angeles: Nash, 1971).

57. See the discussion in Carl T. Schmidt, *The Corporate State in Action: Italy Under Fascism* (New York: Oxford University, 1939), chap. 6.

58. See the discussion in A. James Gregor, "'Totalitarianism' Revisited," in *Totalitarianism Reconsidered*, ed. Ernest A. Menze (Port Washington, N.Y.: Kennikat, 1981), pp. 130–145.

59. See the works of John F. Copper concerning the development of democratic institutions on Taiwan. The democratic aspirations of Sun Yat-sen are unmistakable in the pluralism of the Republic of China on Taiwan. John F. Copper, *Taiwan's Recent Elections: Fulfilling the Democratic Promise* (Baltimore: University of Maryland School of Law, 1990); Copper, *Taiwan's 1991 and 1992 Non-Supplemental Elections: Reaching a Higher State of Democracy* (New York: East Asia Research Institute, 1994); Copper, *Taiwan's 1998 Legislative Yuan, Metropolitan Mayoral and City Council Elections: Confirming and Consolidating Democracy in the Republic of China* (Baltimore: University of Maryland School of Law, 1999).

60. Throughout the regime, Fascists made weak attempts to introduce elements of an elective, representative system in Mussolini's Italy. Very little came of any of it—and it seems that little is to be expected from the "democratic" elections reportedly held in the rural areas of China. See the discussion concerning the Fascist efforts in Francesco Paoloni, *Sistema rappresentativo del Fascismo: Polemica-Storia-Dottrina*, 2d ed. (Milan: n.p., 1937).

61. See, for example, Michel C. Oksenberg, Michael D. Swaine, and Daniel C. Lynch, *The Chinese Future* (Los Angeles: Pacific Council on International Policy, 1998).

62. Richard Bernstein and Ross H. Munro, *The Coming Conflict with China* (New York: Knopf, 1997).

Index

Printed in the United States
24857LVS00001B/163-276